I dedicate this book to,

My mum and dad, sadly now departed but without whom none of this would
have been possible.
Special thanks to Shaun, who taught me how to drive my first crane.
All those wonderful people I met and loved along the way.
Austin Macauley Publishers, who helped me get my first book published.
I thank you all.

Billy Crane

ONLY PASS THIS WAY ONCE

AUSTIN MACAULEY PUBLISHERS™

LONDON * CAMBRIDGE * NEW YORK * SHARJAH

A CIP catalogue record for this title is available from the British Library.

ISBN 9781528937979 (Paperback)
ISBN 9781528937986 (Hardback)
ISBN 9781528969352 (ePub e-book)

www.austinmacauley.com

First Published (2020)
Austin Macauley Publishers Ltd
25 Canada Square
Canary Wharf
London
E14 5LQ

My special thanks to Lesley Young & Ann Austin.

Preface

BORO boy growing up in MIDDLESBROUGH CLEVELAND 21 Bell Street. Born to my father, William RENNISON, also my mother, Flora RENNISON. My father was a bricklayer and a good one at that. My mother was a housewife plus a breeder of good children as they were in those days. As there was nothing else to do, after the war had just finished as I came along and I was told I was born under the stairs just like my brother Norman before me. My father had been demoted from the army as he was in the home guards across the River Tees as it was an army camp and was on the big guns there, the big guns guarded the steel works on the River Tees. I was told later on in life dad could not go in the regular army because he had chest problems. I was born under the stairs I was told as the second world war ended Kathie was out of the pram and started to walk as I got in it there was only Norman and I left in it Kathie sat on front then Norman started to walk that is only when I had the pram to myself for fifteen months as Norman had finished with it, as Norman was two years older than me, then Paul came along, in 1947, he was a noisy brat and was all ways kicking me in the back as he was put behind me in the pram. I was glad when I was two and started to walk. I had two brothers plus two sisters at that time. There was Iren, Ronnie, Kathy and Norman in order. Then there was a problem with Norman as he was not always at home, Mum and Dad would go out after tea as I grow up I learned what was going on Norman was in hospital, I was told Norman was not coming back home again and died with T B after a three months stay in hospital. Then One day there was a lot of people at the house again later on in life it was Normans funeral DATE 1948. Paul followed me fifteen months later as I said we were like a staircase plus more to come .You knew later on in life there was a brother or sister coming as the single bed would come down stairs Mum would ask us for a name if it was a boy or a girl I remember one year when I was six and in the juniors we had picked a name for another brother or sister but when I got home from school Mum had been taken to hospital and stopped in there for the next few days my older sister Irene stayed at home to look after us till dad got home from work , As I got older I learned mum had lost the baby. The house was only four bedrooms. Large bedroom at the front also a small box room next to it. There was a large back bedroom at the back also a small room next to it which became the bathroom four years later on when the council modernised them in the fifties. The kitchen had a new gas stove put in so my mother could cook on it. The heating was a coal fire with a built in range which Mum used to cook on in the down stairs back room, it was a coal fire were I would crawl in the oven to sleep in the first two years, bath nights were on Sundays night, which was a large tin bath that hung in the shed outside it was brought into the front room in front of the fire there was two cast kettles on the fire all the time to make sure the water was always hot, I learnt over the next year or so get in first because my brother and sister would pee in it. Dad put a big fire guard round fire to keep us away from it. I was glad to get out of the pram also because I finished up with one ear larger than the other were mum would straighten me up by it in the pram. I also got a big penis in later on in life, I was told Mum would lift me out the pram by it. When I was three, I fell down the stairs I caught my foot in a dry milk tin, that was the start of my turned left eye as I would always look left. Later on, in life I tried to get it sorted out. In the garden there was a Andersons air raid shelter we would play in it was used in the war every back garden had one our side of the street there was still sand bags outside the entrance, Mum told me later on in life she had a choice of going outside to the shelter or go under the stairs. Dad eventually took the shelter down and made a lawn where it had been. The front room had a cast fire place with a oven on the side were mum would cook in and the kettle was always on the fire grate for hot water upstairs was also two cast fire places in the front and back bedrooms as the coal went down in the coal house my dad would mix cement in the coal dust to make bricks in a wooden shutter on the yard floor he got the Portland cement from work. I would help him later on in life. They burnt great on the fire. In 1950, there was a sign hung in the back room which said SILENCE IS GOLDEN and you knew about it when dad was at home dad would point to it if we were noisy dad liked peace and quiet when he came home from work and would read the evening Gazette paper witch was torn up in to squares for the toilet paper plus Radio times. Then he would listen to the Bush radio, On Sundays we would listen to uneasy head and the Archers on the Radio, Dad liked the radio before going to the Newport Working men s club, Dad was on the committee at the club for a few years and in the summer the club would pay for its members to go to Redcar for the day out. All members children were given ten shilling note each to spend on the day, so on the Saturday morning Mum would dress us up in our best clothes as usual the clothes were hand me downs so my short trousers had patches in them as they were my brothers Ronnie pants he had grown out of. My boots had plenty of studs in and if Dad could not hear you coming down the path the boots were taken off you and put more studs in that day. The big day was here we all lined up in the street as we had to walk to the station we went down Newport road to the Middlesbrough railway station. IT was two and a half miles to the station when we got on the platform I could see our neighbours the Rook crofts were going as well as their dad was a member of the club also, so we loaded up like cattle in to one of the carriage. We went past the steel works there was black smoke everywhere. When we got to Redcar we got off the train and we walked down to the sea front Mum and Dad liked to get a place in the band stand, facing the sea and beach because Mum did not like the sand. Mum could watch us play with our hand me downs bucket and spade in the sand. The four grownups went to the amusements Kathy, Maureen, Ronnie and Andy. I kept Paul amused on the beach, Dad went for a pint with Uncle Charlie, Aunty Rosy stayed at home with Granny Martin. The weather was good to us and that year we all had to be at the station at the same time as I learnt years later the trains were laid on for the club. When I was just over four I had to go to go Archibald Infants school which was at the bottom of the street I remember my first day Mum took me in to school, we went into the class room to meet the Teacher the lady looked down at me and asked what is your name I said William well said the lady would you like to play with the toys first. I said yes as the ones we had at home were broken plus hand me downs, the teacher was a plump lady with an ugly face you could stand her next to the fire place and you would not go near it, the class were mixed with girls as well as boys, I had never seen so many toys to play with tin cars, lead solders and dolls for the girls. After the first day I would go to school with Ronnie or Kathy as they were at the same school Kathy in juniors Ronnie in seniors. Paul followed on a year later worst luck because he was my worst nightmare in years to come, he would pinch a worm out of a blind chicken's mouth you could not leave money down anywhere. At school you got milk once a day when I got into Juniors, I was made milk monitor to look after the milk to classrooms in the mornings.

At home every morning the milkman came with is horse and cart to our house. There was always a rush to get the horseshit up if it shits near our house as it went on Mums roses. Once a week the tea man would come down our street Ring tons and the same again, the pop man came round in an new Bedford petrol lorry Lay cocks was the firms name, Mum would buy four bottles of mixed pop plus one bottle of ginger beer. In the 50 plus early 60s we still had ration books which was still in circulation after the war Ronnie s job was to go to heath shop which was in Linthorp road with the books you brought back was bottles of orange juice plus cod liver oil the taste was horrible plus dried milk in a tin. Every morning we had a line up at the front door for a spoon full of olive oil plus if you could not shit properly you got senna pods seeds to swallow followed by a mouth full of pop before you went to school. You had got to be ready in class as the senna pods worked as you would shit yourself. I moved up classes at school and started to read slowly the times table was hard to learn but got there in the end. Paul came to school to the infants and my nightmares began years with Paul pinching and getting away with it at school till he got found out at home, Kath got half a crown for her birthday she left it down on window sill Paul must have spotted it and took it Dad was told when he came home we had to line up and be searched, Dad went through our pockets and found it in Paul's pocket it had lipstick on it. Dad had a broad belt on his trousers and Paul felt it for days to come. We got the cane in the seniors but in fact you got the slipper on the legs.

The buggy came in to fashion so I asked Dad to build me one which he did out of an old steel pipe it had a slit bend in it Dad put a wooden seat on off a chair plus wheels off an old pram, the steering was a piece of wood with a bolt in the middle on wheels and a peace of rope. I was the pride of the street;

Ronnie and I would race up and down the street as the street was on a steep hill. We would give Paul a go to keep the peace.

Bradley the Butchers was at the bottom of the street as well as the paper shop and Testers the Barbers where Dad would go to get his hair cut, but us three lads had to line up at home Dad would find a bowl to put on your head and cut round it with clippers he had brought it was the fashion at the time. There was also a fruit shop. Mr Bradley the butcher looked after the big family's s in the area you would go in and get two shillings of bones with some meat still on them Mum would boil them up and make a Stew out it the vegetables for the stew came from two rows of potatoes plus greens like cabbages Dad had grown in the garden. We also got pigs trotters in vinegar plus chicken livers, pig's balls and pig's chaps from half a pig's face plus bread pudding and rice pudding with a brown skin on top. So, we did get a good selection of different things. I loved dripping sandwiches on Mondays from the meat on Sundays the jelly was great.

Year 1955

In 1955, I was coming up to TEN YEARS OLD, along came the coronation of the queen and with big street parties there was plenty of food on large tables in the street as everybody had baked cakes plus jelly and custard and lots of lemonade to drink. The radios were on loud in the street so we could hear the coronation from London the food was great the kind you've never seen before we played games all day long. One prize was a metal aeroplane. I ran to the wrong lamppost as I was told to, so I never got the plane I was going to punch the neighbour's lad. The family were called Rush croft they were a big family as well with nine children I think it was a competition with parents. In the street the other neighbours Don Reeve he lived opposite at number 18 Bell Street Don Reeve became a footballer and went on to play for Middlesbrough team. Round the corner of the school lived Brain Clough he also became a footballer my brother Ronnie was in the seniors at that time.

My Uncle Charlie and Aunty Rosy which was my dad's sister lived next door with their children Andy, Maureen and Peter came along the same time as Paul. I think their names coincided with a nursery rhyme the two little black birds Keith came along the same time as my brother Dennis. My uncle Charlie worked at the ICI Wilton; Andy worked with my dad at Hudson brother's builders when he left school as a brickies labourer. Ronnie and Andy went to school together Maureen went to school with my sister Kathy, Uncle Charlie was well in to motorbikes with side car, which aunty Rosy used to ride in the side car. I remember one year going on the back of Uncle Charlie's bike it was a big bike Aunty Rosey went in the side car. I think we went to Middleton in Teesdale to pick blackcurrants to make jam that year. I had to hold on tight on the back of the bike it was good the sun was shining. My Aunty Rosy wanted a piss and got squatted down behind the blackcurrant bushes she pulled down her baggy kickers but she got them caught and yelled to my uncle Charlie to release them. It was the first time I had seen a big hairy pussy and there was laughter all round My aunt Rosy had a red face all the way home. Andy followed with motorbikes as well plus Peter and Keith in years to come. My uncle Charlie he had a new garage put up a bought one, my dad did the concrete floor for him My dad built mine in later years. My brother Ronnie got in to pigeons so my dad built my brothers pigeon loft on the back of the garage. Ronnie had a lot of skims which is northern talk for pigeons. My brother Paul got into pigeons later in life and our neighbour across the back also kept Pigeons, His name was Dave Hewitt so there was a lot of bird shit on the roof as my brother Ronnie got in to racing them

At that time, I lived at home with my sisters Irene, Kathleen, And brothers, Ronnie and Paul. Mum had the belly up again and the bed was coming downstairs Mum gave birth to a lad again the name we picked was Malcolm more mouths to feed more to baby sit and the crying to put up with. When Malcolm finished with the cot it was more smelly feet in bed topped and tailed. Mum liked the family to go to church on Sunday mornings, four of us would go to saint Cuthbert's church in the morning Iren would not go, Mum would give us six pence each to put in the collection box again Paul would hang back but Kathy would watch him but three years on I would put six pence in box and take half a crown out for cigs at school, woodbines or long toms, smoking became popular in the '50s mainly in the toilets so no one would see you.

Christmas 1955 my uncle Harry and aunty Pauline came to see the family he was mother's brother. He brought a second-hand Meccano set which you could build things with he also brought a wooden fort which he had made. Uncle Harry and Aunty Pauline were very posh and lived in the village of Martin outside Middlesbrough. We had to share the toys as it was the only ones we had, 1956 was also the year we got our first radio gram to play 78 records on. Dad brought it at Lloyds radio shop on Newport road. He brought it on chucky a slang word for paying weekly. My dad and I went to visit my aunty Mary she lived at South bank Cleveland we had to go on the bus to North Thorsby then get a trackless bus up to South Bank. The Trackless had overhead lines to run on it had to get the electric to make it work. South bank was a business place as it was a steel works town with black smoke coming out the chimneys the steel works was on the coast. There were five streets of back to back houses approximately sixty in a row. My aunty Mary was another one of my dad's sisters married to my uncle Billy they also had a large family as well. There were kids all over the place you could tell there was plenty of competition in the family, they had a collection of records which were 78's that we got given the name of a couple that we had been given were wheel of fortune and Connie Frances we listened to these quite a bit, plus others later came out on the 45 records. On a Sunday afternoon me, my Brothers and Sisters had to sit around and listen to a progamme called Education Archery and then we could listen to records after this.

At weekends we would go to the River Tees and play on a rope that was tied underneath the Tees Bridge. We also used to stay on the Tees Bridge when we heard the bell go and the road gates would close the bridge would lift to let a big boat go under the bridge it was a great sensation going to the top with a brim-full view of the river plus Middlesbrough town centre. A girl in my class at school Doreen Hunt's father worked on the Tees Bridge in the control room which lifted the bridge up and down. Doreen and her best mate Margaret Millwall were a couple of snotty nose little girls in the infancy school. but as I grew up the two girls filled out in all the right places and in the senior's school the two girls were good for sex behind the bike shed. In the late fifty's kite flying became popular and lads in the area started to make them, I liked to make kites to fly on the recreation ground near our street bell street where I lived. The Wreck as it called was the name of a large piece of land which had houses on before the war and were bombed out. The land was never built on again just tarmacked over. The kites were made of large sheets of newspaper it was stuck with flour and water made in to a paste and put round the garden canes plus string round the outside of the canes the tailings as we called them were made with a long piece of string with cardboard folded up in six inch length and six inches apart going on the size of the kite. You had to get the wind right to make them fly, we had competitions to see whose kite could stay up the longest in the clouds it was good fun.

Dad loved a pint of beer at the Newport working men's club he would go after tea and after reading the local paper, the club was ten minutes walk from home uncle Charlie would go if he was on the right shift. Mum liked a bottle of Mackesons stout most nights. Dad would take the empty bottles back on Wednesday night as there was money back on them. Dad had a friend at club called Sandy he worked on the railways as a fireman he was second man on the loco and he got me in to train spotting with a school pal of mine called George Smith piggy was his school nickname. We bought I spy books and we would go down the side of the Tees bridge to the main railway before the river, sit on the fence and write down the numbers that were on the side of trains. Dad's friend Sandy asked if we would like to meet him after work and show us round the train sheds George and I were over the moon and said yes , the next night after school we both went towards Stockton as the Engines sheds were there Sandy met us and took us round , there was a big turn table where the trains turn round on to go in different parts of the sheds we had a good hour walking around. We were the envy of the class when we told them. A couple of times we got the train with Brother Ronnie to Darlington Station got a platform ticket and wrote train numbers down of trains which were on main line Scotland to London.

On Saturdays I would look after cars in the street as it was a football match on if they were playing at home It was held at Ayresome park football ground, people would park in our street as it was near to the ground we would ask people going to the match if we could mind there car as the match came out people came back to their cars I would ask for two shillings but if they won I would get half a crown for looking after the car pocket money was always wanted as money was short we never got pocket money, my parents could not afford it with a big family to support. My brother Paul was a year younger than me and you did not put any money down where he was. He was like a magpie as far as money concerned plus if I skipped School, he would grass on me. I brought my first bike with my money from the cars I made on Saturdays. I had to go on my bike to collect bottles of orange juice plus national dried milk in tins on Tuesday night after school and for this you had to use the ration book.

I had a school pal called Dennis Manual his parents were well to do as his mother was a Sister at the local Hospital she was German very hard faced and she never smiled his dad was a British doctor at the same hospital they had moved into the area and he joined me in the late juniors class. Dennis had the first Television I had ever seen in my life. It had a colour picture, you had to put slides in the side of the TV you could put two in at a time to make the colour. Dennis also had a bicycle so on light nights we would go for rides out down beside the river. As I was coming to eleven years old, I joined the scouts as a lady in next street used to run it. Dennis joined as well, it was great and we went to our first camp in the Yorkshire dales. My dad provided the lorry from work the drivers name was Joe and the lorry was a Bedford petrol and we loaded it up from the hall as it was used for the Scouts movement in Newport road. The old scouts went in the lorry and we had to go by train to Castleford then walk three miles to the camp. I was told off during the walk for calling Dennis Manual the arcade lady said his name is Dennis and that is what I should call him as it was his first name and what should be used .The tents were up when we got there so the first job was to settle in the tents as the ground sheets were down and you had army blankets to cover you but after the first night you left your clothes on as the blankets were itchy, the grub was next then we sat round camp fire to sing songs before we turn in. The next day there was sports plus jobs to do, I got a job to help the cook and had to peel spuds. There was another group in the next field they were from Derbyshire a mixed group girl guides and scouts and we had to go and meet them. I was not interested in the Scouts just the Girl Guides the girls looked good and were filling out in all the right places, made the mind boggle. The camp lasted four days and we came home on the Friday as it was School holidays and we were back to school on the Monday. When I went back to School I was moved up into the seniors.

I up graded my buggy from wood to make a buggy out of a steel pipe and four pram wheels with an old chair seat on it. I fitted a lever on as a brake. I was the pride of the street Dennis and I would play and take turns each pushing one another.

I heard there was a job on a paper round at a news agents ten minutes away so I got on my bike after school the lady in the shop asked if I could get up early in the mornings to do the paper round as the shop was in Albert road it was the other side of the general hospital it was 15 minutes ride on the bike. I also had a round after school, the mornings were still light but as the night closed in it was dark in the mornings and the same at night, so I had to get some lights on my bike. I fitted a battery light back and front. The paper round was on a long one Hartington road plus Cambridge road. In 1956, my first

Christmas on the paper round, it was cold in the mornings, the pay was six shillings per week ten shillings if I did extras rounds. I got to know the people on the round as the last paper lad did not deliver in the mornings and that is when people want their papers before they go to work. Christmas was good with tips my money growing in the post office. In spring of that year On Saturdays morning after the paper round we would get on our bikes and go for a ride over the Newport bridge we would take our swimming trunks rig a rope up from the railing, we would swing on it and then let go dropping straight into the river We had many a good day playing at the river instead of going to school. Mum knew I had been in the river as I stunk to high heaven.

The School Bobby would not think of looking for us but my Brother was a grass and if I belted him he would tell my mother then Mother would tell my dad and I would get belted with the big wide belt my dad wore. My dad liked a pint of beer at Newport Working Men's Club and even when I left home at fifteen things did not alter. My dad was on the committee in the early years. The club looked after the members with family's where we would go to parties at Christmas and see Santa Claus. The parties were held at the town hall in Middlesbrough the food was good and you had to line up to get your stocking from Father Christmas we got fruit plus a toy. As I mentioned earlier My parents had a three-bedroom house our back bedroom had two large double beds in we were three in the bed with another Baby Brother or Sister on the way. You knew when there was another coming along as the spare single bed came downstairs out of the attic. Over the next four years Margaret came along, when Margaret was finished with the cot she had to go in Kath's room as Kath and Margaret had the box room. Kath was always moaning about Margaret as she was always peeing the bed. My sister Iren moved in with my mother's mum Nanny Readman. She lived downtown Middlesbrough and as Iren had to go to special school as she was deaf and dumb it was easier from Nanny Readman's and then there was also enough room for Margaret in the box room.

On Wednesday we always had the bones from the butchers down the street. The bones order was getting more week by week still had a bit of meat left on them the butcher used to look after the big families in the street. Mum put them into a stew with vegetables out of the garden at the back of the house the sweet was nearly always bread pudding with raisins in or rice pudding to follow. On Sunday was a big day as it was Church first then for dinner we would pull the leaves out on the table so we all could get round the dinner table it was like a party every Sunday in our house. The dinner started with Yorkshire puddings with gravy then the dinner which was meat with vegetables then we had jelly and custard plus homemade bread. My mother always baked on Fridays. I loved the bread and dripping on a Monday and Tuesday dinner times it was from the fat out of the meat from Sunday's dinner. Mondays was always wash day my Brother and Sisters had to fold the washing after school. My mum had a big mangle and a gas pot tub and a scrubbing board to wash with.

My dad's mother lived with his sister which was my aunty Rosy who lived next door. I would go to the shops for her at the bottom of the street she would lift her dress up and put her hand down her knickers and take out her purse and gave me money for the shop. I would get six pence for running the errand. On Thursday nights Dad came from work with his wages then Mum had to go to the Co-op stores which were on West lane at the top of the road from the house it was ten minutes walk. My Sister Kathy and I had to go shopping to carry the bags of food home.

Year 1956

I went from juniors to senior class where I met some lads from Cannon Street School which we called Fox Heads. They were Rough & Ready The Fox Head was in cannon street the road was as long as Newport road and both streets went into Middlesbrough town centre there was always big battles with Fox Heads that divided cannon street especially coming up to November with bonfire night. The Fox Heads wanted to steal it there was some spare land as there was houses on before the war and it was now still empty the fair came twice a year the council put a concrete wall for the local children to play football and ball games up against and the local lads like Robo and I and the gang had a big bonfire on 5 November. I remember in later life (May 2014) I was working in Swanage on a seafront development and got a visitor pass in to the local conservatives club and could not believe it when I was to meet up with Steve who was also a smoggy from Middlesbrough like me and Steve was born at the bottom of Cannon street and was in the Fox Heads gang at the same time as me. Steve was two years older than me we had a great time reminiscing about other boys we both knew even thou we had not been to the same School because we were in the same gang we knew the same gang of boys and just talked about what had happened to them all Dave Rob, Porky Pounds, Ron Ward. Dave Robs who came from a one parent family. His dad died when he was young and his mother went to work in a factory to keep him and his two Sisters and his Brother. Dave became a great pal plus the other two lads. I saw life as it really was.

Ron Ward's family was separated. His dad ran a corner shop. It was just off canon street the girls we knocked about with were called Jenny Goldthorpe, Ann Hall who I would walk home at night as she lived in Acklam which was a good hour walk plus Pamela Davison. Pam became David robs girlfriend. I remember Jenny Goldthorpe getting pregnant with a lad out of the street but she did not let on she could not afford a pram, so she kept the Baby in a drawer in the front room. My first girl I had crush on was called Mavis Wright I got my sex experience up against the toilet wall behind the bike shed it was then called a knee trembler and I never looked back with my sex life. We were always talking to the girls at dinner time we became very good friends Dave Plunder's Porky to us as he had chubby cheeks Porky's family worked in shipyards. He was also from a big family just off Canon Street.

15

Over the next four years, we became very good friends. As I moved on to the senior class, Robs and I started building bikes and selling to the lads at school. I got in good with the teachers as I would repair their bikes and it was good to get out of lessons. The music teacher, Mr Gilligan, had a rally bike that he rode to school on. I would let down the tyres and get the chain off and it got me out of music lessons. The cane was used on a regular basis at School as we always knew how to play hooky. We would go over the Tees Bridge and make a camp to rest in. We had wanking competitions in our camp and it was the first one to come three times that won. A good place to hide in was the old army camp.

One day, we were coming back from the army camp and as we walked down the road, a car stopped, the driver opened the window to talk to us. There were only the two of us Robs and I the driver asked if we wanted a lift. We said yes and set off back over the Tees Bridge. We told the driver to stop at the end of the bridge which he did. Before letting us out the driver showed us photos of naked boys and asked if we would like to have our photos taken the next day. I looked at Robs and he looked for the door handle but there wasn't one. Robs and I agreed that we just needed to get out of the car so agreed. The driver asked what time and we both said the same time as now as we were very nervous. The driver got out and walked around to open the door and we got out. As the driver got back in, we ran down the road as fast as we could to get clear of him. We looked back to see whether he was following us. We said to each other that we had a narrow escape and how stupid we had been to get in the car.

The next day, we did not tell anybody at school about our experience as we would be in trouble for missing school. It would be the cane again. We had to hide the cane, so we went to the classroom early to look for a good hiding place. I hid the cane on the top of the doorframe and as you entered the classroom, the teacher could not see the cane. The teacher called out our names and told us to go to the front of the class. He asked us where we had been the day before as we had no note from our parents for the day off. Mr Robertson was not a bad bloke and he turned out good in the next couple of years. He looked for the cane at the front of the blackboard where it was usually kept and asked the class if they had seen it. Dave and I turned around and looked at the Class but nobody said anything, so the caning was delayed for a while. The cane was there for months.

Once a month, we had a woman to look at our hair for nits. Nora was her name. One day, I was in the queue to get my head looked at. When it was my turn, I stood in front of her; I was at the height of her waist. My penis came up and rubbed against her leg. The woman screamed at the top her voice and told me to go and stand in the corner and control it. It was the talk of the school before the day was out.

There was a lad at school called Jimmy Tate and his brother, Spud. They were both in the Senior Class. Jimmy had left school at the same time as my brother Ronnie. Spud was still at school and would hang out with us some nights. Spud was not all the full shilling and was slow on the uptake but his heart was in the right place. When he left school, the only job he could get was outside a shop in town with a broad back and front and walking up and down on the pavement. We would pull his leg at night when we met him. Then one day, we met up with him at teatime on the corner of the street. He had a big smile on his face as he had a pocket full of money. At first, he would not tell us where he got it from. By the end of the night, he told us. He had stolen the money. There were four of us and Spud said that we would all go to Redcar on the train and play in the amusements. So, we went downtown to the railway station and boarded the train to Redcar. We got off at the sea front to play in the amusements. Spud gave each of us five pounds to play with. It was a good night as we had fish and chips to finish the night off, then back on the train to Middlesbrough for home. The next day at teatime, we heard that Spud had been locked up at the police station as Spud had left his glove in a safe with his name inside the glove, but he did not grass on us.

As television was taking off and was cheaper than before, my dad went to the Lloyd's shop where we had brought the radiogram. Dad bought a TV; it was an eco-model and black and white. The family would sit around and watch. Saturday was the big night as the six five specials was on this was a Rock n Roll music show called this because it was shown five past six every Saturday evening. With all the 1960s' pop groups, it was a great programme. Dad would love to watch the BBC News.

In the early '60s, there was a murder in the carpet shop on Newport Road. It was just down from the Newport hotel. It was a Chinese man who had been murdered. There was a lot about it in the papers at that time. I never knew if anybody got caught or charged of the Murder as I moved on over the years to come and never heard.

1957: Duke House Wood

That year, I went to the Duke House Wood camp at Hexham, Northumberland. The school holiday camp came up and we had to pay so we asked our parents. My dad said I could go but Mum was reluctant to let me go because of the cost. I said I would use my paper round money or my car-watching money. The cost was five pounds for the week. My mates from Fox Heads plus Cannon Street could not afford it so I had to go with Dennis Manual as his parents were well to do so could afford it. On the day we left, I had an old suitcase that my dad had found in the attic of a house he was working on. It was big and clumsy. On Saturday morning we had to line up to get on the bus, Girls on one side and Boys on the other. Two of our teachers were going with us: Mr Robert, the PE teacher and Mr Taylor, our history teacher. Mr Taylor was a sergeant major in Buma before he took up teaching and he was a good crack. He would talk about when he was in Japan. The girls had their own two teachers to go with them.

The bus stopped at the café for dinner and so we could have a piss. Dennis and I sat next to each other on the bus. When we got to the camp, it was late in the afternoon. We got off the bus and lined up to go to the wooden huts dormitories as they were called. We were allocated a bed, which was already made. Then we were told to line up again to go to the dining hall for tea. It was a big wooden hut at the back of the camp. We had sandwiches for tea. Then we had to go to a hall where we were asked about what we would like to join in activities like canoeing, football, cricket or country walks. I put my name in for country walks and canoeing as I was not much into sports but I liked boxing. It was early for bed and everybody was ribbing each other about snoring and farting. It was a long night as it was strange to sleep in a bed that was on your own. I was used to four in a bed.

In the morning, we again lined up in the dining hall for breakfast. It was the first time that I had seen breakfast like that. We had to say grace before we could eat. I was glad when the Amen came as I was very hungry. After that, we went outside and were split up for the day's activities. Dennis and I were in the line for canoeing, which I thought was great. We had to put on lifejackets and then we were taken to the river. We stood and watched as one of the teachers demonstrated how to use the paddle with side-to-side motions to control the boat. Then it was my turn. They pushed me in and you got into a bit of a flow, so it was easy to control. With the instructor at our side in another canoe, we went about half a mile, then we had to turn around, which was hard to do with the flow of the water rushing against us but we all managed to get back to the bank. Then it was dinnertime. The others would have a go after dinner, the instructor said. The dinner was good with a choice of meals, then it was back to the river to watch the others have a go. It was a pleasant afternoon.

We changed for tea with a shower. I had never had one before. We were all in together and I got a lot of looks from the other lads as I was well-hung. Some of the lads were still virgins whereas I had been 13 years old when I lost my virginity. I was hoping to screw some more girls on this camp as there were plenty to go at. We had tea and then went into the games room to play darts and snooker. The girls joined us with their teachers and Robs, as we called Mr Robert, was with us. Some of the girls were a bit chunky. The teachers asked us if we would like to join in a singing competition. My school versus the other school. I put my hand up and my name was added to the sheet. There was going be practice on Wednesday night after tea in the hall. I looked across the room and noticed two girls looking across. *Well*, I thought, *that's a good start.* One was a little fat but I was not very fussy. I plucked up the courage and walked across. I said my name was Billy. One girl was Ann and the other was called Jean. I asked what school they came from and Ann said it was Gates Head for girls. You could tell by their voices that they were Geordies. Ann asked if I was in the singing competition and I said yes. The song was *Rock a bye baby* a lullaby adapted and sung by *The Fortunes.* The rehearsals were this evening in the hall and the girls said that they will have a go. The girls turned and looked at Dennis and told him to have a go as well. The look on his face said it all but he came to back me up. We all went across to the hall with the Girls on one side and Boys on the other. The names were read out and when my name was called, I went on the stage beside the piano. The teacher was an old hag in glasses. I told her what I was going to sing and she looked for some music to match. She could play so I did my bit and got a round of applause, which made me feel good. Dennis said that I was good. The girls' turn was next. Ann was good and Jean packed it in halfway through. We said goodnight to the girls because it was bedtime. On Wednesday morning, we were up and out and after breakfast, we had to line up as it was sports for some and country walks with a packed lunch for the others. The names were called out and I noticed that the two girls were also on the country walks. It was a good time to get to know them as Dennis was too slow at coming forward. Before we set off, we were given a map each to follow. It was the Hadrians Wall that was put up to divide Scotland and England. So off we went.

As we walked along, Dennis and I walked with the girls. Ann gave me her address and I asked her to keep in touch when we left on Saturday. She could not believe the number of brothers and sisters I had as she had only one brother, Malcolm. There was a café cum hut and it had bench tables outside. We all sat down on them and the teacher came around with the lunch, which was sandwiches and a glass of pop each, then we set off again along the side of the wall. Now and again, we would cross from side to side. It was a pleasant day, warm for midsummer. We followed a path away from the wall into the woodland and the teacher kept stopping us to tell us about the birds and bees that we could see, but the only bird I was thinking of was having sex with Ann. I know Dennis was thinking the same with Jean. When we got back to camp, we had to wash for tea, then into the games room to sit around and talk. The teachers were there to keep an eye on all of us. I told Ann to come for a walk and off we went, leaving Jean with Dennis as Jean was into the German language and Dennis's mother was German. Out on the field, we walked to the top corner there were not a lot of Girls or Boys hanging around here. There was a branch on the ground and we sat on it. I put my arm around Ann and as she did not object, I left it there. I knew I was in as I had gotten her address already. Ann said she would like us to be friends for the moment. I just smiled and said OK. We kissed goodnight when the camp bell rung for bedtime. As we were walking back to the hall, there was a crowd of Girls and Boys shouting and screaming. We walked over and in the centre were three boys bullying another boy from our school, so I let go of Ann's hand and stormed in, pushing two of them at the same time. The third was tall and broad and he went for me but he had no luck in landing his punch because the teachers arrived to pull us apart. Robs told me to report to the office so I was marched off. I told the big lad that he hadn't seen the last of it. In the office, I wondered whether I would be sent home or receive a good caning, which I was used to. Robs asked me what had happened and I told him that it was three onto one. Robs asked me if I would like to see the big lad in the ring and I said, "Yes sir.". He told me that he would meet me in the gym for some practice tomorrow. I went back to my dorm and a boy asked me what had happened. I told them that it was going to be a boxing match tomorrow afternoon. Dennis said, "You will kick him." He was the school bully from the Girls' school. The next day, I spotted the lad in the canteen during breakfast with big smiles on his face as he had his friends around him. I thought, *It won't be long before I knock the smile off your face.*

At dinnertime, I did not eat anything as I did not want to box on a full stomach. I went to the gym to practice on a bean bag, which was hung in the corner. Mr Roberts came in to watch. He said, "Rennison, do not let the School down." He had laid a bet on me. I turned and smiled. After the warmup, the gym started to fill up with Girls and Boys from both Schools. I went to change out of my patchy trousers into some shorts. I found the gloves very hard but I found a pair that fit me good. It was time to get into the ring. Robs fastened my gloves up. Robs was the referee. The smiling bully entered the ring to applause from his mates. Robs got us to the centre of the ring and said that it was three rounds for five minutes each. Robs made us shake hands and warned us, "No hitting below the belt." I nodded and went back to my corner to wait for the bell to ring. The bell rang and out I came with my left hand up. The bully came at me with both hands; I just put my guard up to protect myself. A couple of blows slid off my gloves onto the side of my head, but I could see that he was tiring. The bell rang after three minutes and I went to my corner and sat down. I stared across at the bully and I could see that he was being told to keep it up. The bell rang again and out I came. The bully was at it again but he was laughing as he thought he had me. I threw a right in-between his gloves and it landed under his chin and down he went like a bag of shit. Robs started the countdown but the bully was crying like a baby and holding his jaw. Robs counted him out to the cheers of the girls from the school. Robs held my arm up as the winner. I went to change; my head was sore but the bully had to go to the hospital. His jaw was wired up as he lost two teeth and was kept overnight. I was the envy of the Girls' school as well as my own school. I was the talk on the field that night but I had other things on my mind, like getting to know Ann a bit better in the woods, but too many people were watching me now. We had to go to the hall for the singing contest. Both schools were taking part. There were some good singers. Halfway through it was my turn; I was the boxer of the year and got a good applause. It was a good evening and Ann had a smile on her face. It was going to be our last night on camp as we were going home tomorrow. I managed to get a kiss on the field before we were told to make our way to the dormitory. The side of my head was still sore. Next morning, after breakfast in the canteen, we had to assemble in the hall and the teachers dished out prizes for the school. There was one for football, one for cricket and one for canoeing. I got one for my boxing with my name on. I caught hold of Ann and got the number of the telephone box at the end of her road and fixed up to call her on Sunday night at 7 o'clock. We parted with a kiss and then Dennis and I got on the bus to go home. We stopped on the A1 Road Café for food and a drink; we got home on Friday night. My dad had fed the pigs for the week and life went on. I went to the phone on Sunday night to ring Ann but after half an hour, gave up so that was the end of that.

My brother, Ronnie, left school and got a job working for the local Gazette newspaper so I got to go to football matches at Ayesome Park football ground for a whole year! I would park my clients' cars on the street and then dash to the far end of the pitch where the score box was, climb up the steps to the box and look down at the pitch.

Ronnie started to bring in some money to help my parents; so did my Sister, Irene. She got a job in a special factory for the deaf and dumb. This is where my Sister met her future husband, Dennis, who was also deaf. Ronnie joined the TA army on Stockton Road and went on manoeuvres on weekends and was paid for it. He was in it for two years. The lads and I were getting interested in it so Robs, Porky, Ron and myself went to the TA Centre to enrol. We had to pass a medical which we all passed, but I looked left as I had fallen down the stairs and spoiled my left eye. The army doctor said that he could book me into the local hospital, called the infirmary. It was an eye hospital and it would take a couple of weeks to get booked in it. We all learnt to take orders from the officers in charge. We also learnt how to march and use a rifle and we learnt how to clean them and strip them down.

The weeks passed and I got a letter from the hospital to go see the doctor. I went with my mother. It was a Thursday morning at 10:30 am. Mum and I sat in the waiting room and waited until my name was called. I was to read the alphabet on a wall that I did with my right eye. I had to turn my head to see the card on the left side. The Doctor said that I would need an operation to put it right. He would take the eye out, cut the core and shorten it to straighten it up so I could see straight again and it would save me from wearing glasses. Mum and I agreed to it. We went back to the reception to see when I could have it done. There was a cancellation for the next week. The doctor gave my mum a letter for the School so that I could have the days off. The thought of being blind for a couple of days frightened me. Anyway, Thursday was here and my mum had bought me new pyjamas to wear in the hospital as my pyjamas were hand-me-downs and a bit raggedy. I settled down in the ward to sleep as there was no food since the operation was for the next morning.

The next morning, I was given a needle to make me sleep. The next thing I knew was waking up in bed in the ward. I was blind as there was a bandage around my head. So, for the next three days, I had to just lie there with my spinning head and I hoped that the operation had gone right and I was not blind. On the third day, the doctor came around with a nurse. The doctor told me that he will take the stitches out, so off came the bandages. Everything was a blur. The nurse got the scissors and started to cut the stitches from my eye. I screamed with pain. There were four stitches in my left eye. I was glad when the fourth was out and I could close my eye for a rest. The nurse put a patch over my eye and I was told that I could get out of bed. I went over to a mirror and looked in it. My face was all red as they had put oil on my face to go under the hot light. The next day, I was told by the doctor that I could go home and rest but school was out of the question at the moment. My eye got better in the next couple of weeks and I could see more out of my left eye. I went back to the TA to go on manoeuvres.

Year 1958

When I was 13 years old, I got myself an allotment with my dad. It was at the back of the Greyhound track. My dad was into growing vegetables for the family. I got my first pig, Recline (runt of the litter), for half a crown and kept it in a box in the shed and would warm it up in front of the fire. I had to feed it from a bottle with milk. That's what started my interest in pigs. Robs and I became friends with a man called Ronnie Ward; he also had pigs. We would go on rounds to collect his swill; Robs' girlfriend's mother had pigs as well. Her brother, Peter, looked after them. I got hold of an old bike that had been an ice cream bike. It had solid rubber wheels.

I would collect swill from the local fish shops, fruit and vet shops and Woolworth and I would collect the milk from the Northern Dairies Depot in churns. My dad started to build my pigsty with old bricks that I could find. We also got a few chickens so that we could have some eggs as money was short. Dad brought home timber plus old wooden doors in the lorry from work.

I started to go to markets with Ronnie Ward and see how the pigs were sold. I would also help out on the cattle lorries loading up and delivering. This was the start of my farming days as I got to know farmers when they came to the market. I was asked to help out in the summer. I would help the farmers with the harvest. I would catch a bus early in the morning to Stockton, then get another to Carthorne village. I would feed the pig before I would go and, in the winter, I would help with threshing. I always got the job of cutting the stalks on the top of the machine as they went past you—cutting the string and feeding it into the threshing machine. I learnt how to drive a tractor and plough the land. It was hard at first to drive in a straight line and set the plough as you drove but practice makes perfect; I was getting complimented on it as the soil was turned over evenly.

I was hooked onto farming and loved going to the young farmers' club at Stokesley, Cleveland. I met a couple of lads out of the village. Their names were Martin and Lou Reilley, Lou worked on his parents' farm on Stokesley Road; it was a mixed farm with milking cows and arable. Lou and I became good friends and would meet at the pub in the village where I helped out on the farm in the holidays. I would get my dad to feed the pigs when the swill was already boiled the day before. Tuesday nights at the pub were darts and dominos nights. The village Men and Women attended to play the games at the pub. The toilets were outside and they were not flush toilets but a dry pan under the seat. At the back of the toilets was a flap to lift to get the pan out and put ashes in. When we knew that a lady came out of the pub to go to the toilet, we would go around the back and lift the flap and when the lady sat down on the seat, we would put stinging nettles on their backside and run around the farm to hide. The landlord—my boss—Redvis, was always looking for the lads in the village to blame.

22

As my pig was growing, I had to take it to a boar pig to get it serviced. A friend I met had saddleback pigs that had black patches on them. If she fell pregnant, as luckily, she did, my friend would have the pick of the litter, so it cost you nothing to breed. I had six piglets in my first litter. I had to boil more swill with more mouths to feed.

As I was getting older, I traded in my box bike (an old ice cream bike with solid rubber tyres) for a horse and cart. As it was a shared arrangement with a man called Lawrence—Lol for short—he became a good friend. Lol worked for the Middlesbrough Council refuse tip that was along the River Tees. As the bike was hard work with more mouths to feed, I would collect the swill in the cart and friends would sort out the hay to feed the horses, which were 14 hands high. There was plenty of horseshit for Mum's roses and vegetables. I liked riding around town on the cart but not on wet days. I felt like *Steptoe and son* of the TV but it was great to be noticed as you drove around town. Some Saturday mornings, I would feed the pigs early to go to the elite picture house on Ling Thorpe Road. Pictures like *Dick Barton*, *Roy Rogers* and *Tonto* were good to watch for six pennies when I had the time.

For the last three years of school I did not really go much as I had a lot of work. The school bobby was always looking for me but my mum and dad knew that I was out working. I was busy with the pigs and markets—Darlington on Mondays every other week and Stockton on Tuesdays once a month. The pigs were growing and multiplying and money was coming in and I could pay my way at home. There was also plenty of pork which was good. Dad built more pigsties as more pigs came along. The days were long with light nights but soon I had to decide what to do in life as Mum had a bun in the oven again so it was not going to be long before the bed would be coming down again.

When I was fifteen years old, the time came to leave School and find a job. It was September 1960. I tried a couple of farms but they only needed extra hands at busy times so my brother suggested that I should try to get work at the bridgebuilding yard at Dorman Long's Steelworks as a platers mate. Ronnie had a job there as he had left the Evening Gazette and worked as a crane driver at Dorman Long's Steelworks. I got the job as one of Dad's clubmates, Stan, was the head crane driver. Stan drove a big overhead outside in the big yard; he would load bridge sections onto railway trucks and lorries.

I started doing this job, it was an early start so I would feed the pigs at around 5 am and then cycle to work for a 7.30 start. I would work until 4 pm, then I would cycle home to feed the pigs and clean them out before it became too dark.

I went to the Young Farmer's club on some Tuesday nights and one night, I met a girl called Mavis. She would look after pigs for her dad and she lived on a small holding in Billingham just across the River Tees. Mavis's dad got stale milk and rolled oats to feed the pigs with. When I got the bus from the Tees Bridge to Billingham to visit Mavis at night, we would finish up in the pigsty making love over a bale of straw. Mavis was a good shag but I knew our relationship would not last as Mavis was a home bird. I started to think about getting out of the pigs' game as swine flu was getting around the markets locally and I had to get out fast or lose a lot. Over the next few months, I started to sell out at the markets. The price of pork was going down as swine flu took over and the Ministry started to come around the allotments.

In 1960, I got a job on a farm at Crathorne where I had helped out in the past. The landlord was Redvis Bolton and his wife, Hellon. I knew the lads in the village and the landlord at the pub as well. I lived there as it was good to live away from home since there was another baby coming along; it was a lad called Dennis. I had happy times on the farm; it taught me a lot for further life. My duties on the farm were getting up early to milk cows—10 in all—as the milk had to be filtered through a cooler and then into the churns and the lorry came at 9 o'clock to pick up the milk. The pigs were next but they were not fed swill as I used to; they were given meal and rolled oats. Then we had five bullocks to feed; they were kept for the market. The boss and I would set up beer barrels and taps in the pub, ready to pull off to drink. My sex life was good as a girl in the village was always there for a good shag. From the Young Farmer's club, not many townies got the chances that I got in life.

Christmas in 1962 was coming up and it was the first year away from home. The Landlady got the decorations out to put up in the pub. The nights were dark and the cows were let out in the yard after we had milked them. We cleaned them out, then bedded them down for the night—it was another of my daily duties in the winter. The food was good on the farm as the farmer's wife could cook; she made lovely large Yorkshire puddings with mince and onion gravy. The parties in the pub with the locals of the village were good. I went shopping in Stockton High Street for Mum and Dad's presents and then went on to deliver them. Dad was not very well as his chest was playing up again. Mum gave me the same old present—socks. My brother, Paul, was still at home and well into pigeons but had no job. Malcolm was growing up and carried on with the allotment and chickens and he also had a dog Rip. On my long weekend, I would go home and meet up with the lads. Dave Robs got a job as a Refuse Collector for the local council and his love life was good with Pam. Ron Ward was now Accounting. Dave Ponder was going his own way with one of the girls when we were at school—Ann Hall.

I started to go out with two lads from another school. They had moved from the Cannon Street area to the Brambles farm estate. They were named John and Joe Teeny; they were twin brothers, with John as the older one by two minutes. We became good friends and started to go to pubs in the town and listen to good bands as '60s' music was the best. On Saturday nights, we would meet up and set off on the train from Middlesbrough to Redcar as the Coatham Hotel was the place to be on Saturday night. There was plenty of fanny to chat up but you had to get the bus back at midnight or it was a long walk or hitch a lift home.

Over the next few months, I got a chance at getting my own car; it was a Morris Minor. I got two *L* plates put—one at the back and one at the front. I got it taxed and tested plus insurance. I put in for driving lessons with a man on the next road. He picked me one night a week as I had the cash. The man's name was Mr Tom Bell. I also got my licence for the post office. I passed my second test over the next two months. One Saturday, I picked up John, Joe and Dave to take them to the Coatham dance at Redcar. We agreed that I would drive but no drinking. We called in at the Bramble Farm hotel for a pint on the way. We parked in the car park and when we came out, a lorry with steel pulled in. As we were about to leave, a Policeman came into the car park, put his bicycle against the lorry trailer and came over to talk to us. I told the policeman that I was not drinking. Just then, the lorry started up and pulled out but the Policeman's bicycle was leaning against the trailer. It fell and the back wheels of the trailer ran over the bicycle and flattened it. The boys were laughing and the Policeman said that as it made our night, he let us go. We parked and went in to the dance.

By the end of the evening, John and Dave had pulled two birds and were going on the bus home as the birds lived near the boys. Joe and I scored with a mother and daughter who lived in Easton, which was on our way home. The mother's name was Helen and the daughter was called Shelley. We set off and Helen showed us the way. We got to the house and Joe and I went to different bedrooms. The sex was good as Helen was very experienced in bed. It was a good thing that it was Sunday and there was no rush to get up early. I put my hand on her pussy again and it was still purring so I got back on top and shagged away. I was knackered and sore when we got dressed and had a mouth like a shithouse. The kettle was on when we got downstairs and a cup of tea went down well.

I dropped Joe off at home and then called at my parents' house to see if they were all right. Dad asked whether I was coming to the club with him. I said that I had to get back to the farm. Then I drove to the farm at Crathorne. I got back early so I changed to feed and do the milking; it gave the boss a break as he had company for the weekend. The next day—Monday—he said that we would go for a ride as his father also had a pub. His father was in his seventies. The pub was at High Kilburn on the edge of the North Yorkshire moors, which was called Hamilton hills. So, we set off in the boss' Morris Minor Traveller that he had just bought in exchange for his Hillman Husky. It was a good day for a day out. When we got to the pub, I met his dad. He was a nice old chap, ready for his retirement. At the top of the Hamilton Hills, there was a horse carved out of the hill that the boss' Dad looked after every year. It was white and was whitewashed every year. You could see the horse for miles around. I enjoyed a ploughman's lunch plus a pint. Then it was back to the farm. We had to milk and feed the animals. The weather was good as we waited for the corn to be cut. The next day, after milking and breakfast, the boss told me to get the binder out and service it. He showed me the grease points on it. The boss told me that there was a lorry coming for the David Brown as he had traded in the David Brown crop master petrol for a T20 Ferguson petrol TVO. The David Brown would not start and we had to get the Blacksmith across to start it. We were losing the daylight. We also had a Fordson Major that was petrol TVO 27

N. The days were long and dusty with cutting, stocking, leading in and making corn stalks. I was getting itchy feet and was ready to move on but I would see the harvest in before I would look around.

My seventeenth birthday was coming up in September 1962. When things started to cool down, I thought that I would move on. I looked in the farmers' weekly magazine and there was a job for a farm labourer plus tractor driver with experience, which I had two years of. I rang up about the job and got an interview. The farm was at Great Broughton, which was a village under the North Yorkshire moors. The farmer's name was Edwin Bainbridge. I turned up to see the job and take a look around. The farmer was a Fordson Major man as the tractors were not very old. The farm was a thousand acres. The farmer's wife was Irish and was called Katherine—Kath for short. They had two children—John and Anna. John was away at college and the girl was still at school and was a spoilt brat. I went back to the farm at Crathorne as the farmer had someone else to see and was to ring in a week's time.

All week I thought about the move as the job was to live in the big house plus a bit more money. I met up with Lou at the Young Farmers' club as it was the Hutton Rugby show that weekend. Lou and I were there in a contest with other clubs to drive a tractor with a four-wheel trailer at the back. You had to reverse with a milk churn full of water and you had to go over obstacles. If you spilt the water, you would get penalty points against you. I was not too bad but Lou won for the club as he had been practicing a lot on his farm.

The weekend arrived and I had to ring up about the job. The wife answered the phone and told me that I had got the job. I told her that I was pleased but I had to put in a week's notice. On Sunday, I told Redvis that I was leaving. He was very understanding and wished me luck with my life. I went across to the Blacksmith's shop to say goodbye. The blacksmith's name was Erine Hallsop and he was a good engineer plus he was good with shoeing horses. As the week came to an end, I said my goodbyes and drove to Great Broughton to the farm. I settled in and got to know my duties as there was not just corn but this farm had a combine too. It was a Massey Harris plus a Bedford lorry to lead off to the corn bins. It was all new for me to learn, which I enjoyed. After a week, I settled into a new way of life. I felt proud to drive new and big tractors like Fordson Major and Ford Dexter. We also had an old Case hand clutch. At night, I was on my own in the kitchen, so I bought myself a small radio to listen to. The top ten was good to listen to on Sunday nights. My favourite song at that time was *Tell Star*, which was number one that year.

When the work died down to normal, it was great to plough with a new tractor and new machinery to sow wheat with the weather still dry. The days were getting dark early. I would drive down to the end of the road and then walk to the pub in the village. The first pub was called the White Hart Hotel and it was owned by the Cameron's pub ales franchise. The next was a free house pub called the Coach and Horses and was run by a father and daughter family, who were good to talk to. Over the next few weeks, I got on well with the locals and even got in the dominos school, here we played five and three games and it cost a penny a spot. On Sunday afternoons, four of the locals were long-distance lorry Drivers who worked for a local haulage firm. The firm was called Arthur Sanderson's and they would run local jobs as well as long-distance with steel from Dorman Long's Steelworks to Cardiff in Wales. One night on my long weekend in the winter of 1963, I went with one of them called Bob. We became good friends and it was a good two days out and an experience. It was coming up to Christmas and most of the ploughing was done and the winter wheat was in. I got the job of cutting the edges by hand and the tool to cut the edge was called a bill knife. It was a good job to keep you warm on a cold day. I would take a flask with me and a pocket watch to check the time to knock off and do the feeding. One day, I was in the field doing an edge, looked at the time, put the watch back in my pocket, or so I thought. When I went to return the watch to the boss, Edwin, I found that I had lost it and I had to buy another one. In the spring of next year, I went back to the same spot along the edge and—lo and behold! I found the watch at the bottom of the edge. I wound it up and it worked and did not lose a minute, so I kept it. I got on with a local family called Bradley. They had a small holding and bred large rabbits to kill for the butcher. They lived at the end of the village. Brian Bradley was a farm labourer and would help on the farm with me. They were a large family, eight in all. Two of the girls were of my age. I got to take the girls to the dance in Stokesley town hall. Ann was the oldest and Mary was two years younger with no experience in the sack. We had a good Christmas and a good new year as well in the pub. The year was 1964. I called at my parents' house to see whether they were all right and to exchange presents and see my mates, John and Joe, and catch up on the local gossip.

Year 1964

One day, I heard about a job at Thornaby Old Airfield, so I took a ride up there to see what it was. It turned out that they were turning the Airfield into a new Industrial Park.

The plant was so exciting to watch. I got talking to one of the men on the site. He operated a crane that was on tracks called a 19RB. It was crane work to lift the pipes down the trench. The pipes for the drainage system was being installed at the side of the road. The man was Irish and Shaun was his name.

I was so impressed with the machinery that I asked if I could learn to drive it and Shaun agreed to teach me. He showed me how the crane operated and the sort of things that it could lift. He taught me how the controls worked—the levers, main clutch and, perhaps more importantly, the brakes!

There were a lot of grease nipples on the moving parts. These were tools to pump grease into all of the moving parts on the crane to keep everything lubricated. You had to make sure that the wire ropes did not go slack and bird-nest (a construction term for tangle). There was also another 19RB excavator onsite to dig the trench for the pipes to go in.

There was so much to remember and I was really nervous at first but after three Saturdays, I started to get the hang of it. Shaun was really impressed with me; he said, "One day, you'll be good at all this; you're a natural, son."

The bug had gotten hold of me and I started to leave the farming life behind me.

At just over eighteen years old, the novelty of the pig's life had started to wear off and the plant and travel bug kicked in. I had heard all the stories of big money, meeting new people and going to new places. I heard about a job at Richard Wallington Plant Hire who had just opened a yard on Port Rack Lane, Stockton on Tees. The firm had just opened the yard and were looking for men. The plant manager was called Rubin Walter and the second manager was Freddie Higginbottom. In the '60s, you had to start at the bottom of the ladder and work your way up. I applied for a job and got it. I put my notice in on the farm and said my goodbyes. I told Ann that I would keep in touch. I looked around for a new place to live so I went to Stockton as it was near the yard. It was a daunting experience but the men in the yard and onsite made me feel at ease. My first was going out on a Jib Lorry, 40 feet, with jib sections from Coles Cranes. They were coming in new from Sunderland Works where 30 had been made.

This was the start of my travelling life and I left home. It felt good with no sweaty feet in your face when you woke up as our bed had four of us in it. It was good to have a bed to yourself. I would stop at a different place most nights and the lodge money which was around ten shillings per night. It was a good feeling to get away from home and meet more people and have new things to talk about.

One of my first jobs was at the shipyards at Newcastle on Tyne, unloading ships at night with a new 100-tonne Coles mobile crane. The crane driver was Billy Saunders, affectionately known as Big Billy to his mates. He was a huge man, easily twenty stone and 6 feet 3 inches in height with curly black hair and he was strong as a bull.

The second on the team was Lou Riley and I was the gofer of the team, the grease monkey. We had to put a hundred feet of jib in, so we built with a smaller crane. It was a Tailor hydro and the driver's name was Taffe from Cardiff in Wales. We had to wait for the lorry with two lifts on so we would go for a drink in the pub just off the quayside. After a few drinks, we would go back to derig the crane and load jibs back on the lorry. I jumped in with Taffe in the passenger seat and went back to the yard. I had booked the digs already and it was 7 o'clock when I got to the yard. Billy told us to be back at the yard by dinner as we would be paid at double time. The digs were good and so was the food. The digs were just off the high street and we would meet up in the club on Portrack Lane or the Prince of Wales pub across the road. The Landlady was very attractive and when I went in, she was always eyeing me up with a big smile. It would get me thinking of having sex with her.

I got my chance on Wednesday night when the Landlord was on a games night and rang to say that he would be late as the games were taking longer.

There were only two customers and when they went at 10.30, Nelly asked me to give her a hand in the cellar with the barrels. I did not need asking twice so I followed Nelly to the cellar but barrels were not on Nelly's mind. Nelly took me from behind with her arms around my neck and kissed me. It was an experience to have sex over a barrel and it was not a night to forget. Over the next week, every time I went on my own, Nelly served me free beer. When I went home for the weekend, it would be the Blue Post Hotel in Stockton high street. Big Billy and I became good friends as I felt safe with him. We worked well together and I soon became his second man on big jobs at ICI Wilton and Billingham.

Big Billy got into a spot of bother with the police and ended up getting a two-year stretch in prison. When they were trying to arrest him, they had to handcuff him to the railings in the high street and this was not before he had floored a few of them.

Back in the yard in Portrack Stockton, Christmas was coming up. I called around at Mum and Dad's to see whether everything was all right. Dad was poorly with a bad chest and off work as a bricklayer at Hutson brothers at Middlesbrough. Malcolm had started at Prudential insurance at Darlington, Durham. Kathy got a job in a hotel in Caterrick, Durham, off A1 Road. Ronnie was still working at Dorman Long's Steelworks. Dennis and Margaret were still at school. Irene was courting Dennis who was living at Darlington. Mum had bought me socks for Christmas, as usual. I did not know what to get Mum and Dad for Christmas, so I gave them 20 pounds each. I was earning good money as I was on 40 pounds per week. I wished my parents *Merry Christmas* and drove back to Stockton to the digs on Hartington Road. Back at the yard, the boys had lined up a party at the Portrack Lane club. The Boys in the yard were called Tom Beanie, foreman fitter, and Bob Bates. Bob and his wife took over the Rose and Crown pub up the road.

The new year—1965—was approaching. We went back to work on the third of January. I was in the yard in Portrack when a mobile crane came into the yard. It was a Coles 25-tonne from the Liverpool depot. The driver had come to the workshop. He introduced himself as Jerry Sledick and he was going to Billingham ICI to work. He was also looking for digs for a few days. I told him that I would ring up and meet him back in the yard at 6 o'clock that night. I took Jerry to the digs with me. He got himself sorted and then we both went for a couple of pints. I soon found that Jerry was good crack to be with. Jerry had been with the firm for a couple of years and was a union man at heart.

The next day, I had to take a 10-tonne roller out on hire to the local council. I had to scarify the surface of the road with tarmac and a man would walk behind the roller to turn the screw at the back. The hire was only five days a week. On Thursday night, Jerry asked me to take him to Stockton station so that he could go home for the weekend. He would drive back in his own car early on Monday morning as the job was going to be for three or four weeks. I went to the club on Friday night and then across the road to the Prince of Wales pub. Nelly was on her own and had a big smile on her face when I walked in. I stood at the bar so that I could have the crack with Nelly. She told me that her husband would be late and asked if I would stay back and lock up with her. I did not need asking again so when the last costumer had gone, it was down to the cellar for a kneetrembler over the barrels. We had just come up the cellar steps when the landlord opened the back door. Nelly let me out of the front door.

I met up with Jerry again on Monday night after work. He told me that he had a good weekend at home, we really got on well. I was still on hire to the council with the 10-tonne roller for the next couple of weeks. Three weeks later on Thursday night, Jerry said that he was off hire. On Friday night, he was told from the office that the crane had to go back to Liverpool depot that weekend as it had another job. On Monday, Jerry asked me to drive his car down to Liverpool. On Friday night after work, I told the plant manager, Freddy Higgingbottom, who told me that there was a 7-tonne lorry coming back from Liverpool yard and if I would fetch it back to Stockton, I would get paid travelling time plus expenses. I agreed.

Jerry filled the crane up and I filled the car up at the garage. I followed Jerry in the crane to Liverpool as Jerry knew the best way. The journey took three hours. Jerry drove the crane to the yard down on the docks. I look around for the lorry that I was to take back. It was a Ford Thames trader. Jerry and I got in the car and set off for Jerry's home. We were met at the door by his twin Daughters, both with ginger hair. Jerry's home was a bottom flat. We had tea and I washed up and changed. Jerry said that we could walk down to the club as he was on the committee as a consort chairman. In the club, I met Jerry's friends and as it was Saturday night, there was a good group on. On Saturday morning, I was up early and made a cup of tea. I called at the paper shop, got a paper and walked to the park as it was still the end of March. Monday was April fool's day. I walked back to the flat; Jerry and his family were up and breakfast was on the table in no time at all. I told Jerry that I could do with a suit to wear. Jerry's wife, Ann, said there was a Burton's tailor in town; they would drop me off and pick me up later in the day. I walked down the high street until I came to the shop. I told him to measure me up as I could do with two suits—one made by Meier and the other off the peg. I tried on a mohair suit and the jacket fitted but the trousers needed altering a bit. The made-to-order one was going to take long so I settled for the one off the peg. It would take an hour to be altered so I said I would be back. I walked down to the pub for a pint. I walked back to the shop and tried on the suit. I looked good. I paid the man and got a taxi back to Jerry's flat. We had tea and watched a bit of television. Soon, it was time to get ready for the club. Ann was coming too as she had a babysitter coming to look after the girls. I felt really good in the suit and Jerry and Ann said the same. We got a taxi to the club and met up with Jerry's friends. As the night rolled on, the group was good with Jerry as the compere. I noticed that there was a woman looking at me. She looked all right so I went over to ask her to dance to which she said yes. After the dance, I went for the drinks and sat down with her. She told me that her name was Sally and we seemed to get on all right. I walked over to Jerry and Ann and told them that I had scored and would get a taxi back to their flat. Jerry gave me Ann's key to get in. I went back to Sally. We had the last waltz and then Sally said I could take her home and we got a taxi back to Sally's place. When we got there, I paid for the taxi. Sally had a two-up and two-down terraced house. I sat down on the sofa and Sally came over and sat down next to me. We talked some more and the kissing started to get good. We went upstairs, I was as horny as hell. The sex was good with Sally and then there was a big noise. Sally jumped up and said it was her husband coming home early from the docks. I did not have time to argue as he was coming upstairs so I had to think quickly. I looked out of the window to the backyard and lifted the sash, grabbed my clothes and climbed out. Throwing my clothes down in the yard, I got hold of the drainpipe down to the outhouse. By this time, the man was at the window, shouting and yelling. The back door was locked so I put the dustbin against the back door and climbed up the wall. I threw my clothes over the wall, which had glass on it and was bad on my hands. Over I went down the alley. The man was in the yard by this time, so I gathered up my clothes and ran down the alley to the bottom. I was still naked. I put on what was left of my clothes the trousers were badly torn and I had left my shoes behind. It was a bit cold to my feet but I had to make fast tracks as I headed for the main road. I was looking for a taxi. I had lost my watch as well but my money was still in my side pocket what was left of it. I looked down the road and there was a car coming up. I put my hand up to stop the driver, who looked at me a bit strangely. I told him the address as we drove off. I arrived at Jerry's flat, let myself in, washed up in the bathroom and then went to sleep on the settee.

In the morning, I got up early to put the suit out on the road. I had put it in a bag, ready to dispose of it. I went down to the paper shop and back to the flat. Jerry and Ann were up and the breakfast was on the go. Jerry asked how I got on last night. I replied, "Not that good; I will tell you later when we are on our own." Jerry said that we will go to the club for a pint. As we were walking down to the club, I told Jerry what had happened the night before. I asked Jerry if he knew Sally or her man and Jerry said that he had never seen her before in the club. Jerry's friends also said the same, so I felt at ease. We had a game of bingo, then it was time to go back to the flat for dinner. After dinner, we watched television and had a nap. After tea, I went to a pub down the road for a pint. I could not have a lot as I had to get up early on Monday morning to drive the lorry back to Stockton yard. In the pub, I started talking to the lady at the bar; she told me she was the Landlady. Her name was Jenny. She asked me where I came from and I told her that I came from up north Durham way and was going back in the morning. I bought Jenny a drink as closing time was coming up and Jenny told me that her man had left with his girlfriend three months ago. Jenny asked me if I would like to stop back for a drink plus a bit of supper. Jenny closed up and we had a drink and a talk. I told Jenny that I could not stay too long as I had to get up early in the morning. I was soon in bed with her; she was really good at sex. It was 1.30 in the morning and I had to go. I told Jenny that I would ring her during the week. I left and went back to Jerry's flat. Jerry knocked when it was time to get up. I told Jerry that I had scored at the pub and might be coming down more.

Jerry and I set off to the yard. At the yard, I got the lorry ready and checked the diesel and the oils and water. I set off the way we had come. I called in at a café for some breakfast which I enjoyed. I set off again for the Stockton yard. Back in the yard, I parked the lorry and got in my car and went to my digs. I changed and went to the Blue Post pub to see if Big Billy was in. I heard that he was in town. Billy told me where he had been working and that he was still in the ICI Billingham with Jimmy Tune, Billy's mate on the crane, which was a 100-tonne Coles crane. We had a couple of pints and then I went back to my digs.

In the morning, I went to the yard early because I had a job to go to as the 10-tonne road roller was off hire this Friday. I went out on the jib lorry for the rest of the week all over the northeast. I came into the yard on Thursday night. I was told that I had to go to the office. The yard manager, Freddy Higgingbottom, was in the office and he told me that there was a 19RB crane coming up from the Birmingham depot. It was going to the NCB at Seaham Harbour Colliery. Fred asked me if I could drive it and I said that I could. I was told to go to the pit tomorrow. I set off in the morning to the pit. It was up the A19 road to Seaham Harbour as the pit goes out to sea. I offloaded the crane from the low loader. There was a ten-foot section with a cat head which is the name for top of the jib. I lay it out on the road to bolt them together, put pennant ropes on, put pins in, then reeled the hoist rope out and got in the crane to lift the jib and slew around to where the ball was that I was going to use. I was then ready to work; I went to the office to see what I had to do.

I followed the instructions that Shaun had given me when we first met. I did not have to load it up as it came from Birmingham yard at Cocks Green, which was where the main office was.

We were breaking up concrete on a weigh bridge with a half-ton ball. It was a Saturday and the NCB pitmen and I went down the shaft to test for gas. The pitmen asked me if I would like to go down. It was an experience unlike any other. After signing in, I collected my lamp and helmet which had a small light on the top. I made my way over to the cage and climbed inside. The cage went down at some speed, especially as I was not used to it. My skin felt as if it was coming off my body. When it reached the bottom, I got out and stepped onto the Paddy Train, which went out over three miles under the sea. It had huge steel doors at each mile just in case there was a flood and you needed to shut off one of the sections. If you did not make it, you just put your hands together and prayed. When we came back up in the cage, I asked the men if there were any digs in the village. One of the men told me to try the pub. I got digs in the village pub for one night as I could not be bothered to travel back to Stockton since I was on again on Monday.

Saturday night was not too bad in the miner's club but all eyes were on me as I was a stranger and you had to watch who you talked to. On Sunday, I got up, had breakfast, went for a walk, got the paper and sat down on the seafront as the fishing boats went out. When the pub opened, I had dinner and then upstairs to bed for a couple of hours. That night at the club was bingo plus turn. In the morning, I was back at the pit, breaking up concrete. On Monday night, I parked the crane, got my timesheet signed as the crane was off hire and waited for fitters to strip it down and load it up. I rang the office and I was told to go to the yard in the morning on Tuesday. I drove back to Stockton that night back to the same digs on Harrington Road. I called around at the Blue Post pub to see if Billy was in. I had a couple of pints and then back to the digs. I was in the yard on Wednesday. A 3c had come to the yard from Liverpool depot and had to go on hire to the earth-moving division on A66. It was Richard Wallington's job. I had a day to learn the levers as it was going out the next day. They were complicated at first but after an hour, I got the hang of it. The next day, I drove the JCB to A66 Sadberge. The job was making a dual carriageway. The JCB was for drains. There were two more on the job. This one was a spare as one of them kept breaking down. I got a lift back to the yard. The plant manager, Freddy, came across the yard and asked me to go to Wallsend-on-Tyne. I was going on hire to the earthmoving division, so I had to go to the digs and book out. I told the Landlady that I would be back soon and off I went to the A19 Road to Newcastle-on-Tyne. The job was on the coast road which was being widened. I met up with one of the section foremen on the job and he told me that he wanted a driver for the 22RB on the drag line and I had to load the lorries. I was slow for the first couple of hours. It was good that there were two of them on each side of the dig. John Kelly came over at dinnertime; he was an artist on a 22RB. He said that I was picking it up very quickly, which made me feel good. The driver of the 22RB that I was driving was called Shaun. I told John that I had met him at Thornaby Airfield and was back the next day. I was looking forward to seeing him again.

The clay that we loaded up was used to make road fill. On formation, it was rolled out into six-inch layers. When I finished, I heard that there were digs at Wallsend. It was a Salvation Army B&B so I booked myself in. The next day, I went to work and met with Shaun again. I had to go to the offices at Ancestor where I met up with the site agent called Mr Joe Herrherd. He told me to go to the Seghill NCB Colliery to drive a 951 CAT, which was a loading shovel on tracks. I went to the pit, found the machine, checked it over and made it ready to load with red ash. The lorries were starting to line up to be loaded up with 951 tractorvator. On Wednesday, I was loading a lorry when another lorry came down the road. The driver ran over to me and said that the driver on the 22RB needed help. The red ash tip had come down on the machine. I put the 951 in top gear and set off down the road. When I got there, the 22RB was buried with the Driver still in the cab. I started to dig around the tracks so that I could get the Driver out of the cab. The red shale was still coming down the side of the machine. It was very hot and the stench was bad. The driver was burning as the front window was open. The sliding door was open too. I got most of the shale away and could hear the sound of an ambulance plus a lorry full of men. By this time, the stench was really bad. I cleaned up the ground around the machine so that the ambulance men could do what they could but it was too late. I pulled back and let other people get on with the job. The fire brigade arrived as well. I was told by the site agent, Joe Herrherd, to park the 951 tractorvator as the day was over with the NCB calling in the health safety. I jumped in my car and went to my digs. I was staying at the Salvation Army hostel in Wallsend-on-Tyne. I had a room on my own, which was ten shillings per night with breakfast. I went to a pub called the Penny Wet. I drank Newcastle brown ale and got talking to the barmaid, Winner. She lived locally and had an Irishman lodging with her and I could meet up with him later in the week. Winner said that she would look out for digs for me. The next day, I went to work at the pit where the foreman told me to go back to the main offices on the coast road and wait to be told what to do. I went to the fitting shop to meet the lads and was told to come back the next day. I would be paid for the two days, so I went to the pub. Winner told me to go down the road for digs as she had sorted it out. I went to the house; there was an old couple. The couple's name was Gordy and the woman's name was Efal. Gordy was retired from the Wallsend shipyards. I said I would be back shortly with my bags. I got a key and went back to the pub. Winner's lodger, an Irishman called Tommy Kane, was there. I told Winner that I got the digs. Tommy was with his mate, Patsy. Tommy and Patsy told me that they worked for a subcontractor on the coast road job, the same as me. It was a Mitchell's construction job who they were subbing off. Tommy and I had a couple of drinks and then went back to my digs. In the morning, I went to the office and was told to go back to the pit and start work; the job was for seven days a week.

I was lodging in Wallsend where I met some good guys who worked on the job with me. One was called Dennis Moseley, a lorry driver, who turned out to be a great mate. There were also Pete Mallory and George Capper who were both plant fitters. Dennis and I would go to the Wallsend Miner's club with his family. Newcastle brown ale was always flowing and it was here that I met up with two more Irish guys named Patsy O'Donnelly and Johnny Doyle, two great blokes. They were great friends of Tommy Kane, the man who had introduced me to Guinness and Whisky chasers! Some mornings I would have the 'shakes', what with all the drinks. I would chase after the milkman, get the bottle of milk and end up spilling most of it.

Over the next six months, as the job got underway, I had to drive various machines—from 951 to D8 plus 63G scraper boxes. I was working on a red ash tip at Seghill Colliery with a big cat dozer and blade. It had a Kelly ripper at the back and over the weeks, it became dusty and hot. I would put a hanky around my mouth. The machine started to overheat so the plant was called and another machine was brought up to do the job. We loaded the machine onto the same lorry to go to the fitting shop to be serviced. The next day, I was in the fitting shop to help the service fitter. The fitter's name was Peter Morley and later in life, he became a great mate. We had to take the belly plate off so that we could get to the fillers. We jacked it up, took the bolts out and then loaded it down.

The job went well but I ached. The machine was ready for work again so back to the digs I went. In the morning, I woke up and one of my testicles was large and it was hard to walk. I asked the landlady where the doctor was. I went down the road to the doctor. The doctor opened at 9 o'clock. The girl at the desk asked me what was wrong. I just bypassed the questions and waited for my turn with the doctor. My name was called and I went in. The doctor was a Lady; she asked me what was up. I told her and she told me to drop my pants to look. I was so used to this that it was not a problem. She picked my penis up on a pencil to look at it. I told the lady that it had been some places but never on a perch. The doctor said that I had strained myself lifting or having sex in a bad position. She gave me a prescription to fill out at the chemist for some tablets. As I was going out the door, the Doctor said that if I did not cut down on the drinking, I would have trouble later on in life. I thanked her and left to look for a chemist for the antibiotics. At night, the tablets got to work and my ball started to go down. I met up with the lads at the pub. The next morning, I felt better and went to work. I got a bit of jib at teatime when I told them. I met up with a man called Billy Hunt who drove the lob lorry that went around the site servicing the plant. Billy had a car for sale. It would replace the one I had, which was a Morris Minor. Billy's car was a Sunbeam Rapier convertible. In the months to come, this car would be a fanny-puller. I paid 120 pounds for the car. As the job for the big machines was coming to an end on the coast road, there was talk of a job starting at Gretna Green on the A1 north.

There were approximately five months of summer left. Dennis and I were asked to go. I said my goodbyes to the lads in the pub and set off up the A1 to Gretna Green, where I met up with Dennis on the job. There was a big transport café on the main road with a car park at the back. We called in at the café because we heard that there were a couple of caravans to let. Barry Smith met us there as he was the agent of the coast road job. He also brought his caravan with him.

Dennis was on the lorry and I was put on a 19RB loading clay up to form the dual carriageway. At the car park at night, there were lorries parking, so the girls of the night were around. The lady in the café was called Big Mary and a fine wench she was. She had big tits and an arse to go with them and was always up for a ride. The job was going great. We would meet up in the pub after work in the local village for a couple of pints and then back to the caravan or café for a feed or if horny, Big Mary or one of the other girls—Alison or Jane—was available if the price was right. We came back one night from the pub, had a feed and Big Mary was still there so we asked her if she could take all of us. She said that was no problem and we went out to Dennis' car, which was a Ford Zodiac with plenty of room for five. Down the road, we got a blanket out in the field. I managed to go second; otherwise, it would have been wet and sloppy.

Winter started to set in and it was the end of October 1965. All of the earthmoving jobs closed down for winter and we said our goodbyes to Stan and Ann who owned the transport café where we had rented our caravan. Dennis and I were asked to go back for the coast road job for the winter so back we went. I went back to the digs in Wallsend and met up with Tommy and the lads in the pub. I drove a JCB 3 and Dennis was on a lorry on the drains on the coast road job. On the weekend, Dennis and his wife plus Dennis' brother-in-law would go to the club. One night, I was at the bar and a lady stood next to me and we got talking. I asked if she wanted a drink and she said that she was with her friend, so I bought them both drinks and went to sit with them. The lady said that her name was Mary and her friend was Gail. Mary said that she was divorced. I thought, *Here we go again*, with Liverpool in mind. Then she said that she had two kids with her husband. Mary had a fine body and I was not ready for marriage yet. I went over to Dennis and told him that I would see him on Sunday at dinnertime in the club as it was a six-day-a-week job. I could sleep over if the matter was on offer. So, at Mary's flat, we had to get the babysitter home, which was not a problem as she lived three doors down on the same floor of her flat. The two children were asleep, so we got down to the nitty gritty. Mary was very good at sex. In the morning, I was up early and had a nosey around the kitchen to make tea as I had a mouth like a shithouse. I turned around to see one of Mary's children by the door, looking surprised. It was a lad, so I asked what he wanted for breakfast. He told me that his name was Jack and his sister was called Lilly who had just got up. I took a cup of tea back to Mary and I told her that I had just met her children. She seemed to be pleased. I went to the paper shop and when I got back, the food was on the table. I ate it and read the paper and then got ready for the club. I got a taxi to the Miner's club and met up with Dennis. He asked me how I had got on and I told him that Mary had baggage, meaning children, and that I would keep Mary at arm's length for now, as a friend. In the next few weeks, my sex life was good with Mary. The children were going to her sister's for Christmas and I was going to spend Christmas in Wallsend-on-Tyne.

The year was 1964. Mary asked if I could take her and the kids to the smoke outside London. I said that I would. Next week, I got the car ready—the Sunbeam Talbot convertible that I had bought from Billy. Mary had packed two cases and I was to leave on Friday night to drive south. We set off down the A1 road with a full tank of petrol. Mary had put up a flask for drinks and soft drinks for the children. An hour into the drive, there was a noise coming from under the car. I pulled over on the side of the road, got out and looked under the car but could not see anything wrong. The exhaust was all right so I got back in and set off again but the noise was still coming. I pulled into a laybye and got out again. This time, I looked around the wheels and noticed that one wheel was loose and hanging off. The wheel studs were coming off and making the holes large. I looked down the road and I could see a farm. I told Mary to stay where she was and I walked down the road to the farm. I knocked on the door, a man came to the door and I told him what had gone wrong. The farmer said that he might have some bolts in the shed down the yard, so we went to look. I found some bolts that would do the job. I asked him if he had a welder and he said that he had but his son was the one who could use it. I said that I could use it in a fashion. I went back to the car, jacked it up to get the wheel off, then put two bolts through the wheel with washers on and tightened the bolts with spanners from the toolbox. I got the wheel on and tightened it. I put the jack and toolbox away, then drove the car to the farm. I met the farmer again and asked if he had a welder. I got the welder out and tacked the wheel on. The welding looked good, so I asked the farmer if I owed him anything. He refused and said that he was just glad to help so we got on our way. The two children were asleep in the back. The back wheel was a bit bumpy as the wheel was not too square but near enough for a paddy so on we went.

We got down outside of London an hour later. I stayed at Mary's sister's house for the night. I was up in the morning, got some breakfast and set off back to Wallsend. I got back at teatime and went to my digs to shower and get ready for the pub. I went to the Penny Wet pub and the lads were there—Tommy and Patsy. I told them what I had got up to and they just laughed and said that the things I got up to. I went to the club to see Dennis and his wife. He also laughed. I told Dennis that I was going to get a taxi to North Shields—the Jungle as it was called—a nightclub with a difference. I got out of the taxi and into a queue to pay to get in. It was packed as it was Saturday night. I got myself a bottle of brown ale and looked around to see what was free. There were a couple of very large girls waiting to be hired so I went across to talk to them and have a couple of dances, but as the night came to a close, the price was to dear for a ride. I went outside to get a taxi. As I was about to shut the door, a lad got in and said that he was also going to Wallsend and would share the fare. Going along the road, the lad put his hand on my knee and said that we could get together. I told the taxi driver to slow down at the lights. He did and I leant across to the door, opened it and pushed the lad out and told the driver to drive on. I told the Driver that I was not gay. On Sunday, I was up early and down to the paper shop and back for breakfast. The Landlady and Gordy were getting the house ready for Christmas and asked if I was staying back. I said yes. I got a card at the shop for my parents and posted it while going to the club. I told Dennis that Mary was coming back on the bus from the smoke. It was holiday and party time in Gordyland.

New Year came and went. The year was 1965. Mary came back from her sister's. Dennis and I went back to work on the coast road, which was coming to an end. On the weekend, I set out to go to my parents in Middlesbrough. It was a two-hour run in the car. I was hoping I would not get a puncture as I still had the back wheel welded on. I drove on the A19 and started to go on the Tees Bridge. A police car followed me with blue lights flashing. I stopped and the bobby got out and came to the car. He asked me if I owned the car and I said yes. The bobby told me that the car still belonged to the finance company and he was going to repossess it then and there. I told the bobby that my parents' house was just up the road and if I could just get there. He said yes and he would follow. I drove around to Bell Street and got out. My dad came out of the house to find out what I had done and I told him that I will explain shortly.

I got my gear out plus my toolbox and one bobby got in the car and drove off. I took my gear into the house and my dad gave me a hand. I told my dad that the car was still on finance with some 200 hundred pounds to pay. I asked if I could stay for a couple of days and he said yes. I had to sleep downstairs as another mouth to feed had come along—Dennis. Mum made tea and I changed to go to the Newport Working Men's club. Ronnie was working at the Steelworks, Paul was still at home sometimes and still in trouble, Kathy had started courting, Malcolm had just left school and started working in insurance, Irene was on the verge of getting married and Margaret was still at school. When I was ready to go out, Mum was going to the club as it was Saturday night with a good turn on plus bingo. Ronnie came as well as he was courting in the club. We went upstairs and found a table for six. In the northeast, women were not allowed in bars, only in pubs. I met Ronnie's girlfriend, Chris. Her mother was also there—a big woman and plenty of rattle. It was a good evening out as Mum won a full house on bingo.

On Sunday morning, I had to walk to the police station to sort out the car. I knew I had to buy another one. After that, I walked back to mum and dad's and got ready for the club with Ronnie and my uncle Charlie. In the club, there was cheese and biscuits, cow heel and black pudding. It went down good with a couple of pints, then back to the house for dinner. Dad and I went to the club at night.

On Monday morning, I got the local paper to search for a car. There was a Ford Consul 357, five years old. I walked to the public phone and rang the number. A woman answered, I got the address to go look at it. It was not far to walk so I told her that I was on my way. The car was blue and white and in good condition. It had a big bench front seat and column change gears, so I made the deal as I was desperate. I drove it back to the house. I changed my insurance to this car; it had ten months plus four months tax. I said my goodbyes to Mum and travelled back to Wallsend-on-Tyne.

On Monday afternoon, I went to the office and Joe said that I had to go to the yard in Birmingham at Acocks Green. I had to be in Rotherham to use a Bio Drott crane it was on hire to a Cementations piling firm. The job was just off the town centre. I drove back down the A1 in my new car. It was late when I arrived and stopped the car to ask if there were any digs in the area. A man said that there was a B&B just past the football ground, so I went further down the road. The Molders Arms was the pub's name. I went in and asked for digs; yes was the answer from the man behind the bar as he was the Landlord. He took me upstairs to show me the room; it was a single and it was all right. I put my bag in the room and went back downstairs to the bar. The landlord's name was Alan and his wife was called Sandy. Alan asked me how long I would be staying. I told him four or five weeks and the job was just off the town centre. The crack was good but sleep was catching up on me, so it was bedtime for me. In the morning, there was tea in the kitchen, so I drank a cup and off I went to find the job.

The machine had arrived the day before, which the German foreman on the job—Carl—told me. The lads were Patsy and Noel and the crack was going to be good. Both the lads were stopping in a café up the road. I checked the Drott over for oil and water plus diesel then started it up. The gravel started to arrive and Noel was there on the tip lorry. A low loader turned up with a piling rig on it—a 22RB with a power pack on the back plus a fitter's van with two fitters to rig it up. There was a flatbed lorry with a rocket type Vibro on the back. It had to be lifted off with a rig. The jib was all put together ready to start. I gave Noel and Patsy a hand to set the pins out for the piles to be drilled out but the driver had not yet turned up for the rig. The fitter had gone to phone. When he came back, he came into the cabin and asked if I was Billy Rennison. I said yes. The plant manager had spoken to my plant manager who said that I would drive the rig and they would get a driver from Rotherham yard for the Drott. The German foreman said that there would be a good bonus for me. I said that I would go for that. I showed Noel how to drive the Drott for now so that we could start after dinner. I went to the shop across the road to get a sandwich. The lady behind the counter had a big smile on her face when I walked in and straight away I noticed her tits did not look bad at all.

"Are you working across the road," she asked.

I said, "Yes. Can you make me a ham sandwich?"

"Yes," she replied. Her name was Pauline and I told her my name. I took the sandwich back to the cabin, ate it with a cup of tea, went out and got started. I soon got the hang of the rig with the Vibro on it and worked off the power pack on the back of the machine. The water to clean the pile was from the hydrant in the road, which was good as we had to do many piles a day. When we finished work, I went back across the road to the shop. Pauline was on her own and I asked if she would like to go out on Friday night. Yes was her answer so it was a date. I went back to the pub to meet Noel and Patsy; the Guinness was good and it was soon bedtime.

In the morning, I picked up the paper on the way to the job. Noel had told me where the key was for the cabin, so I started the kettle. The lads turned up for a cup before we started. No driver for the Drott had turned up yet so it was Noel again. We got plenty of piles drilled but the next day I was shown how to test them to see which pile would carry the bearing load for buildings to be built on. It was a very interesting day and I learnt new things.

It was only a five-day week and it was soon Friday; I had a date with Pauline and went to the shop to see if she was working. She had a big smile on her face as I walked in. "Where should I meet you tonight?" she asked me.

I told her to come to the big pub in town called Gresham Hotel; it had Stone's beer as most of the pubs in the area did since the brewery came from Sheffield. I went back to my digs, had a bath and walked back downtown to the pub. Pauline had not yet turned up but I was early. The beer did not look good as I looked around to see who was drinking and it looked flat, so I ordered a pint of stones; the taste was not bad. I got a tap on the shoulder; it was Pauline and her poison was a gin and tonic. We found a table and sat down. Pauline told me that she had a three-year-old girl named Jenny and Pauline said that I could meet her tomorrow if I liked. I said yes and asked where she was tonight.

"I got a neighbour to babysit tonight. Do you want to come back for coffee?" Pauline said.

Pauline had sex on her mind you could just see it in her eyes. Our last orders were called and we drank up and had a steady walk home to Pauline's house, which was around the corner of the shop she worked in. We got to the front door and the neighbour was about to go. Lynn was her name and she said that Jenny had not moved all night. The kettle went on and two coffees were made. Pauline went upstairs and came back down in her nightie. I knew sex was in the bag. The coffee was on the table and we sat on the settee with the lights out. We started kissing on lips and I worked down to the tits kissing and caressing the sex was great and we were both very satisfied. I had to leave thou because Jenny was in Pauline's bed, so it was back to the digs. The first thing that I did was wash my penis in the sink.

I was up the next morning, got the paper and went to Clifton Park to read as it was a nice day. Then I went to the café to meet the lads for breakfast and I was asked about my date. "Good," I said, "sacks are empty now."

We decided to meet at the pub for dinner and said that we would walk uptown because the football match was on and we would not get that in the pub; so uptown it was and we met up at 11.30. It was a good dinnertime drink and to the café for tea before it shut down. A good feed inside you sucks up the drink and I went for a lie down in the digs.

It was ten past seven when I woke up. I tidied myself up, got a shave and a good spray to smell good and then went downstairs to the bar. Noel and Patsy had just walked in and the drinks were on the table. We sat and talked about the jobs we had been on in the country. Noel had been with Cementations six months as a training foreman and had been with the firm for over two years. He had been on different piling jobs in the country and it sounded good for the future. The pub started to empty after the match. The man at the bar said hello to the lads as he was their Landlord from the café—Roy. He came to join us and was an interesting man to listen to. There was a phone call for me and I took it at the bar. It was Pauline and she asked me if I wanted to come around for supper as she had enjoyed last time. I said yes. I went and told the lads that I had a woman to service and I would see them tomorrow. Then I walked around to Pauline's house; she must have been at the window looking out as the door opened as I reached it. I was dragged in and my clothes pulled off. The electric fire was on in the room and the light was out. The sex was good and she was full of it. I hoped that Pauline was on the pill; if not, she would get pregnant because she would not let me pull out. Pauline said that I could sleep on the settee, so she got me a blanket and gave me a kiss goodnight.

In the morning, my first job was to wash my penis in the sink as the lads on the road were experienced. I made tea from teabags and next I heard a voice behind me saying, "Are you my mummy's friend?"

I said yes, looking down at a little girl, Jenny. "Would you like a drink of tea?" I asked. I found a plastic beaker on the side and washed it out. "How old are you?" I asked her.

"Three," she replied. "Are you staying with us?" she asked.

"Well, you never know," was the reply from behind me as it was Pauline dressed and up, so I put the kettle back on the gas. "So, you have met my daughter now; what do you think so far?"

I replied, "Not bad." But in my mind, I was not ready to play happy families. "I will see you later."

"You know, you can come around for dinner after the pub shuts down. Do you like Yorkshire pudding?" Pauline asked. "I will do a big one in the meat tin and onion gravy with it."

So, I went back to my digs, calling for a paper on my way. When I got in, the cleaner was in the bar. "Late night?" she said.

"Yes," I said. "I stayed with a friend."

The cleaner was an old lady but had a good neck for her age—about 50. She had a ring on her finger which is what you look for unless you got a partner. "I am putting the kettle on," said the cleaner. "Do you want a drink?"

"Yes," I said. "I will read the paper in the bar after I get washed and cleaned up."

I came back down with the paper and I sat down to read but the cleaner was more interested in where I came from. She said that her name was Alice and she was divorced. I thought to myself, *What a fast worker you are, Alice!* She was very chatty; I think Alice was lonely and needed someone to talk to. *Well, if I get a spare night, I will fit you in*, I thought.

"I work here six days a week," Alice said. The landlady walked in at that moment and Alice went on with her work.

"Were you out all night?" she asked. I said that I stayed with a friend. She smiled and I carried on with my paper as it would soon be opening time and the lads would be in; Noel was in first and then Patsy and we had a good drink. I got the landlord to get me a taxi to Pauline's for dinner. When I went in, the table was all set and Pauline and Jenny were in the kitchen. Jenny came in to keep me company. Pauline came in with the Yorkshire pudding with the jug of gravy and it was spot on. I was full as a butcher's dog. I sat on the settee and told Pauline that I would wash up but I was told to sit back down. I must have gone to sleep. When I woke up, it was dark and I apologised to Pauline and Jenny. "Don't worry," they said, "you must have been tired." I went into the kitchen and washed my face to liven myself up. The kettle was on and a cup of coffee went down well. "I will see you in the shop tomorrow," Pauline said. "I will sit and read to Jenny for an hour before she goes to bed."

"Yes," I said, "I will be off." I gave a kiss on the cheek to Jenny and got back to my digs. It was nine o'clock and the lads had not yet been in. Roy was at the bar and so was Alice, who smiled when I got a pint of Guinness. I asked Alice to have a drink and we sat down.

I did not want to know Alice's past but I had to sit and listen, no matter what. I got two more drinks before the bell for last orders.

"How far do have to go to get home?" I asked.

"Up the road," said Alice.

"I will walk you home if you like," I responded.

"I had hoped that you would," said Alice, so we drank up and left. Alice was a bit unsteady on her feet. "I am not used to drinking," she said. Her house was four streets up but she held onto my arm like glue. She fumbled in her bag for her keys. I had to put the key in the lock and we went in. I put the light on at the side of the door and sat her down. It was very clean but then, she was a cleaner. "Can you manage now?" I asked her.

She said no and told me to put the kettle on. I found the coffee and made it, then sat down next to her, which was a bad move because Alice was all over me and I was getting raped at last and it felt good. She pulled my trousers down and took my penis in her mouth and gave me the best blowjob that I could remember. Then off came her clothes and the sex was great on the settee but we finished up on the floor. There was a mat on the floor but it was a bit rough and the skin on my knees was almost rubbed off as it was a coconut mat in the front of the fire. My knees were burning and were red as I walked back to my digs. I got undressed to look at the mess. I went to the bathroom, put cold water on them but I had no cream to put on. Sleeping was out of the order as I could not stand the covers on my knees and legs. I was up early with no sleep. It was six o'clock and I thought I could get some cream to put on my knees from the paper shop. So, I went to town, asking myself if it was worth it. I smiled to myself and thought, *Yes, but don't be too greedy from now on*. I managed to get some ointment, went to the cabin, put the kettle on, then took my trousers down and gently rubbed the ointment.

The lads turned up and I told them what had gone on. They had stayed back in the pub and went straight to bed at teatime. "How was the dinner?" Noel asked.

"Good," I said, "but I came to the pub for the last hour and got fixed up with the cleaner, Alice, and serviced her at her house up the road and I knew about it on the knees." The lads just said that would teach me.

It was hard to get through the day as I needed both legs and knees to drive the rig. I put more ointment at dinnertime to ease the pain. When I called at the shop, Pauline asked me what was up as I was limping. I said that I caught it at work. "It must have hurt," she said. If she only knew! So that was the end of that and I got my sandwich and limped back to the site and back on the rig. It was a good day but slow and we had to do some testing, so I was pleased to knock off early and rest my knees. I limped back to my digs, all three of us. "Three pints," I told the Landlady. She smiled and took me to one side and whispered in my ear, "You have made a lady very happy."

"Do you mean Alice?" I whispered back and I got a nod. I took the three pints to the table and sat down to work it out in my head. Then in walked Alice and came and sat with us. "Did you have a good night?" asked Noel.

"Yes," said Alice, "great." The lads giggled. I told Alice that I was having an early night and a bath to ease the legs plus knees. The lads drank up and went to get food in the café. I said goodnight to Alice and the Landlady laughed as I went up to bathe my legs. I got the bath running and put my towel around me. I went into the bathroom, got in the bath and relaxed. To my surprise, in walked Alice. I did not cover up my dick as Alice was going to wash me. I just shook my head and let her get on with it but my penis did not rise even when played with but the experience was great. I got a big kiss and she left so I dried myself and went to bed.

In the morning, I felt a lot better and rubbed ointment again before going to work. The job was going well and we got the first 25 piles drilled so we had to test the ones that we had done while the engineers set some more out and we could move the rig. The rest of the week was work and no interruptions from women. I knew I had brought it on myself as my penis rules my brain sometimes and my knees and legs were getting better towards the end of the week. I hoped to have a quiet weekend as Noel was going home for a long weekend so it would be Patsy and me to drink together and have a crack. Patsy was on about going up to Sheffield to have a look around and I said that I would take him in the car on Saturday morning. I called at the shop and Pauline was on but she had her mother coming for the weekend. She asked me if I would come around on Sunday for dinner and meet her. I replied yes and that I was looking forward to it. She told me not have too much to drink before I came. On Friday night, Patsy and I were in the pub and got the Guinness down and talked with Roy, Patsy's landlord. The crack was good but in walked Alice with a smile on her face. Roy bought the drinks as it was his turn and got Alice one. "I will not get drunk tonight," she said with a smile, but she did scrub up well and made my donkey sit up. Sex on the carpet was out of the question tonight; bed only if offered on a plate. The bell rang for last orders and Patsy did not want any more. Roy said the same. They left. Alice said, "I have got you all to myself now." The Landlady looked over and did not mind Alice going upstairs as she did the cleaning. So, I went up and left Alice talking at the bar. I got into bed and the door opened; it was Alice. Off came the clothes and into bed she got. The sex was great again. She said that she would stay the night as it was work for her in the pub in the morning. I was sore but satisfied as I let Alice be the jockey to save my knees. I got up in the morning and Alice was still in my bed. *Well, you won't be late for work*, I thought as I went to the kitchen to make a cuppa. The landlady, Sandy, came in the kitchen. "Was the night good this time?" she asked me.

"Yes," I said. I then knew that the women had been talking about last week.
"Has she gone home?" Sandy asked.
"No," I said. "I will make her a cuppa." But in walked Alice, fully dressed.
"Had a good night?" Sandy said.
"Yes, great."
You could sense that these two got on very well together. "I will let you two ladies get on and I will see you both later," I said and went out to the café.

Patsy, who was just about to have breakfast, wished me good morning. Roy popped his head into the room. "Breakfast, Billy?"

"Yes," I said.

"How did you get on last night after I left?" Roy asked.

"Well, I went to bed but Alice followed me up." I answered.

"I bet you did not turn her away."

"No," I said.

"How are your knees today?" Roy asked.

"A lot better, thank you. I think I was set up by Alice and Sandy."

The landlord, Alan, said nothing. "I can see you living in Rotherham," Patsy said. I smiled, we ate the food and I went to get the car and picked up Patsy, then off we went to Sheffield following the road signs. We found a car park; it was an old railyard. There were a lot of cars so it must be all right. Then we walked uptown. I got socks, a pair of jeans and a denim jacket to match. Patsy bought a work coat and socks. The pub was open in town—The Black Swan. The Guinness looked good, so we tried a couple of pints. They went down good and then we walked back to the car and went back the way we had come—along Attercliffe Road, past the steelworks, back to Rotherham and the Molders pub. Patsy took his coat to the café and I took my shopping upstairs to my room, which had been cleaned and had new bedding on. I guessed that Alice had done it. When I came back down to the bar to order two pints, Sandy told me that my favourite cleaner had cleaned the room for me. I sat down at a table and thought, *I am getting deeper into this with two on the go. I will be glad when the job finishes to jib out and move on.*

Patsy came in and the TV went on as Patsy had put a bet on the horses on Friday afternoon. Alan, the landlord, was also into the horses so the crack between them was good. I asked Roy what was for tea in the café. He said that there was some nice rump steak in the fridge with fried or boiled potatoes. The steak went down well and I went back to the digs in the pub and up for a bath. I sat down on the bed but must have dropped off as it was eight o'clock when I woke up and I could hear noise in the kitchen. I got up and saw that it was Alice. "Hi," she said, "I brought Sandy some food from the shop as I have been shopping for both of us. Alan took me in the car as Sandy was busy with washing and drying. What are you up to?"

"Getting a bath now and then down to meet Patsy in the bar for a pint." I replied.

"I could wash your back, if you want," she said. We went into the bathroom, undressed each other as the water was running, then the door was locked and the sex was good—doggystyle over the bath. Then I got into the bath and got my back washed. When I got out, Alice got in, so I washed her back. I went to the bedroom and got dressed. When I came out, Alice was dressed and we both went down to the smiles of Sandy. "You have been a long time upstairs," said Sandy to Alice.

"Well, I did not want to waste the bath water," Alice said with a smile. I sat down with Patsy and Alice brought my pint over to me.

I whispered in Alice's ear, "Please, can I have a rest tonight?" Alice nodded her head. After an hour, Alan rang the bell for last orders and I asked Patsy if he wanted another pint but the answer was no. So, we said goodnight as Patsy went out the door and I went upstairs but I was stopped to get a kiss from Alice.

In the morning, I had a cup of tea and was out to work. When I got to the cabin, it was open as Noel was back and the kettle was on. I told Noel about the weekend and he just laughed. In walked Patsy with a smile on his face and then we were out and starting the rig up, filling it up with dev. We got the drilling going. A new man turned up to drive the Drott so that left Noel free to do the paperwork as it left the German to help the engineer set out more piles. At dinnertime, I went across to the shop, Pauline was on but there was no smile on her face. I asked her what was up. She asked me to come around to her house after work. I agreed. On the rig in the afternoon, I was thinking what was up, then it dawned on me. I guessed that she was pregnant and that was what she wanted to tell me. At the end of the shift, I told the lads that I would meet them in the pub later on. Off I went around to Pauline's house. I asked Pauline where Jenny was and she said that she was at the neighbour's while we talk. Pauline had a test and she was pregnant and I was the father. "Well," I said, "what are you going to do?"

"I want the baby so that Jenny can have a brother or sister," she said. In my own mind, I was set up but I would face the music.

"Well," I said, "get on with it." I smiled and we agreed to have it. I got a big kiss.

"We will go out on Friday night if you want," Pauline said.

"Yes, it's a date." I left and went to the pub to meet the lads. I thought I would keep it to myself for the time being and the drinks went down with the thought that I was going to be a dad. It was Monday and I had all week to think about when I was going to tell the lads or should I keep it to myself for a while. I had Alice to contend with also. The more I thought about Pauline, I knew that I was set up and it went over and over in my mind. The next day at work, I had to concentrate on what I was doing and push it to the back of my mind for now but I knew it would not go away. At the end of the day, I went across to the shop. Pauline was working and said hi as I walked in. "There are some friends that I would like you to meet this weekend," she said. I agreed. "I will get a babysitter for Friday night, if it is all right with you," Pauline continued.

"Yes," I said, "I will see you tomorrow."

I was then off to the pub to meet the lads. As I walked in, I was met at the door by Alice and got a big kiss on the lips that felt good. I hoped Alice was not pregnant and all. I asked her and she looked at me with her big eyes and said that she could not have children. That was a bit of a relief. "Why did you ask that?" said Alice.

"Well, we have been having unprotected sex, that's all," I replied.

"You have nothing to worry about, sweetheart," Alice said with a smile.

The next day on the site, we were in the cabin and Noel told us that there was one more week to go with 55 piles more to drill out and test. Then it was the end of this job and time to move on.

While we were drilling on Wednesday, we caught a big electric cable, which was dead. The site had houses on it before and it fed the old houses. We asked the site agent and he could not see why we could not pull it out and strip it and weigh it in for beer money but we had to strip it out of work hours. So, we agreed to stop back at night to strip it. It would take a couple of days. We cut it up into short lengths to handle it and came an hour early in the morning. Towards the end of the week, we had got it done and weighed it in for a going-away drink.

On Friday, I met up with Pauline's friends in the pub in town. Pauline's friends were from Liverpool and had moved to South Yorkshire for work. George was his name and his wife was called Ann. You could tell by their patter that work was a no-go as they lived on the dole and had been on it for some time. Ann asked me what it felt like to be a dad for the first time and I said OK. I noticed that it was me buying the drinks as Pauline's friends were a bit short and I was conned again. After two drinks that I bought, I said I had no more money left so we made it last until last orders. They asked if I was working tomorrow and I said no. I was glad when the time was called so that I could get away from them but Pauline said that she would like to go for a meal. I told her that I would take her tomorrow night. "Yes," said Paulie, "I would like that." We walked home to Pauline's house but her friends went straight home, thank God. Jenny was in bed and the babysitter went home. I told myself that I could not do any more damage so I might as well bang away at it to my heart's content.

In the morning, I had a cuppa and then walked to my digs to get changed. I brought the car back to put the cable in to take to the scrapyard. We had to do two runs, then we shared the money out with the agent. I called in at the shop; Pauline was on. "You were up early this morning," she said.

"Yes; early bird catches the worm, you know. Are we on our own tonight or have we got company?" I asked.

"On our own," Pauline said.

"Good," I said, "I will see you tonight. I will call around and I will fork out the babysitter's money, OK?" I took the car back to my digs and parked it. I went in the pub and told the lads that I was taking Pauline out tonight. The next thing I know, Sandy said that I was wanted on the phone. It was Pauline; she could not go as Jenny had a temperature and she was not going to leave her so we will go next week. I went back to the table and told the lads that I was off the hook tonight, so it was drinking night. But I spoke too soon as Alice walked in.

"It's not bath night," Sandy said and laughed. I had to smile at that. The lads asked Alice if she was going to grace our company tonight.

"Yes, if you want me to," she answered.

"We will be away this time next week and we are having a going-away drink on Thursday night as well," the lads said. Alan called time as it was the second week and football was away, so we all went to the café for something to eat a nose bag as we called it. I was hungry and steak was on the menu again, so I got that down. I knew it was going to be a long night with Alice on hand. I decided to get a catnap while I could, so up I went and lay down on the bed. When I woke up, there was a noise in the kitchen. I got up and it was Alan, the Landlord. "Hi," he said, "I did not know you were in."

"What's the time?" I It was 8 o'clock. "Well, I will clean up and come down."

"Your mates are in the bar plus your girlfriend, Alice," Alan said.

Thank God it was Alice and not Pauline, I thought, as I could not handle two in one night. I got a wash, put my smellies on and went down. There was a pint in so Sandy pulled it and I sat down with the lads plus Alice. "Catching up on sleep?" Noel asked. I said yes and Alice smiled; the look on her face said that it would be the only sleep I would get if Alice had her own way. Noel and Patsy were going to another job in South Wales. "Are you going with them?" asked Alice.

"No not to my knowledge. I work for another firm and I am only on hire." The crack was good with Roy and the locals. Sandy had made some sandwiches, so we got supper as well. The time was called so when the locals had gone, Alan locked up and it was goodnight. When we all started to get tired, the party broke up as it was after two in the morning. The lads went and Alice was in top form. I could see that she was going to sleep with me somehow and up I went with Alice on my tail. We undressed each other and got into bed and cuddled up as I had too much to drink to know anything better and would not be able to perform.

In the morning, I had a mouth like a shithouse, so I started the kettle. Alice was still in slumberland but I made a noise in the kitchen and as I went back to the bedroom, Alice had woken up. I sat on the bed with my cuppa. "I hope you are not getting up yet," she said. *Yes*, I thought. But Alice had other ideas; she took the cup from me and put it on the bedside table and the covers went back to reveal a naked body. We had sex and it was great and then I had to recuperate and we talked about what would happen after next week. I said that I would keep in touch but I always say that and move on. I had a lot to see in the world and more people to meet but there was one problem Pauline's baby. If it was true, I would go into that next week before I leave. Alice got on with cleaning, so I went to the paper shop up the road and read the paper in the bar with a cuppa that Sandy had made. I was not into breakfast at the moment. There was a good crowd in for Sunday dinner but I thought I had better go around Pauline's to see what was happing about the baby. When I called, there was nobody in and she had not said that she was going anywhere for dinner. I walked back, calling at the pub in town where Pauline's friend was. I asked him if he had seen Pauline; he stuttered and said that he was not too sure. I could tell by his speech that he knew but was not letting on and I was sure that it was one big con. I did not have a drink or else I would have had to buy him one.

I left and walked back to the Molders pub where the lads were and so it was drinking, then to the café for dinner and then a lie down on my own as Alice had gone home after cleaning. I got up, tidied myself up and went down to the bar. Roy was in and the lads were not coming back as they had told me in the café. So, it was two pints and bed for an early night as it was the last week.

I walked to the job and the lads were there, so we got on with the last of the piles to drill out as Wednesday was the day to derig the rig and Thursday, it was to be loaded out. On Monday, at dinnertime, I went across to the shop to see Pauline. I told her that I had come around to her house. She told me that she had heard and she and Jenny had gone out for the day to a friend's place. I asked her, "What are we going to do about the baby that you are having?"

"I am going to have a scan on Wednesday morning, so I will tell you on Wednesday night," she replied.

I broke the news that the job would be finished by the end of the week. She said, "Well, I hope you are coming back."

I had been on the phone to the yard and had to go to White Mare Pool on the other side of the tunnel and report on Monday morning. So, it would be back to Wallsend-on-Tyne and back to the digs in Wallsend. I would see Dennis again. I had told nobody about Pauline and her pregnancy. We had ten more piles to drill out on Tuesday and on Monday night, we had a couple of pints at the pub, then food and shower and bed on my own. We were getting ready for the Thursday night party and I had not mentioned it to Pauline, which was a good thing. We got through Tuesday and we got the job finished. I went to the shop but Pauline was nowhere to be seen and the man in the shop said that he had not seen her all day.

On Wednesday, we started to derig the rig as the fitters turned up and the man on the Drott levelled the site and then parked the Drott, ready to go home. I went again to the shop but still no Pauline. So, I went around to her house but still no joy. On Thursday, I wrote a note and put it into the letterbox. The note told Pauline to ring me on a number, which was Dennis' at Wallsend. We loaded the rig up on Thursday and then we all went to the pub. Alan and Sandy did us proud as the agent and engineers were staying the night so the food was good and the people in the pub gave us a good send-off. But the night was not over as Alice was full of it, so I kept the drinking down. We had a lock in and we turned out at one in the morning. Alice wanted a sex double dose and would not let me out of the bed I was exhausted. I eventually got to work and the cabin was full. We said our goodbyes and I went to the shop to see Pauline, but she was not there. I went to my digs to say goodbye to Alan and Sandy and Alice gave me a big kiss. I got in the car and set off back to Wallsend. I got back at teatime and went to my old digs, where I was welcomed back with open arms. Gordy and Lily were in fine fettle and were pleased to see me. I unpacked my bag and went to the Penny Wet pub. Winner was on and I asked about Tommy. Winner went to the phone and rang Tommy, who said he was indoors and would be out shortly. I got a Newcastle brown down my throat and Tommy came in, all smiles. It was good to meet him again after six weeks. I rang Dennis from the phone in the pub to tell him I was back and was in the Penny Wet pub with Tommy. I asked him if he was coming for one. He asked me where I was working and I told him that I had the White Mare pool job for a few weeks. He said that he would pick me up in the morning as he had been out last night and Ann was not too good today. We decided to meet in the morning at 6.30 outside the Penny Wet pub. I went back to the bar, Patsy joined us, the crack was good and the whisky went down a treat. I had a bit of a speed wobble as I left the pub. It was a good thing that my Landlady was in bed. I was out in a flash.

I had the alarm on for 5.30 and was up at that time. Lily had made me a packed lunch to take to work—my favourite cheese and onion and a cuppa. It was a good thing that I was not driving as I was still shit-faced and even Dennis noticed. "Good night?" he asked with a smile. "I am back on a lorry for now; I have a Case 1000 shovel that was the one that was delivered on Friday. Well, that's what we will be on."

We pulled up at the site offices and went in. The ganger man (foreman) or slasher as he was called, was on muck-shifting jobs and he told us where the job was and he would be down shortly to show us what to do. He told us to get a cuppa in the canteen before going down to the job. Dennis went to the lorry that he was to drive; it was a six-wheeler Dodge dump truck. He checked it over for oil and water plus dev and we set off down the road to the job. The ganger came up and showed us what to do. I checked the Case shovel and started it up and put a load on. Dennis was off up the road as it was going to be used as a backfill behind kerbs on the centre reservation on the main road. There was a café up the road so on the second load, I went with Dennis in the lorry and had a good feed of bacon and eggs. Dennis dropped me at the pub where Tommy and Patsy were at the bar. The mug of nukey brown was put on the bar. I asked Winner for a menu as I was feeling peckish and I ordered ham and egg chips. I ate it at the bar and Patsy ordered the same. The crack was good and Tommy said his job was coming to an end and there was a pipe-laying job for Murrey's local. The job that Dennis and I were on was just tidying up as the job was nearly done and would take four or five weeks at the most, then move on again.

The week passed quickly as we only had a five-day week. On Friday night in the car while coming home, Dennis said that it was a wonder I was not going around to see Mary. I thought about it but did I really want to go there just to get my leg over. Dennis smiled and asked me, "Are you out tonight?"

"Yes, I will see you in the pub at 8.30," I said. I went to my digs and had a bath. Lily asked if I was hungry and I told her I could eat a sandwich if there was one going on. I changed, put on best smellies (I might score tonight, you never know!) and ate the sandwich while going to the pub. The lads were at the end of the bar, which was the main standing place for Tommy and Patsy. Then Dennis walked in with his brother-in-law, Alan. We were all going to the

Miner's club down the road as there was a turn on Fridays. The last orders came and Tommy had already gone back to the Penny Wet pub to be with Winner when she finished for the night. All three of us got a taxi to South Shields to the Jungle Night club to finish the night off. We got there and stood in a queue to get in. There were some big girls waiting in the queue and I would have had a job tackling them in a sexual way. I had a dance with one big girl but it was 20 pounds for sex. I told her that I was out of work and money was short. I went back to where Dennis and Alan were standing. "How did you get on?" Dennis asked me.

"Too dear," was my reply. In the end, we all got into the same taxi and decided to meet up on Saturday night in the club.

The next morning, I went to get the paper and had breakfast at the café down the road. I went back to my digs as Gordy wanted some jobs to be done. After that, it was time to go for a pint, so I called in at the Penny Wet pub. Winner was not on until 1 o'clock so I carried on reading the paper at the table. Tommy walked in with Winner. I paced myself with the drinks as I was going out in the evening to the club. We talked about the people I had met on the jobs and Tommy knew some of them too. It was a good dinnertime session and I then called at the café for some tea. I went to my digs to watch TV with Gordy as he liked the racing. I bathed, changed and walked to the club. Dennis was in with his wife, Ann. The turn was a comedian and was not too bad and made the night. I did not fancy the night club again, so it was digs for me, early for a change. Sunday was a quiet day.

Dennis was there on Monday morning. I said that it was my turn to drive my car but Dennis insisted it was his, so I gave him half the petrol money. It was a busy week at work and the crack was good in the pub at the weekend with Dennis and Ann. On Monday, I was told to ring the yard in Birmingham and I had to make my way to the yard by Tuesday afternoon. When Dennis and I got back to Wallsend on Monday night, we had a pint together in the pub, then I said my goodbyes to Tommy, Winner and Patsy. I went to my digs to tell them that I was leaving in the morning and I was not sure whether I was coming back or not.

Next morning, after tea, I set off for Birmingham. I looked at the map and drove a couple of hours, then stopped at a café for a sandwich and a cup of tea on the A38. When I reached the yard, it was 4 o'clock in the afternoon. I parked and went to the plant office. The plant manager told me that there was a job in Coventry at the Royal show. It was a CAT 951 tractorvator and would be dropped off in the morning. I asked the manager about some digs and he told me to go to the pub at the end of the road after work where the lads would tell me. I went to check the machine over. As it was knocking-off time shortly, I went to the pub. There were a few fitters in the bar, so I asked them about digs. An Irish lad named Patrick Glimpse also worked for the same firm and was on hire to Wimpy. Pat said that there was a room at his sister's as there were two beds in his room. Pat rang up to find whether it was OK. We finished the pint and I followed Pat to Smallhearth. Pat took me to meet his sister, Monica, and his brother, Michael. The tea was about to be set on the table—it was boiled bacon and cabbage and pottages and a pint of milk to wash it down. Pat told me about an Irish club that he went to the one called the Gary Owen. We changed and walked around to it. The club was big and it was darts night. I got introduced to Pat's friends and the Guinness was good as well. Pat told me how to get to Coventry in the morning. We drank up as we had to get up early. Pat was on hire to Wimpy construction and was driving a 933 CAT tracktorvator shovel. Up in the morning and I set off to Coventry. The job was at the Royal Show Ground. It was also called the Royal Agriculture College. I went to the office to see the man in charge. He introduced himself as Jim and took me to show the job, which was filling low-lying ground to another level with topsoil. The first job when the machine arrived was to fill it with brick rubble as they had a lot of building work done and the brick rubble was heaped all over the place. As Jim and I were talking about the hours to work, which was nine hours a day, the low-loader turned up with the machine, so I took off to start work. I got on with the job on hand; it was dinnertime and I had nothing to eat but I knew where I could scrounge a drink. I met up with Jim and he took me around the farm as I had told him that I had worked on a farm and had been in the Young Farmer's club. I was impressed with the new ideas on pig farming. I met young people who were living and working on the agriculture farm. I got on with the job for the rest of the day and went to the Black Swan pub to have a pint. The lads were there and they asked how my day had gone and were the digs all right. I said everything was great. Alan, one of the fitters, said that he had stayed there and the grub was good. Pat walked in and the crack was good. We went back to the house for a feed of boiled bacon and cabbage with a pint of milk.

The next morning, I got up at the same time as Pat. Tea was on the go. If you were hungry, you could get a sandwich on the way to work as the café opened early and Pat usually called to get a sandwich plus try to get the knickers off the girl who worked there. We both called at the café and had the crack with the girl, Ann, who had a good body and tits with a skirt around her well-formed arse. I ordered two ham sandwiches to take away and so did Pat. Monica and Pat were going out early so I had to find my own tea and then we both went different ways to work. When I arrived at the job, there was police all over the place and at the gate of the showground. I had to get out of the car to be searched and was asked what my job here was. I told them and they let me in. I had to prepare myself for more talks as the day went on. I reached the machine and got on with the job on hand until break-time. I went to the canteen where Jim was and asked what had happened. Jim told me that there had been a murder in one of the houses on the estate and it was the chauffeur's wife who had been killed. I got my sandwich with a cup of tea and then went back to work. After some time, I was asked by a Policeman to go to the office. I was questioned about where I had been and where I lived and what time I left last night. Then I was told to go and I went back and got on with what I was doing. I then set off to Birmingham and then I would go to the pub.

The lads in the pub asked me what had happened at the showground as it had been on the radio, so I told them the bits I knew. Pat walked in and I told him too. We had a couple of pints of Guinness and then it was time to put to get some grub so down the road to the café we went before it shut down. Ann was on but I was told by the lads that Ann was a lesbian and had a partner who worked at the chemist down the road and both lived together in a flat, so that was that. I had steak, egg and chips, which went down well. Pat had the same and we went to our digs to shower and then bed.

In the morning, I called on my own at the café. Ann was on and I chatted with her to check whether she was a lesbian. She said yes and told me that her partner was called Mary who worked at the chemist in Smallhearth. Ann asked me, "Have you been to the Irish club yet?"

"No, but my mate was on about it at Friday night. We might meet you there if you go, Ann," I replied.

"What would you like this morning?" she asked.

"I think I have time for some breakfast," I said.

"Well, sit your arse down and read the paper because it will be ten minutes or so," Ann said.

I thanked her and read the paper until the grub came, which went down a treat. I was full for the day and off to work I went. When I got there, the Police were at the gate and I had to go through the same as the day before. I got to start work after half an hour and I heard at teatime that it was the chauffeur who had committed the murder for the love of the secretary but they were gone at the end of the day. My job would last until Friday so I asked Jim, the manager, if I could use the phone to ring the yard. The plant manager came on the phone and told me that when I got signed up on Friday, I should park it and it would be picked up some time on Monday. He asked me, "Will you go to the big park at the side of Brum and drive a D4 CAT and scraper box from Monday 7.30 on the site?"

I agreed and on Friday night, I left the digs and Pat got in Michael (Pat's brother-in-law) who worked for J Murrey, laying cable in and around Birmingham. As Pat and myself were not working on the weekend, we decided to go to the Irish club. Pat had a hot date so I would meet him there. Pat changed first and I walked down to the local pub for a pint. There were not many people in, so I walked to another pub where the Barmaid was very chatty. I got on well at the pub, which was called the Malt Shovel. I did not get her name and I told her that I would call in again. I walked to the club and I had to get signed in. Michael was just inside the door and came across and vouched for me. Up to the bar I went as the Guinness was very good in the club. I got talking to Pat's friends but you had to watch what you were saying because of the troubles in Ireland. I knew I would not score in the club as they were all Catholic. It was a good night as the group was the Dubliners. As the night came to a close Pat, Michael and Monica plus friends were going to a Casino in the town. Monica told me where the spare key was. I went outside and started to walk home when a girl who had been with Pat's girlfriend, started to talk to me. She said she would feel safe if I walked her home. Molly was her name and she held my hand. Molly told me that she had a little girl called Emily who was three years old and she had a babysitter so that she could have the night out. Molly asked me in for coffee after the Babysitter left. I said yes as I had nowhere to go. I waited at the end of her street while Molly went in. The door opened again, Molly was at the door with a girl and when the girl had gone down the street, Molly waved to me. I was off down the street and into the house. Molly had a downstairs flat and I sat on the sofa as she made the coffee. We had a good talk and one thing led to another. Molly checked on Emily who was asleep in the next room. Molly was good in bed and we had brilliant sex but she said that we had to keep our friendship a secret. In the morning, I was up early and I went back to my digs, calling at the café on the way to get a cup of tea. I packed up my clothes and put them in the car, got in and set off for Holyhead. It was a good day for this time of the year.

March 1966: Travelled to Holyhead

It was a good four hours from Birmingham. When I reached Holyhead, there was a lot of traffic as Holyhead was one of the main ports to Ireland. I got in the town centre and stopped the car to ask a couple where the job was. The BICC Cable factory was going to be built. Apparently, it was out of town and I followed the directions I was given. As I approached the job, I saw a lot of buildings going up on my right. It was a camp for the workers to live in. I went to the security at the gate. I told the man that I was going on hire to BICC to lay the road with a machine. The man took me in and told me to park and come to the office to see about a room in the camp. It was £1 and 10 shillings per week for a bed and breakfast and the evening meal was to be paid for. After looking at the menu, it was cheap—2/6 per meal. I got my bag to the room in a wing of the campus. There was a big hall where there was a snooker table, a dartboard and a bar. There were men at the bar as it was Sunday plus cards school was going on. There were a lot of Irishmen around me. I started to talk with an Irishman who had come over to work on the site for J Murrey's cable-laying firm. He told me how to get to the site as it was all unions on the site. I thanked him. The Guinness went down well and off to the room I went for a kip.

The next morning, I was up and out by 6 o'clock and in the canteen for breakfast, which was really good. Then out of the camp and down the road to the job, which you had to walk to. At the gate, I gave the man the paper I had with me and was taken to an office to get my pass. I had to keep the card pass on me at all times when I was on the site. When all the paperwork was done, I went and found the CAT 933 on the side of the road. I checked the oil, water and diesel, then started it up and waited until someone came along. A Land Rover drew up alongside me and as I had no cab, the driver asked if I was ready for work and I said that I was. Two Irishmen opened the back door of the Land Rover and took out two shovels ready for work. I got down from the machine and introduced myself as Billy; they said their names were John and Pat. The job was to make all the roads around the site out of stone. The stone had to be laid to levels plus it had a camber on the road. Then the stone would be laid, the curbs would be set out and laid for ash and felt and rolled. There was a lot to do. The lorries started to come in and lined up with the stone; it was a busy day and I was exhausted when I finished. Then, I got a phone call.

Aberfan 1966: Disaster

I was told to go to the office as there was a call for me; it was from the head office in Birmingham, Acocks Green yard. The call was from Mr Roy Richards and I was told to drop everything and travel to South Wales on Monday night. The low loader would meet me there from the yard. Roy told me to assist in moving the slurry from the School yard as the slurry tip had come down on the school. I went to pack again; the office had already made arrangements with the BICC Cable company for a replacement until I got back. I did not have time to go back on the site, I handed my pass in, grabbed my bag, got in the car and looked at the map to find the easiest way to South Wales. It was a good run; I filled up with petrol at the first garage I came to as my car had a big tank. There were not a lot of garages open at night on some roads. The map told me to drive back inland and then go down the country on the A40 towards Newport, South Wales. It was dark, cold and wet as I got to Wales. I stopped again to look at the map. I came to a main road; there were a lot of byroads from it. As the interior light was not that bright, it was hard to read the map. Then I took a pot-shot and followed a byroad. I was in luck when I found a sign to Aberfan. Most of the road signs were in Welsh. The time was now 1 o'clock in the morning and I was down to less than half of the tank and I had not seen a garage for the last 50 miles. I came across an army fleet of lorries heading the same way, so I followed as they had an escort in the front with blue lights flashing. After a few miles, I could see a mass of lights and I knew that I was on the right road. The army vehicle pulled over to the side of the road and I did the same. The army sergeant was shouting orders to his men to unload the lorry with picks and shovels, then he marched them down the road. I parked the car and followed with my work boots and flying jacket on as it was windy and cold.

There were people everywhere, crying and digging with bare hands. The Army had the shovels out; I stopped a Policeman who looked in charge and told him that there were low loaders on the way from Birmingham with tracked shovels. I could see blue and orange lights following. The blue lights were coming fast and then I heard the air horns blasting out. I knew the machines were here because Richard Wallington's low loader was a Yankee Mack with big air horns. I ran back down the road and met the driver of the lorry. Both lorries had Cat 933 tractors with no cabs on. I came off the side of the trailer as usual, dropped onto wooden blocks and set off down the road with lights on. The Army Sergeant put me to work moving brick rubble, which was the wall around the school. I moved into the road and the army lads got shovels and rakes into the front bucket. As we moved forwards, it was 3 o'clock in the morning. I learnt that the children had been in the classrooms when the slurry came down and the Teachers had no time to get them out. Lorries from all over South Wales turned up in force to take the slurry to tip on spare land; it was a long night. Doctors and nurses were everywhere. When dawn started to break, it was clear that no one could have survived unless they were in a classroom with no windows. At around 8 o'clock, another Manager told me to take a rest and he put one of his men on the machine. I showed the army lad the controls and I climbed down to walk towards my car. The house on the road was open and I was told to go in as there was hot food and drinks. The people were consoling each other. I was given a mug of hot tea and there was a pan of vegetable soup. I wolfed down a big bowl as I had not eaten since the day before. It was time to sleep so I went to my car and with it being a bench seat, I lay across the front seat and closed my eyes.

The noise woke me up; I looked at my watch and saw that it was 10.45 in the morning. I got up, walked down the road past army trucks where people were still working hard to dig the children out. I could now see one half of the building open. There were bodies being carried out. I went across to an army sergeant who was helping to fill the 933 shovel with diesel I asked if they had got anybody out alive and a shake of his head said it all. I got back on the machine and was directed to continue where it had left off. I carried on as before with the army lads shovelling and raking into the front bucket of the track shovel. When the bucket was half-full, I had to reverse and drive to the waiting lorries to be taken away to NCB Colliery. I was directed to the other end of the school while the medical teams got the bodies moved out of the way. It was a horrendous sight to see children this way; this would always remain in my memory for the rest of my life. It was another long day and the army sergeant told me to take a break and one of his men took over. I went down the road and to a different house. I used the toilet and was given tea and a couple of sandwiches. As darkness was falling, I had to try to ignore the crying all around me. It was now Wednesday night and lights had been brought in by the army to the colliery. I finished my grub and got back on the machine. We carried on from one side of the school to the other. It was a long drone, out of practice and it was very hard not to say anything. This was my job; my stakes were on the job doing what I was good at—driving the machine. Wednesday night came and went.

It was Thursday and dawn approached. I did not dare ask how many children were taken out plus their teachers. It was time to take a break again and the army lad took over from me. I walked down the road to my car again for some kip on the bench seat. The time was 7.15 and when I woke up, it was 10.35. The noise of police cars and fire brigade had woken me up, giving me just over three hours of sleep. I got out of my car and walked across to an open door of a house and asked where the toilets were. I was shown out to the back where I washed my face to liven myself up. There was tea and bacon and I sat down with the tea and enjoyed the food, then it was time to walk back to the school. By now, most of the dead children had been uncovered as well as the teachers. The army lads were cleaning up as I went over to the machine, which was to one side of the once-schoolyard. I stood next to it and waited for my orders on what to do next. I was told that the church hall was being used as a mortuary. It was dinnertime when I was told that the machine was not needed now as the NCB Colliery were bringing their own from another colliery. They would be moving the slurry from the back of the school; it would take months to move it away from the village. The overhead bucket that brought the slurry from the pit would be taken down. I walked down the village to find a phone. There was a phone box at the end of the village. I looked at the time again; it was just past 2.20 in the afternoon. I dialled 100, got the operator and asked for a reverse-charged call to Birmingham Acocks Green. The operator wanted the phone box number before she would put me through; I got through to the office switchboard and asked for the main man, Mr Roy Richards, himself. I waited for a minute and then Roy came on the phone. I told him what the score was and he told me not to book the 933 tractorvator out as I was on television and on all the front pages of the papers since the name was on the back of the dev tank. Then Roy told me to go back to Holyhead over the weekend. I put the phone down and went to the car; I thought I could head out towards the A40 so I looked at the map to decide where to go for the night. I drove down the valley to Neath and got some petrol at a garage. It was teatime when I arrived in Neath and I asked the garage were there digs for the night as I was ready for a good bath and proper sleep. I found one just off the town centre and it was good to get a good bath as I had not had a bath or wash for nearly a week. The Landlady in the guest house gave me a funny look when she took me upstairs to show me the room as it was 6.25 in the evening. I got into bed after having a bath for an hour and it was 9.30 when I woke up.

I got dressed and went down. I asked the Landlady when the pub shuts. The Landlady said 10.30 so I went out. There was a pub on the next corner so in I went. I got served with a pint of Guinness and sat down; there were a few people in the pub and the conversation was about the disaster up the valley at Aberfan. I kept quiet about it; one person asked if I was working down in the town and I said I was just passing through. I asked about a late-night club in town. There was a late-night dance until 12.30; you could buy a ticket in the club early. I thought I could go to that as I was not due in Holyhead until Sunday afternoon. I had to remember to ring in tomorrow—Friday—as I had no timesheets to send in. I got another pint before last orders as it would help me get a good night's sleep. The second bell rang and it was time to go back to my digs. It was not long before I was asleep again.

I woke up; it was just breaking dawn and it was cold and wet. I put on my clean working gear and I needed a launderette or something like that. I went down and breakfast was from 7.30 onwards and as it was only 6.45, I thought I would go to a paper shop. It was a good job that I had my coat in the car so I put it on and walked to find a shop. When I got back, it was time for breakfast, which was good because I had not eaten properly for a week. I settled down in the front room with a mug of coffee and the paper. There were pictures of the disaster on the inside pages and pictures of myself and the army lads. I thought at the time that I would keep this paper, The Daily Mirror. The lady walked in the room and said it was a bad job up in the valley. I nodded yes. She told me that she had realised who I was this morning from the TV and that the army lads, locals and myself had worked hard, but in vain. I said that I would be stopping another night here if it was all right.

"Of course, you can, and it will be an honour," she said.

I said it was good to be appreciated now and again. I carried on reading the paper and I must have dropped off for an hour as it was nearly dinnertime when I woke up—11.45. I thought I should ring up the office weekly, so I went out to find a phone box. There was one in the square. I dialled 100 for the operator, asked to transfer the charge to Birmingham and got through. I asked for the plant office, the assistant plant manager came on the phone and I gave him my name. He said that Roy Richards had already booked me in for the week plus double lodging to cover any expenses. If the expenses were not enough, I should write it on next week's timesheet and send in the receipts. I said thank you and rang off. It was time for a pint in the pub that I was in last night.

It was Friday and I went to the bar to order a pint of Guinness. The Landlady said that it was on the house and the Landlord came over and shook my hand as I was recognised from the TV and morning papers. I sat down. I wanted to keep my thoughts to myself about the job I had just done. My mind just wanted to move on. I could see people looking across at me in the pub; I just smiled, had another pint and read a local paper but it was in Welsh. However, the pictures were the same. I wondered if it was a good idea to stay so close to the disaster but the man in the pub said that if I could not score in the club tonight, I must be gay and my balls must be full. Well, I was hungry and I saw a café open as I drove around town last night, so I thanked the Landlady and Landlord for their hospitality, shook hands again and left for the café as it was time to put the nose-bag on again. I reached the café, went in and sat down. There was home-made shepherd's pie on the menu. The girl came over and I ordered; I got more looks again. The shepherd's pie went down a treat and I swilled it down with a pot of tea. It was nearly teatime when I got to my digs. I looked at the car to see if it was all right and still locked up. I would have a lie-down for a couple of hours before changing. It was just before eight when I woke up. I jumped into the bath and put on my aftershave to smell nice. I felt that my luck could be in tonight as I was popular at the moment, some split asses were going to get a good shagging! I got to the club, which was a Working Mens Club and I still had Dad's membership card on me. It was out of date but the man at the door did not look inside so I signed in and bought a ticket for later. I got a pint of Guinness and stood at the bar. I could see people sizing me up. I sat down and noticed a skittle alley at one side of the bar, so I went over for a look. I watched for a while, then a man and woman asked if I wanted a go. I said yes. It was hard to start with but I soon got the hang of it. I had to partner up with the couple's friend, Jane. The couple's names were Tony and Alice; we lost the first game as Tony and Alice had played in the league for the club and knew how to bowl the ball. Jane and I were a couple of amateurs at it. Jane said she liked my accent from up north. Tony said that he had seen me somewhere but I did not continue with that conversation. I noticed that Jane had no ring on her finger and was a bit older than me but her tits looked firm. *Middle-thirties*, I thought. It was time to go upstairs as Jane and I could not win at skittles. Tony and Alice plus Jane had tickets; we found a table and sat down because the big hall had started to fill up from the pubs. The band was quite good and the dancing started. I got Jane to dance and we had two dances together. Jane was drinking gin and tonic and it was all going well so I thought I was in with a chance. As the night drew to a close, I got the last dance, which was a slow one. She came close. Tony and Alice also got up to dance. We all went back to the table and the hall started to empty and Tony and Alice got up to go. Tony said to Jane, "Will you be all right with Billy to walk you home?"

Jane said, "Yes, he will walk me down the road, two streets away." We got out of the club and started to walk down the road. Jane and I got to the door and I got a peck on the cheek. As I had just met her, I thought I would not get sex on the first night. I asked Jane if she would like to go out on Saturday night for a drink and Jane nodded and said yes.

On Saturday morning, I had breakfast, picked up the paper at the shop, went for a walk around Neath, and then went back to the digs. I sat in the front room, watched the news, read the paper and nodded off to sleep in the chair. When I woke up, I went to my room, washed my face and thought that I would go out to a pub for a pint of Guinness. There was racing on the TV but I was not into racing; however, it passed the time of the day. I drank my second pint and thought my belly needed filling. So, I went around to the café and Spaghetti Bolognese was on the menu so that's what I had. Then I went back to my digs for a good bath and put my best clothes on and smellies on in case I scored with Janet. I met up with Janet at the pub at the end of her street. I got some strange looks when we sat down together as people knew her; you could see people talking about me.

But I just smiled and asked Janet where she would like to go. Janet said that there was life around town on Saturday nights, so we went to the Shoulder of Mutton to start with. There was more looks again but I was getting used to being popular. Janet asked me when I was leaving, I said I had to be back at Holyhead to start work by Monday morning. The music was loud so Janet said that we will go to the Lion pub down the road. When we got outside, Janet held my hand and I knew I was in for a good night. In the Lion pub, the music was not that loud and you could talk. Janet was quite chatty as the drink was going down and she suggested that we go back to her flat as she had drinks there. We walked around to her pad; the place was neat and tidy. The wine bottle came out, red and white; and I chose red to suit the Guinness. We sat down next to each other and carried on with the conversation from the pub, but Janet was into the physical side and in no time at all, the clothes came off as we undressed each other and we were at it like animals on heat. The sex was good on the floor but not good for the knees on a coconut matting, so we got into bed. I could tell that Janet had not been screwed for a long time; it was multiple orgasms for Janet and she was full of it. The sacks were empty and donkey was sore. I got out of bed to bring the drinks to the bedroom. As we lay back to take a break, I looked at the clock—it was two in the morning. We kissed and turned over to sleep. I needed it as I was so shagged. I woke up to daylight and looking at my watch, saw that it was nearly 7.30. I went to the kitchen to put the kettle on as I had a mouth like a shithouse. I took the tea to the bedroom. Janet was awake; I sat on the bed and we talked some more. I said that I would keep in touch and ring her when I reached Holyhead tomorrow. I kissed her and said that I had to go and pack and move out of the digs.

I had a bath at my digs and packed. I went down before breakfast in case the Landlady had a smile on her face; she knew I had not been home for the night. As I left, she shook my hand and made me sign the book for memory and wrote Aberfan. As I got into the car, I thought it was a good job I was going as my prick (donkey) would have ruled my brains. As I drove out of South Wales to Holyhead, Janet was on my mind. I thought that maybe I could have settled down with Janet but, was I ready for it yet? It was three o'clock in the afternoon when I pulled up at the gatehouse on the BICC job. The man at the gate rang the camp for a room. I got a room, not the same one, but it would do.

End of Aberfan and Back to Holyhead

Year 1966

I ate a meal, then went to the games room where the bar was and had a couple of pints of Guinness. Then I went back to my room to get some well-deserved sleep. I got up in the morning, dressed, went to the canteen and had a good breakfast. I got on the job and Pat and John were pleased to see me and shook my hand. They had seen me on TV. I rang Janet on the number that she had given me but there was no reply. The job was for seven days a week. I got on well with everybody on the site. One day, I forgot my pass at the gate and the security man told me to go back for it. He told me that I would not be late as he had already clocked me in. The job rolled on and I got to know everybody. On Sundays, we finished at 12 o'clock so we could do our own thing like shopping in Holyhead or games in the games room. I gathered my washing, got my car out and went in search of a launderette. I was told where it was. I found an empty washing machine and put my clothes in. There was a woman in the shop and I asked her how to use the washing machine. She came around to me and told me to put the money in and washing powder as well and let it do the job. While the washing machine was running, we got talking. I could just about understand the northern Welsh accent. I asked her if there was a club in town where you could go to get you off the camp at night. She said that Saturday was a good night as many of the men from the camp usually went there. Wednesday was games night with darts, dominos, snooker and supper. Kathrin was her name and she was in her mid-thirties; she was slim, tall, with tits in the right place and no more than a handful, long brown hair and no baggage (no kids). I told Kathrin that I would be at the club as it was not far to walk to town. By that time, my washing was done and next was the drying but I had to wait until Kathrin was done with her drying. She opened the door on the dryer and put my clothes in, so I gave her two shillings to dry the clothes. When the clothes were dry, I thanked Kathrin and said I would come to the club on Wednesday night. I went back to the camp to put my clean and dry washing in my room and then went to the games room. I saw Pat playing cards and from the look on his face, I could see that he was losing badly. Pat borrowed a few pounds off me until the next week. I went to the bar and had a few pints of Guinness, watched the television for an hour or so, then went to the canteen and had my dinner. I decided to go back to the bar for another pint.

In the morning, it was work as usual. The days were long and I was looking forward to Wednesday night and meeting Kathrin again at the club for darts. I also wanted to meet Kathrin's friends and see if I could make a date for the weekend and get Kathrin to the camp on Sunday night.

On Wednesday night, I finished early, washed up and changed. I went for a walk into town with the club in mind and a set of darts in my pocket. As it was still light, it was a good evening for a walk. I got to the club where I had to sign in and put a couple of bob in the box. I got to the bar and looked around to see if there was anybody I knew from the camp. I noticed a group of women in the corner of the room and there was Kathrin. I waved and she came over. She said that I should come and join her and her friends, so I went across. Two of the girls were quite buxom and were practising on the dartboard. They said that I should have a go so I did and we all got on quite well. The team that the girls were playing with was from a village outside Holyhead and were so good at darts that they were unbeaten up until now. After the darts, I sat down to watch with my pint. They were good chuckers and good at scoring and as the night went on, they won. To a big applause, Kathrin sat down next to me and I got the feeling that I had scored for myself. I had screwed in South Wales and now it was North Wales' turn! Kathrin was very chatty and I asked her out on Saturday night to which she said yes. I was surprised but over the moon. I walked to the door of the club as she was with her friends. Kathrin came with me and I said goodnight, then walked back to the camp. The bar was closed so I went off to my room.

In the morning, I had breakfast in the canteen, still excited about Saturday. I could barely concentrate on the machine but it was a good day at work. The weather was good for this time of the year.

On Saturday morning, I told Pat, the foreman, that I did not want to be late and I had a big smile on my face all day. 4 o'clock came and I was like a jackrabbit on heat. I showered and put on my smellies. I smelt like a whore's handbag; I was told in the canteen when I went for tea. I walked to the club but I was early so I called at a pub in town for a pint of the black stuff (Guinness) to give me the energy that I needed. I was told that the pubs did not open on Sundays because of church and the Welsh. I came out of the pub and walked to the club corner. Kathrin was there with a smile on her face and I could tell that she was happy to see me. In the club, we had to sign in and put a pound in the box. There was bingo and also a turn. Kathrin and I got a table as it was filling up very fast as it was the main night out in Holyhead. We chatted about things in life and her job at the shop in town. It was a fashion shop and she was well on fashion. The turn was a comedian and he was not too bad, then came bingo. I got the books but with no luck. It was a good night out. At the end of the evening, I told Kathrin that I would walk her home. She still lived with her parents on a housing estate on the outside of town. Kathrin said that it would be hard to get a taxi on a Saturday night, so we walked. She held my hand and I felt real good about it. We talked as we walked; it was a good summer's evening. When we got to her street, she put her arms around me and I gave her a big kiss on the lips and said thank you for the night out. I asked her if I could see her again and she said yes. I told her that I could get her to the camp as there was a group on Sunday night to keep the lads happy. I told her I would get her a temporary pass. I walked back to the camp and went to the bar as it was still open and had a pint before turning in. On Sunday, I went to work at 8 o'clock till 1 o'clock and then went to the office for the temporary pass for Kathrin. I was told that the temporary pass would run out at 11 o'clock and had to be off camp as they would go around and check. I had to give my room number.

I went to the canteen for dinner. Then I walked to town. Kathrin was in the launderette doing the washing. As I had not much to wash, I did not bother this week. As I walked in, she was surprised to see me. I told her I had a temporary pass to get her into the camp and would see her at about 7 o'clock. Kathrin said OK. I left and would see her later at the top of the road. I walked back to the camp, went to my room to get showered and put my smellies on. I put on a new pair of jeans and then went to the bar for a pint of Guinness and sat down with the lads I worked with. I told Pat what I was up to. Pat said that they check the rooms to see that you do not have woman in the room unless I could give the security man a backhander to turn a blind eye. It was time to walk up to town to meet Kathrin; she was there waiting and we walked back to camp as it was a lovely evening to walk. At the gate, the security man looked at me and smiled as if to say that he would not check if I got him a drink. I had a 10-shilling note in my hand and as I showed him the pass, I slipped the note into his hand. He just smiled. There was a back entrance to the camp as the lads had told me and I managed to get a table at the back of the room. The games room was full as gambling was going on. The Guinness was going down well, Kathrin was very chatty and was telling me that she had a brother three years younger than her. The turn was not too bad and the gin and tonic that Kathrin was drinking said that I was on a promise. It was time to wrap up and the lads drifted off with their girlfriends. Kathrin asked me if she could see my room, which did not come as a surprise to me. We went to my room. Kathrin was good in bed but we could not stay too long before we had to get out the back door and take Kathrin home. She held my hand very tight as I walked her home.

The next day, the lads ribbed me about the woman I had. The job was good and I was meeting Kathrin on Wednesday night again after darts. It would soon be coming to an end and I would be moving on. On Wednesday, the foreman on the job came across to me and said that I had to ring up the office. At dinnertime, I went to the office and rang the yard in Birmingham. The plant manager asked if I would be done by the weekend as he wanted me to go to Dublin inland on the ferry. The job was on a 22RB crane as the driver had taken bad and gone home.

On Wednesday night in the club, I broke the news to Kathrin. She was sad at first but came around when I said I would keep in touch and write but I was not ready to get tied down yet with so much of the world to see and things to do. I enjoyed the night out as the supper in the club was good and we had a game of darts with Kathrin's friends. There was no match that night. At the end of the night, I said goodbye to Kathrin's friends and we walked to Kathrin's home. I thought about sex but it was of no use because her mother and father were at home so I had to settle for a kiss and cuddle at the end of the street. I told Kathrin that I would see her again before I left. On Friday night, we could go for a drink as I was leaving on Saturday on the ferry. On Thursday, I tied up all the loose ends on the job, got the timesheets signed and said goodbye to the lads on the job. I went back to the camp early on Friday so that I could have a shower and a meal, then a pint with the lads in the bar before I went to go meet Kathrin. I met her at the corner where the club was. Kathrin suggested that we walk to the seafront because there were some nice pubs where we could sit outside on the balcony overlooking the sea. It was a nice evening. I got a few gin and tonics in her and she was very chatty. Kathrin went on about coming over to the island to join me at the weekends and I just smiled and did not say anything but she was full of ideas with drinks in her. Kathrin even suggested that I should meet her mother and father; that was when I knew that I should put the jib out—in travel talk, move on. By the end of the evening, Kathrin was quite drunk and tipsy as we walked back to her house. We said our goodbyes and cuddled and kissed. She had tears in her eyes as I walked away but I said to myself that it was another near miss.

In the morning, I got up and packed, had breakfast, handed my key in to the office and put my stuff in the car. I had not used it for a couple of weeks because of the police always around. I drove to the docks and found the booking place to get to the ferry to Ireland. I had to wait in a queue for half an hour to load up on board. I could not have a drink because I was driving. I also had to find out where I was going; it was a Wimpy site I was going to outside Dublin. The job was just a two-week relief and the machine was a 22RB.

Dublin

I found the job. Next was to find a pub or digs as it was Sunday teatime. There was a couple at a bus-stop. I parked, got out and asked if there was a B&B or a pub. They replied, "Down a side street."

I thanked them, got back in the car, reversed and turned down the side street. The pub was called O'Malley. I got some funny looks as I walked in and I went to the bar and asked for the Landlord. It was a single I was looking for.

The man took me upstairs and on the first floor; it looked all right and the price was 10 shillings per day. The Landlord's name was Shamus. I asked him if the car was all right outside and Shamus told me to put it in the car park around the back so I did that. I took my bag upstairs and then it was down to the bar for a good pint of Guinness, which went down a treat. Shamus said that breakfast was at 7 o'clock. I told Shamus that I was on the Wimpy site down the road on the crane. Shamus said that some of the boys off the job used the pub at dinnertimes and called in on their way home. It was a great pint of Guinness as it was brewed in Dublin with different water to give the taste.

In the morning, I had breakfast and then walked down the road to the site. I was told to meet Mr Kelley on the site. I found my way to Kelley's office. Mr Kelley was a well-rounded Irishman in his 40s. I said that I was the crane driver from England on relief for two weeks. Kelley took me on the site and down to the crane. I checked it over for oil; it was an air-cooled engine so there was no RAD and no water to check. I started it up. I got out to see what I had to lift. The crane had a 100-feet JCB on, so it had a good reach. The ganger man came across to me. His name was Mick and he told me to look after the chippers plus steel fixers. The job was steady with no rush at all. At 10 o'clock, I was made a cup of tea, then I noted the lads had got steak and it smelt great and they had a small loaf of bread to put it in. The tea man said if I wanted it tomorrow, it would cost £1 per day. The tea man cooked it on two large gas rings with two large frying pans. I said yes and I wanted onions as well. I was given a piece; it tasted great. They asked me if I knew the other driver as he came over from Birmingham and I said no. At dinnertime, I was going to the pub as I told them that I was living there. I had moved in the night before. Three of us went in but I found the office staff already there. I got the round to show good faith. God, the Guinness was good but I said to myself only one pint was enough at dinnertime and very filling. The Landlord was pleased that I was getting along with the other men. Shamus asked me if I wanted a meal at teatime as he was cooking boiled bacon and cabbage and there was plenty. I said yes and the lads piped up and said they would have some as well. Back to work we went and it was a busy afternoon. 6 o'clock was upon us and we all knocked off. I got the grease gun out to grease the crane, then got my hands washed and made my way to the pub. The lads were stuffing their faces with boiled bacon and cabbage which smelt good. Shamus brought mine over and I stuck in. I was full as a butcher's dog. I wanted to have a bath but the idea went out my head and I slept like a log that night. I got up the next morning, Shamus had breakfast on and off to work I went. The crack on the site was good. With all the trouble going on up north with the army, the job was going well and I got on with a lot of people on the site. I was living with Irish people in Birmingham and the Gary Owen club was well-known in Ireland. On Wednesday night, I went to the pub after work with the lads. I was asked by Shamus if I was interested in dominos as it was games night. I said yes. It was a doubles game and I got a good partner—an old dish chap called Mick. All I had to do was watch what he played. He was good and we won the first two games, which took my partner and myself into the next round. Mick and I got to the final and won. The prize was four pints of Guinness each but I left mine in the pump for another night. I had to work on Saturday morning, so I went for a look around Dublin town centre, bought a pair of trousers but the length in the leg was too long. The man in the shop said that he could shorten them for free within the hour, so I left them and went on walking. I had a pint on my brain, so I called at a pub for a pint of Guinness. To my surprise, there was a good-looking barmaid; tall and slim and her melons looked good. I asked for a pint of Guinness which she pulled half and then let it stand. I paid her for it—two shillings at the time. The barmaid asked me what was a goodie bloke doing in Dublin and I told her I was on a crane on the site outside town on relief for a fortnight with one week to go. Her name was Bridget and she was very chatty. I said I had to go back to the shop to pick up my trousers. Bridget said that she was working that night and if I wanted to come in, there was a group on. I said yes, I would come in. I drank up and went back to the shop and got my trousers. Then I walked back to the digs; the pub was quite full, so I had another pint of Guinness and stood at the bar talking to Shamus about the local town. It was good to learn about Dublin's history. I went upstairs to lie down on the bed. I must have dropped off because it was 7.30 when I woke up. I ran a bath and thought I might score with Bridget, so I had better smell nice. I came down to the bar and there was a new barmaid on who I had not seen before. She had a pleasant face with a well-rounded body and was in her early 30s. There was no ring on her finger. I got only half a Guinness as it could be a long night. The barmaid was called Maggie and was surprised that I was English. She had a twinkle in her eye as she smiled; if I did not score with Bridget, I would with Maggie. I drank up and walked back towards town and to the pub. I went to the bar; Bridget saw me and smiled. The music was loud from the group. Bridget gave me a pint and I sat myself at the end of the bar where I could talk to her when she got a minute as there was two other bartenders as well. I drank the pint slowly as it's no good if you can't do the business. I was glad when the bell rang for last orders, then Bridget could talk. When last orders were over with, the band started to wrap up. Bridget said that we could sit down at a table. We talked about where we came from and Bridget told me that she was living with her grandma in town. She said we could have a late drink after most of the people had gone. I had another pint just to be sociable and then it was time to go. We walked down the road together and when we got to where Bridget lived, she turned and kissed me on the cheek and asked if I would come down to the pub tomorrow as she was working. So, I walked home on my own and the pub was still open. I got in by the side door as I had the key. Shamus was still up with friends and he asked if I wanted a pint. I said yes and a Glenfiddich whisky went down well. Maggie pulled the Guinness and got the whisky. I paid and sat down. Maggie came and joined me with her drink. Maggie worked in a solicitor's office and bartending was only a side-line to kill the boredom and to meet people. Maggie talked about life in Ireland and the places I could go and see. I looked across at Shamus as his friends were ready to leave. Shamus said that I could take my drink upstairs if I wanted. Maggie was all for it and went and got another drink of gin and tonic. I decided to have another whisky as it was Sunday now and no work. So off we went after saying goodnight to Shamus and his friends. I put the telly on; it was black and white. I sat next to Maggie on the sofa, we kissed and it was electric in no time at all. Maggie was very experienced in the sack.

In the morning, I got up and made tea as Maggie was still asleep. I put the tea down and got dressed to go for a walk and get the paper as it was a nice day. The time was 7.30 and I made my way down to where the shops were, got the paper and bought a pint of milk from the milkman who had a horse and cart. My mouth was like a shithouse from the whisky. I sat down on a park bench to drink the milk; it tasted good and I started to read the Irish Times. After about half an hour, I made my way back to my digs and let myself in as I could hear the cleaner out and about. I went upstairs to the room; Maggie was awake. I said good morning and asked if she wanted tea or coffee. She said coffee so two coffees it was. I put her cup on the table. Maggie looked so delightful in bed with a big smile on her face that I could not resist. So off came my clothes and I jumped straight back into bed. Maggie said she could not be long as she had work at 12. After doing the business, I got breakfast on. Maggie only wanted a bacon sandwich, so I had one too. Maggie got dressed and gave me a kiss and said, "I hope we can do it more often."

I smiled but knew in my heart that I did not want to settle down yet. I had a bath as the water was very hot and put on my new trousers. They fitted well and I put on a new T-shirt I had bought. I washed the pots in the kitchen and went out for a walk.

1967: Coming up to 22nd Birthday

It was a nice day in September and I realised that it was my 22nd birthday on Wednesday. My mother would send me only a card but she did not know where I was. There was a park and I had the paper with me for a read and sat down. Sex was a mucky and tiring job but someone had to do it, so I sat and read the paper for an hour. Then I walked back to the pub which was full. Maggie made a beeline to serve me with a big smile on her face. She whispered in my ear that lovemaking was beautiful and we could do it again shortly. I thought I would skip it. I threw a Guinness down my throat. I think Maggie was a sex maniac. Two of the lads from the job were in the pub so I went and sat with them and wondered what I wanted for tea. Maggie thought about sex again but she had drained the sacks for now. When the pub closed, Maggie came over and sat down with a drink; she said that we could go into town tonight as she knew where there was a live band playing. I said yes; otherwise, it would be bed again. I washed upstairs and she came up to meet me and we had oral sex before we went out. My dick, by this point, was getting quite sore. The pub we went to was a big one in town and the band was good. We had a meal in the restaurant to take my mind off sex. At the end of the night, Maggie said she was going home so I put her in a taxi. I gave her a big kiss. What a relief it was to sleep on my own!

On the site, the lads pulled me at break-time about the matter; I just smiled and left well alone. The job was going well and I enjoyed being in Ireland but like the rest, Maggie wanted wedding bells. On Wednesday, I joined the dominos school again and had a good game with Pat's partner. Good food for super. On Thursday, the boys had a wipe around and brought my dinner. The steak was really good and tender. I was coming off the site on Thursday night and Maggie was coming towards me with a big smile on her face. She gave me a going-away present as I had not told her it was my birthday on Wednesday. I did not want all the fuss. The present was gloves and a scarf. We walked to the pub as she was working because Shamus was going out to the town. I went upstairs, changed, made a sandwich and took Maggie a cuppa downstairs. I stood at the end of the bar and had a pint; Maggie stood with me when she was not serving. Maggie wanted me to write to her every week and come over when I could. When the pub closed, Maggie was keen to get upstairs and into bed. We had great sex that night.

I had one more day left on the site. I heard loads of jokes about when is the wedding and all, so I just said maybe. When we finished work, I got the timesheet signed and said goodbye to Kelley. Two boys came to the pub with me for a last drink. Maggie turned up at nine for the last ride of her life as I knew I had to move on. Shamus said there was a phone call and the message was to ring up the office in Birmingham. I asked if I could use the phone and rang the office. I was told to come back to the yard as there was a three-week job in Birmingham at a park. I was to report to the yard by Monday morning. I told Maggie what I was doing and asked if she could come across before Christmas as it was only September. I said that I would keep in touch as I had Shamus' phone number. I enquired about the ferries in the morning. 11 o'clock was the second one out which would do me fine. I would then drive to Birmingham from Holyhead. I was hoping to be back at Patrick's sister to stay again as I had a card for the Gary Owen club in Smallheath. I used the phone again and left a message for Pat Gillespie with the number of Shamus' pub.

Patrick called back and I told him what I was doing. He said no problem and I said that I hoped to see him by teatime. On Saturday morning, after breakfast, I put my car into gear, said goodbye to Shamus and said that I will keep in touch. Shamus had thought Maggie and I were an item but it was time to move on. I drove to the docks, got on the ferry and read the paper with plenty of coffee.

1967: Travelling Back to Birmingham

It was just gone teatime when I arrived at Pat's sister, Monica's, house. I went in, put on the kettle and she told me that Pat was working all day in town. I told Monica that I would go to the café for tea as it would be open until seven on Saturdays. I put my gear in the room and then walked to the café. To my surprise, Janet was still working in the café. When she saw me, she smiled. I asked how she was and I ordered ham, egg and chips as I was hungry. I told Janet that I was going to be around for a couple of weeks, then left to go back to Pat's house. Patrick was home from work and we got to talking about work. I said there was a job outside town in a park. It was a four-yard scrapper with a D4 Plus box on the back. Patrick asked if I was going to the Irish club down the road. I told him that I would meet him there as I was going for a walk first. I changed and went around to Molly's to see her. She was surprised to see me and invited me in. Her daughter was still up and Molly said that it was too late to get a babysitter but she would get one for Sunday night. I got a kiss on the cheek and told her that I would call tomorrow night to take her out. But Molly said she would go with her friend and meet me there as it would stop the gossip. I walked back towards the club and called at the Queen Head pub on the way, got a pint of Guinness and stood at the bar to drink it. There were quite a few people as it was Saturday night but nobody I knew; none of the lads from work were in. I then walked to the Gary Owen club, got straight in and went into the bar. Pat was there with his brother-in-law; the girls were upstairs in the lounge. The talk was good as it was all about work. There was a group on upstairs; we could hear the music. At the end of the night, Patrick and his girlfriend plus Michael and Monica went on to the Casino in town. I went home on my own for a change. It was good to get an early night now and again.

In the morning, I got up early and made tea because I had a mouth like a shithouse. I went for the paper, then on to the café as Janet was working. I had coffee first, then a good breakfast and a read of the papers. Janet's partner, Ann, came in and sat down and we had a good conversation about life in general. The day passed and it was club time again. Patrick, Michael and Monica went to mass on Sundays like all good paddies, then on to the club to get pissed before dinner. It was a good dinner and then back to Monica's for boiled bacon and cabbage and sleep for a couple of hours. Patrick was up first and washed, then I woke up. He was going out early with his girlfriend. I got ready for the club and met Molly there. At the club, I went upstairs to meet Molly plus her friend. I sat down at a table with the girls, then went to the bar for drinks; there was a singer as well as bingo and it was a good night. I walked Molly home after saying goodnight to her friend. I told Molly that I could not be late as I had to get up early for work in the morning, but Molly had other ideas. She got the babysitter out as I stayed around the corner of the street, then waved me in. Before I could sit down on the sofa, Molly was taking my shirt off and into bed we went. The sex was always good. It was a good thing that I knew where the key was when I got back in the morning to get changed for work. I found the park where the job was. There was a D4 Dozer and a scrapper box parked. I parked the car near an office and the manager came out of the office. I told him that I had come to drive the machine. The manager took me across the field; there was a large dip in the field and in wet weather, water would collect in it. I was to take the topsoil off and heap it up with the box to one side of the park. I got the manager to get labour to line the hole up for the pin, which was in my toolbox. I set the winches up, then got the grease gun out to grease the box as it had not been used for a long time. It was a good day's work stripping the topsoil off. The manager's name was Stewart and he said there was a haulage firm that would be tipping clay and brick rubble when the land ready to build up. It took nearly two days to strip the land which had been pegged out on Wednesday. I told Stewart that I was ready for the lorries to come in and by dinnertime, I had ten loads to do, so round and round I had to go levelling the spoil out. David, the labourer, was saving the tickets for the lorries to save me from stopping. I took a couple of sandwiches to work from Janet's café; she made them up for me at night. I was hoping the weather would hold up. Some days, I would have a good audience as people walking their dogs would sit down on the seat and watch. It was now late October and it looked like I was going to be in Birmingham for Christmas. Patrick and I got on like a house on fire. Molly had load-offs for the both of us; sometimes it was hard to keep her at bay. The job was going well as it was six days a week and I worked on Saturdays from 8 o'clock to 12 o'clock. Then on Saturday, I would take my clothes to Janet at the café and she would take them to her flat to wash them; I would get them back on Sunday or Monday. In November, I got the job finished and on good dry days, I managed to put the topsoil back and got signed up at the end of November. The D4 plus scrapper went back to the yard; I stopped at the yard for a week helping fitters. I was their gofer and would run about in a Ford pickup.

1967: Oaken Gates

The second week of October, there was a job in Oaken Gates, Telford, Shropshire, on a 951 CAT Track Shovel for a demolition firm. It was time to pull out again, say goodbye to Patrick, Janet and Molly and set off to Oaken Gates. The weather was moving in when I arrived at Oaken Gates. The job was for a local demolition firm called PUG. I pulled on the site and the machine had been delivered over the weekend. It was Monday morning and I got up early to travel. It was not that far, but far enough to travel home daily so I had to find digs again. I was told that the Railway Tavern up the road had a B&B, so I called there at dinnertime.

The job was at a gas works. I checked the machine over. The foreman's name was Tom and he showed me around the job. There was a load of single-storey buildings to be pulled down and load onto his own lorries plus he had a 22RB on the site with a ball on. I told Tom if he wanted me to drive the 22RB crane, it would not be a problem. At dinnertime, I walked up the road across the railway crossing to the Railway Tavern to book in. The Landlord was Brian and Lily was his wife. I asked the Landlord for a single room and he said yes. He asked me about Christmas and I said that I did not know at the moment. It was £2 per night—£14 per week. I told Brian that I was working at the gasworks down the road for a couple of weeks and I had a look at the room before going back to work. I bought a sandwich off Brian. I walked back to the job and Tom asked me if I got fixed up. I said yes. I asked him how long the hire was for. Tom said probably until the end of January, so it looked like I was going to spend Christmas in Oaken Gates, Shropshire.

When I had finished at night, I drove the car to the pub's car park and got my bag out; the car could stay in the car park. The meal was a nice piece of steak, chips and mushy peas and it went down well. The Guinness looked good and it was a good pint. I took my bag upstairs and got a bath as the job was very dusty. I enjoyed the bath and put on men's perfume to smell nice. As it was a Monday night, I did not think there would be any fanny about but the rest would do me good, but not for long. I went back down to the bar, got another pint, had a talk with the Landlady, Lily, which was a good conversation about where I came from and my love for travel as it's a big wide world out there. Lily was a middle-aged lady in her 40s with a figure that was not bad. I got the impression that things were not that good with Tom as Tom looked like a lady's man and made a fuss of lady customers. I could see that it was going to be a good Christmas plus New Year. Tom said he was putting the decorations up tomorrow. Time for bed because it had been a long day. Up next morning, Lily had breakfast on, I ate that, walked to the gasworks; it was a busy day as the lorries were on a short haul and back. In no time at all, I was going back to the pub for tea. Tom had made a good job of the decorations and Lily had a smile on her face for me. I went straight upstairs, got a bath to get the dust off me, then down for dinner—shepherd's pie, made by Lily. The meal was very good, followed by a good Guinness to wash it down. Tom asked me if I would like to join in on games night—darts, dominos and crib. I told him that I did not mind, dominoes five and three or penny a spot and darts if you are stuck. So, when I got in on Wednesday night, I went straight up for a bath, changed and had a dinner of fish and chips that was on the menu. The pub was filling up with people for games night. I partnered up with an old boy called John; I could tell from the way he lay down the dominos, he was good at it. We won the round of darts but lost at crib, so it was a good night all around. Thursday was another busy day; Tom the foreman asked if I would work on Saturday until dinner to load the lorries for Monday to get an early start. I could not see a problem with that. I got home on Friday night and Lily was on her own at the bar but had brought a friend in to help her. Tom had to go away to see his mother as she had taken ill and was staying the night with his dad. As usual, I went upstairs for a bath, changed, and then down for dinner, which was ham, egg and chips followed with a pint of Guinness. There were quite a few in the pub as it was Friday night. Jill, Lily's friend, was an elderly person and was good with the Guinness and a shamrock at the top. I stood at the end of the bar and Lily would come over when she got a minute to talk. As the night wore on and the drinkers started to leave, we sat down at a table and when the bell went at 10.30, Lily's friend said goodnight. Lily said she would clean up in the morning when the cleaner arrived. While Lily was locking up, the phone was ringing. Lily answered it and she told me that it was Tom asking if everything was all right. I went up to bed and I was just about to drop off to sleep when the door opened. It was Lily in her birthday suit. She came over to the bed and I shoved the covers back to let her in. Lily's body was warm and tender and she loved to cuddle. The sex was really good as it had been a long time since she had had any. Tom did not know what he was missing and Lily did not know how or when to stop she just kept going. I was glad when she had enough so that I could get some sleep. In the morning, I woke up to find that Lily was awake. I went to the kitchen, put the kettle on, Lily walked in with a smile on her face, got hold of my arm and whispered in my ear that it had been really good and she hoped to do it again over Christmas.

I went off to work until dinner. When I finished, I filled the machine with dev and greased it ready for Monday. I went to the pub to get the washing so that I could get it cleaned ready for Monday. There was no launderette in Oaken Gates, so I washed it myself in the sink with the help of Lily. Then, I put it up on the line to dry and borrowed some pegs from Lily. She asked me what I would like for tea as Tom was not coming home again until Sunday so I would need all the energy I could get if Lily wanted servicing again. Steak and chips would go down a treat. I went downstairs again for a pint before tea; Lily's friend was behind the bar again. I sat down beside John, my domino partner, and just talked about Christmas. I had Christmas Day, Boxing day and New Year's Day off as Christmas day fell on a Monday and it would be a long weekend. I thought of going home to Middlesbrough or Stockton to see Big Billy or to Liverpool to see Jerry and his family but I would wait and see the weather and traffic. I went up, got washed and changed and Lily had tea in the kitchen with Tom absent. The smile on Lily's face said it all as she told me she felt like a spring chicken again, so I knew I would have to screw her arse off. The steak was well done and I was full, so I told Lily that I was going for a walk. I had not bought a paper in the morning, so I called for one at the shop to sit in a pub to read. I noticed a pub called the Malt Shovel and in I went. It was the pub that we had played in on Wednesday. I got half a Guinness and sat down to the read the paper and rest myself. A man sat down beside me and said hello as he had come with the team on Wednesday and started to tell me about horseracing, which I was not into because I had seen a lot of paddy's skint themselves. But the conversation was good. I told the man where I was working and where my accent came from. I had a pint again and I knew I had to pace myself because Lily would not want me to get pissed like Tom would usually get. The evening passed quite companionably.

I walked back to the Railway pub; Lily and her friend were busy serving. Lily asked me to give her a hand in moving a barrel to the cellar. In the cellar, Lily put her arms around me and we kissed; her breasts were hard up against me and I could feel the donkey going hard but Lily said that I would have to wait. I told her not to tease me so the barrel never got moved. It was a busy night again in the pub but I just lay back. It was a sleep-in day tomorrow as it was Sunday. The night moved on, the jukebox was loud, it was soon over and Lily and her friend could relax again. Lily had asked her friends to stop back when Lily closed up. I just joined in the conversation and the night dragged on and it was soon one in the morning. A taxi was called for Lily's friends and then I made my way upstairs to bed. It was not long before Lily come in wearing her nightie and got into bed with me. Lily apologised that her friends stopped back but it was a thing Tom and she did most Saturdays nights and it would have aroused suspicions if she had cancelled. We got down to some serious lovemaking, then Lily got up and went to her room in case Tom came home early. In the morning, I was up, made tea and dressed. When Lily came into the kitchen, she was very chirpy and all smiles. I told Lily that I was going for a walk before I had anything to eat so I went out, got the Sunday papers and walked to the Railway Station as there were seats outside. It was a bit cold but dry. I went back in an hour and saw that Tom's car was in the car park. I went in the back way and upstairs. Tom was in the kitchen and I asked him if everything was all right. Tom turned and said it was his mother and she was not so bad now. I got on with breakfast—bacon and eggs. Tom went downstairs as he had some work to do in the cellar.

I finished my round and read the paper on the bed until dinnertime; I must have fallen asleep as it was just before one when I woke up. I cleaned up and was ready for a pint of Guinness. The bar was quite full. Lily pulled me a pint with a smile and I sat down with John, my dominos partner. Football was his speciality. All I knew about football was from Mr Don Reeve who lived across the road from me plus Brian Clough who lived around the corner in Middlesbrough. I went to the bar and got John and myself a drink. Tom served me plus I got some cheese and biscuits off the bar and sat down again with John. Two thirty was the closing time on Sundays. Lily had gone upstairs by now to prepare dinner and the pub was thinning out now. Dinner was good and I settled down in my room. When I got up, it was nearly 9 o'clock. I washed up and went down. Tom was busy and Lily was sitting with friends. I just stood at the bar; Tom came across to me between customers to talk. He was telling me what he had got lined up for the New Year's Eve party and that he had gotten a late-night licence for two nights. It was a bit lonely in bed that night but I needed the rest.

Monday was upon us again but work was for only half a week. Christmas Day fell on a Friday, so work stopped on Wednesday night. The job was going great but it was dusty loading lorries. All the small outbuildings were down and cleaned up. Tom, the foreman, asked me if I could drive the crane in the new year to knock the other buildings down as he was going to be busy on another job. The crane was a 22RD I CD 15-tonne and I was new to this crane. They had a 100-foot jib and the buildings were four-storey high. Tom said that he would like me to drive it before Christmas to break some concrete up on a big slab, so on Tuesday, I looked around the machine, greased it, checked the oil, dev and water, took it over to the concrete slab and started to drop the steel ball on it. Tom was watching me while I worked my way across and made sure that it was all broken small enough to load onto the lorries on Wednesday. I loaded the concrete that I had broken onto the lorries as it was the last day. We had to make the site safe over Christmas. I was still wondering what to do and where to go; no matter where I went, I had to pay for the digs. Tom knocked us off at dinnertime and took us all to the pub for a drink when the site was locked up. Tom said that we would go to the Railway Tavern where I was staying, so in we went. Lily got Tom downstairs as we went in as it was going to be busy. We got served and sat down. Lily came over and said she would put some food on. The foreman said that was good of her. The crack was good and with £50 on the table, it was even better. The lads started to drift off at 4 o'clock so I went up to my room to wash and sleep. It was late when I got up—9 o'clock. I thought I had better get up or I would not sleep tonight. I went down to the bar and Lily was on her own. I had missed the games night; the team was playing away at another pub, so it was quiet. I stood at the bar and talked to Lily; she asked what Father Christmas was fetching me and I said the same as last year—nothing. If I called at home on my parents, it would be socks as usual. I told her that I would go shopping in the morning. The phone rang and Lily went to answer it. Tom was needed on the phone as his mother was not too good and he would have to stay over again. Lily smiled at me. It was the last day before Christmas and I could do with some more clothes. Lily was just about to ring the bell for last orders when the games crowd came in with solemn faces as they had lost. John looked at me and I told him that I had slept in after a good dinnertime session with the lads. He smiled and said that you cannot win them all. The bell rang, I got another pint of Guinness and sat down with John. He told me that the Jolly Sailor have a good team and are well up in the league. When I drank up, John said goodnight and I made my way up to bed. It was not long before Lily came in with her nightie on and got into bed. The sex was great. She put on her nightie again and off she went to her own room. I got up early and put the kettle on; Tom came into the kitchen. I had not heard him come home and it was a good thing Lily had gone back to her own bed. Tom said that his wife was very chirpy these days and I thought, *Only because I am screwing her*. In walked Lily with a smile on her face. She had brought the morning papers up, so I sat down to read. Tom said that the road into town will be busy today and if I was going, I should go by train. I thought that was a good idea.

The town was Telford, not a big place, so off I went on the 10 o'clock train. It was cold but dry and I had a good walk around. I called at the post office to get some money for Christmas plus some dig money. £50 would last until the new year. I got a statement off the woman in the post office as my wages were on a post office draft. I thought I should call at Pat's in Birmingham but the weather forecast was not good and the sex was good at the pub, so I decided to stay where I was. I got a couple of cards for my friends plus Mum, Dad and family and posted them while I was in the post office, I put £40 in Mum's card for a present. I knew Mum and Dad would be all right with the rest of the family around them. I went to Woolworth's and British Home Stores and got what I wanted—clothes and socks. I called at a pub for a pint as I was not driving but the Guinness was not as good as in Tom's pub, so I left half of it and walked out. I got the train back to Oaken Gates, I went to the Railway pub and went upstairs to get shot of the bags I had brought back with me, then went down for a proper pint of Guinness. Tom was serving, I told Tom about the bad pint I had. Tom said Lily was out doing her last Christmas shopping, I did not want to drink as it was Christmas Eve and it was going to be a long night. John was in the pub, so I sat down with him, I listened to John going on about his football again. Up I went to the bedroom again for some kip; the noise woke me up as the jukebox was loud, I looked at the clock and it was gone 8 o'clock, so up I got, bathed, put my best clothes and smellies on and went into the kitchen. Lily had left me a ham salad with a plate over it. I ate it, then washed the pots and went downstairs; the pub was busy. Lily, her friend and Tom were behind the bar. Lily came across to me and asked me if I ate the tea she had left me and I said yes. I got a pint and sat down next to John again. He carried on about his beloved football but he was good company. The jukebox played out '60s' music and it was good to listen to. Tom and Lily had a licence until 12 o'clock and I had to pace myself with the drink. I got up to buy John a pint and myself a whisky chaser to help the Guinness down. The night rolled on and soon it was midnight and the bell rang for last time. Lily and Tom stayed back for a lock up and I said goodnight and went to bed.

On Christmas Day, there were no papers, so I took a walk. It was cold and wet outside, so I did not stay out too long. I had breakfast and Lily came into the kitchen, smiled and told me to close my eyes. I did and she put a present in my hand. I opened my eyes. Lily had bought me a watch for Christmas. Lily put her finger up to her mouth. *Well*, I thought, *this was for services rendered*. After breakfast, I went and cleaned the car and checked it all over, oil, water and tyres because in the new year, I would be moving on. Christmas dinner was good with Lily and Tom. The pub was not open at night and I watched TV with a pint of Guinness that Tom had brought upstairs with him as well as a bottle of wine for them both. Tom and Lily could relax and put their feet up.

Boxing Day was another busy day in the pub. I started with breakfast with Tom and Lily, then Tom went down to the cellar to do his daily chores. Lily and I had a good talk about life in general. Lily said that she would miss me when I left; especially in the bed and sex side of it. I told Lily that I would keep in touch and call in when I was around this way. The conversation ended with the cleaner coming upstairs and in the kitchen. It was a good morning all around. Boxing Day was bitterly cold and wet outside, so I read the construction news that I had bought days earlier. It was the wrong time of the year but there were a couple of jobs I was interested in for the coming year. I went for a walk to get some fresh air and as it was cold and wet outside, the fresh air cleared my head. I walked to the park to sit down but everything was wet, so I walked out again. I noticed that the Jolly Sailor pub was open, so I walked in. The Landlord looked at me when I asked for a bottled drink to settle my tummy. His name was Jim and he wished me a Merry Christmas. I had met Jim on games night at the Railway pub. I asked for a pint of Guinness but it did not taste very good; it must have been the first one out of the pump, so I just sipped it. When I got it down, I walked out. It was a good thing Jim paid for it. I walked back to the Railway pub and there were a few people by now. John was in so I got a pint of Guinness from Lily. I sat down with John and his friends and listened to the conversation; it was on sports as usual. Lily came over to the table with drinks on a tray. I could see that mine was a double whisky. Lily smiled as she turned around to go back to the bar and John noticed it. Some people in the pub had noticed that Lily had perked up in the last month. I went to the toilet past the bar and Lily asked me if cold meat and mash was all right for tea. I smiled and said yes. After tea, I had a lie down on the bed and I must have dropped off as it was 8.30 when I woke up. I got up and went to the bathroom to wash. Before I could shut the door, Lily was there in her dressing gown. She shut the door behind her and put the bolt on. She said that Tom had gone out to see his mates around other pubs. It was good sex over the bath and on the toilet seat. When we had finished, I unlocked the door to see if the coast was clear. Lily was off to her own room to get dressed for the bar downstairs. I got dressed, put some scent on and went down to the bar. Lily was down before me and a pint of Guinness was on the bar. Lily would not take the money for it; instead, Lily leaned over and whispered in my ear that the pint was for services rendered. There was a big smile on Lily s face. I stood at the bar as Lily s friend served. Just after ten, Tom rolled in—a bit worse for the wear. Tom said to Lily that he was going straight upstairs and said goodnight to all. Lily called last time and when everybody had gone, we sat down at a table with drinks. Lily's friend said goodnight and left. When Lily came back to the bar after locking up and putting the lights out, lovemaking was on her mind. Lily took my hand and we went across to the bench seats. It was sex again and it was great Lily was insatiable and seemed to want it whenever she could and I was now sore. We kissed goodnight and I went up to bed as I had to get up early for work.

On Monday morning, I got a cup of tea and went out to work. I carried on with the crane and ball on the five-storey building as there were now lorries to load until the New Year. The foreman said that he would leave the building to me as I had four days to work the top down to make it safe. With the weather being wet, the dust was not bad at all. The building was coming down a treat. It was a post-war building consisting of four layers of blue bricks but when you cut a hole in it, it was all right. The roof had already been stripped off the slates and stored as there was a good market for them. When I got to the end of the building, I moved the roof timers and let them fall into the building. Two of the lads took a steel sling and put it around the timers and lifted them out to be stacked and sold. At dinner, myself and the lads whose names where Colin and Brian—they looked as though they had had a rough night and could do with the hair of the dog—so we went to the Railway pub. Lily was behind the bar and I got a pint of Guinness for myself and two pints of bitter for Colin and Brian. It would swill the dust down. Lily got me to one side and said that Tom had to go to his mother's again so I should not be home late for tea as she might bathe me. I winked at her. It was dark at 5 o'clock and Lily said that she would fetch her friend in if needed. We drank up and I went back to work with the thought of screwing the arse off Lily again.

The lads and I made our excuses for the night as Tom, the foreman, was on another site. I went in at the back of the pub as I was a bit mucky and full of dust. I took my boots off, then I heard a voice say, "Billy, is that you?" It was Lily upstairs. I got upstairs and Lily was running a bath for me. I was taken in, undressed and I got in the bath. The door was locked behind Lily and off came her clothes. She got in the bath, washed me all over first and then gave me the best blowjob I had had in years. The sex was good again. Lily washed me all over again. We had to stop as her friend could only stop behind the bar for a couple of hours. Lily said tea would be on the table in a minute. I wrapped the towel around me, got changed and then had tea. By now, my dick(donkey) was sore but I was very satisfied. I sat down to read the papers after I had washed the pots. I needed to get my energy back. It was quiet when I went downstairs. Lily was on her own, a big smile on her face again. I told Lily that Tom had told me that he had noticed the change in her and Lily whispered in my ear that I was a good lover. I just winked. John came over to the bar and asked me if I was available on Wednesday. I said, "Yes, I will try not to sleep in." Lily got talking to her lady friend who had just come in, so I went and sat down with John and his friend. The second bell went so John left and I went up to bed. I had just reached upstairs when I heard Tom's voice at the back door. Oh *Well*, I thought, *I will at least get a good night's sleep tonight.*

At work the next morning, Tom, the foreman, turned up to see how we were getting on and was very impressed on how fast it was going. Tom asked me if I wanted a permanent job with him and I said that I would think about it. It was another good day on the site. The building was coming down good and we cleaned up as we went. I folded the walls into the centre, then lifted more roof timbers out of the middle and stacked them. We had a sandwich at the shop down the road and the cabin on the site had a kettle and cups and a gas stove in it. We cracked on with the building and it was down by Wednesday. It was games night in the pub and I had promised John that I would play dominos with him as his partner. I bathed and had the dinner Lily had set out—egg and chips and ham. I could smell the food for the games league tonight. Tom's team was at home. The evening went well and the dominos won. John and I won darts and the team lost at crib. Lily said that it was a night for the pub in the league. I told Lily that I could do with an early night; I got a big smile from Lily.

I was up early the next day and put the kettle on in the kitchen. Lily came in while I had the frying pan on. She carried on with breakfast and I said to Lily that I would see her later around dinner. Thursday was a tidying-up day on the site as it was New Year's Eve and no more work until Monday. When it was 12.30, the lads said that they would come to the pub with me for a drink for the New Year. Tom was behind the bar and it was three pints of Guinness as we sat down for the crack and the talk was about work next year and where we would be after this job. Lily came to the bar with a plate of sandwiches. I did not want too much to drink as it was going to be a long day plus night. The lads drank up and we shook hands and wished each other all the best for the new year. I made my way upstairs to have a bath—undisturbed this time. It was good to lay in the bath of hot water and Lily's bath salts and have a good soak. I heard a noise in the kitchen; I covered myself in Lily's spare dressing gown and came out of the bathroom. Lily was coming out of the kitchen. She asked me if I enjoyed my bath with a smile on her face and if the bathroom was free. I just nodded my head and went into the bedroom. I lay down on the bed, which was a bad thing as I dropped off. When I woke up, I could hear music downstairs. I shot up, got dressed, sprayed some aftershave on and went down to the bar. Lily said, "I thought you were sleeping the New Year in!" Lily, Tom and Lily's friend were behind the bar and a late night was in hand. The group Tom had booked were not bad and really got the pub rocking. I had a few whiskeys and they went down well. I could see Tom drinking and thought that Lily would be wanting a ride, so I eased off on the drink a bit. At 12 o'clock, it was 1968. We made a ring in the room with all the customers and sang *Auld Lang Syne*. Then I shook hands with the men and had a peck off the women but for Lily, it had to be the lips to the smiles of the customers. Tom was about pissed but shook hands with me. When the main people had gone off to party, the four of us sat down to relax with a drink. I had a double whisky but sipped it. Tom got up and said to Lily that he was turning in and would she lock up. He would clean up in the morning and said goodnight and off he went. The barmaid said that it was time to go as it was 1.30 in the morning, so Lily let her out and locked up. She sat down on my knee, put her arm around me and said, "I will miss you when you go; it was good to have a toy-boy around!" We put the lights out and the sex was good on the bench seat but I was sore again. Lily was satisfied and that was the main thing. Then it was up to bed with a big kiss at the top of the stairs.

In the morning, my head was a bit heavy. Coffee was on and I had it in the kitchen. Tom was up doing the cellar duties; Lily strolled into the kitchen still in her nightdress and dressing gown. Tom came up for breakfast that Lily had made. There was no work until Monday. Tom said to Lily that he would ring up his dad to wish him *Happy New Year*. Five minutes later, Tom came back to the room and said that his mother had taken ill again and was on her way to the hospital. Tom said that he would get a taxi to his dad's to look after him as he was too hungover to drive and I was just as bad. Tom told Lily to show me what to do in the cellar and I said that I would give her a hand. There was a taxi outside so off Tom went. We both went down to the bar to clean up and Lily showed me how to clean the pumps out plus the pipes. We got on like a house on fire but Lily was getting too close and I did not want to settle down yet. When I got the jobs sorted out, I said to Lily that I was going to get some fresh air. Lily smiled and said that she was going to run a bath and have a good soak in peace. I went out the back door to the car park. Tom's car was there and so was mine. I thought, *In the next couple of weeks, I would be finished and off again.* I walked down the road past the station; the air was fresh but cold. I went to a phone to ring home. I had my Brother's phone number on me. Malcolm's voice came on; he was surprised. I asked about Mum and Dad and did they have a good Christmas and New Year? Malcolm said that Dad was not too good with his chest and was off work again. I told Malcolm that I could not get home because of the weather and that I would put some money in the post for them. He also told me that he was courting and it was going well. I told him to tell Mum and Dad that I had rung up. I walked back to the pub and let myself in the back door. As I passed the stairs, I heard Lily ask, "Is that you, Billy?"

I said yes and Lily asked if I wanted a coffee. I said yes and upstairs I went and to the kitchen where Lily was. I told her that I had rung home to ask about my mum and dad. I told Lily that my dad's chest was bad and he was off work. I sipped my coffee and we talked some more about life and where to go from here. I thought about where I would be this time next year. Lily said she would be here as she loved the job and liked living in Oaken Gates. "Well," said Lily, "it is time to open up the pub. You can stand at the other side of the bar for a change and I will keep you right."

Down to the bar we went and I got behind the bar; my first customer to serve was John on Guinness. Lily was an expert at pulling it, so I watched the first one being pulled. I enjoyed my four hours behind the bar and I brought drinks in the pump. Lily had made tea, which was egg and chips. We both watched TV in her lounge and Lily kept her distance in case we fell asleep and Tom came back early. Lily got some dinner—fish and chips. I got the pots washed while Lily got changed and went down to open up. I then went down to the bar to serve; it was a good night. I had a few more drinks and was getting good at pulling the beer plus getting a head on the Guinness but no good at putting the shamrock on top. The phone rang and Lily went to answer it. Lily came off the phone and told me that it was Tom and his mum was not too bad but he had to stay in the hospital for another week. Tom's sister was going to stop with his mother from Sunday afternoon. Lily smiled and I thought my prick would be sore again in the morning. We called last time and Lily looked up when the last people had gone. I took a pint of Guinness upstairs with me and Lily came up with a bottle of red wine. We sat on the sofa and Lily put the TV on but that was a waste of time. We kissed and then it was to the bedroom while we had the chance as this could be the last bed job I might get. The sex was great again. Lily got out of bed and went back to her own room just in case Tom came home early.

The next morning, Lily came into the kitchen and I got a peck on the cheek and a good morning. I went down and brought the papers up and Lily had got food on the table, which was two eggs on toast. I ate it, read the paper and I could hear the cleaner downstairs, so I got up and went down to the cellar to sort the barrels out and clean the pipes. I was at the bar when Tom came home and said that his sister was staying with his mother for a week or so. Sunday dinner was busy and I went for a lie down after a couple of pints. It was 8.30 when I woke up. I got a wash and went down to the bar. Tom and Lily were behind the bar. Tom pulled me a pint and I sat down with John. I told him that this could be my last week, then I would be moving on to where I did not know. John asked me if I would partner him on Wednesday night at dominos and I agreed as we were to play at home. Tom came over to the table and sat down with us. He that it could be my last week with them. "You have been a good friend as well as a lodger; thank you," Tom said. If he only knew! I thought that sex was great with someone else's wife.

I was up on Saturday morning, had tea, and then out on the job. Tom, the foreman, was on the site and he wanted eight lorries' loads of brick rubble for another job where he had to lay a road. When I got the lorries away, Tom came over and asked me again if I wanted the job full time. I asked about the money plus lodging, tax free. He said that he would talk to me later and then off he went. The post office was down the road, so I went to get some money out for my digs and beer tokens while the lorries were gone. I walked back and the lorries were back; I got them loaded again and the lads and I cleaned up the site. I parked the machine and we locked the site up. "Are you coming for a pint to wash down the dust?" I asked the lads.

"If you are paying," the lads said. I agreed and we got to the pub. Tom was behind the bar. I paid the digs money and asked for three pints of Guinness and sat down. Colin, one of the lads, asked me if I was going to take the job Tom offered. "Well," I said, "if the money was right, but I feel like travelling at the moment and meeting people so we will see." We drank up. "I will see you two on Monday as I am going to get a bath," I said and off I went upstairs. I got my towel out of the room and went into the bathroom. Before I could shut the door, Lily was there and the bolt went on. She stripped me and her clothes came off and into the bath we got. I could see that Lily was horny as hell. We washed each other and the donkey stood up to the action. We dried each other, then I took Lily from the back. I had to put my hand over her mouth as she orgasmed to kill the noise. Lily unlocked the door when the coast was clear, then she went off to her bedroom. I finished drying, then got changed and went down to the bar. Lily was down behind the bar as Tom had just left; Lily had a big smile on her face and winked at me. I sat down with John and we got the dominos out and got the school going. It was an enjoyable afternoon.

Lily made egg, ham and chips for tea when Tom got back. I went to my room to lie down as I needed the rest. When I woke up, it was 8 o'clock. I went to the kitchen and the chips were ready for the pan, so I got on with it. The food was good and went down well. I went downstairs to the bar; Lily and her friend Anna were behind the bar as Tom had gone out with his mates. I stood at the bar and Anna said to me, "Lily said you will be leaving next week; do you know where you are going?"

"Not until I ring up the yard next week," I replied.

Lily suggested that I take Anna out as she was divorced and did not get out very often. Anna was in her early 30s with her tits in the right place—a little big but it would be a change, I think. "Where will you take me?" I asked Anna.

She said, "It is a surprise. Eight o'clock all right?"

"Yes," I said. The night ended with Tom coming back and we locked up for a good night's sleep. In the morning, I had the kettle on. I could hear the cleaner downstairs and Tom talking. Lily came into the kitchen and I got a peck on the cheek and a good morning. Tom came upstairs and said, "Good morning. I hear you have a date tonight."

"I think so," I said.

"Well, good luck to you, Billy. Have a good night," Tom said.

I ate the breakfast and went to get some fresh air; it was cold but dry. I got the paper; the news of the world always had plenty of sex in its stories. I sat on the station seat and read until 11 o'clock. I walked back to the pub and looked at my car; it was all right. Lily was coming down to open the bar and she whispered in my ear not to use up all my energy as I might need it on Monday. I smiled and got a peck on the cheek. John was in the bar, so dominos were got out and we had a good game of five and threes. Last orders were called and dinner was nearly ready so I told John that I would see him on Wednesday night—games night. The dinner was good—Lily could cook as well as fuck. I lay down for an hour to let the dinner go down, then washed and put plenty of scent. Down in the bar, Anna was early. "Where are we going?" I asked her.

"The Labour club. There is a good turn on and bingo," Anna replied. So off we went. I had to get signed in. Anna told me to find a seat and I went to the bar. I noticed the barmaid pulling a pint of Guinness; it did not look too good so I had a Newcastle brown ale instead. Anna was on gin and bitter lemon. *Well*, I thought, *a double might do the trick and sex may be on offer at the end of the night*. I sat down with Anna; she had a drink which was a bit strong but I just smiled. The turn in the first half was not bad as I loved sixties music. I went and got the bingo tickets. I had no luck on the bingo, the turn came on again and they played the waltzes. I got Anna up to dance; her breasts were rubbing up against me and I knew the donkey was going in tonight.

We left the club and Anna said that I had better come to her place for coffee. "Well, that sounds good," I said. We walked to Anna's house. Anna went to the front room and poked the fire and added some more coal. The kettle was on and coffee came. Anna sat on the settee and she told me about her marriage. She put her arms around me and we kissed. The inevitable was to happen—the clothes started to come off we fondled and then it was sex on the floor it was great in front of the fire. When we had finished, the coffee was cold but the donkey was sore. "You are a good lover," she said. I knew the girls had been talking and I was set up but not to worry; it took the heat off Lily. I got on the settee, put my underpants back on and Anna got a blanket to put over me. I got a kiss for my services as Anna had only a single bed.

It was still dark when I woke up. I looked at my watch and saw it was 6.30 in the morning. I got dressed and looked in the bedroom—Anna was sleeping like a new-born baby. I left and walked home to the pub; it was a good thing that I had the backdoor key. I went upstairs to the kitchen and put the kettle on. There was a noise on the landing; it was Lily. "How did you get on with Anna?" she asked.

"Good," I said, "she is horny as hell and I am knocked out."

"Well, you made a good friend happy. Do you want breakfast before you go to work?" Lily asked me.

I said yes and got changed for work. The coffee went down well. At work, we got on with the job and took the last building down. After an hour, I started to clean it up and load the rubble om the lorries. It was a dusty day and there was no dinner so we could knock off early. It was 4 o'clock when we went to the pub to wash the dust down. Tom was behind the bar. "Did you have a good night with Anna?" he asked.

"Yes," I said, "it was great." I thought, *That will take the heat off Lily*. The lads went and I went up to take a bath. Lily was out. *Good*, I thought, *I will not be disturbed in the bath*. I had a good soak for half an hour, then dried, dressed and went to the kitchen. Lily was in. "Are you hungry?" Lily asked. I said yes. "I got two pieces of cod for you and Tom with fresh bread and homemade chips," she said.

It went down a treat. I just hoped that I would not have to return the favour tonight as the donkey could do with a rest. I went down to the bar, got a pint and then sat down with John and his friends. "Well," John said, "your last week; we have to win on Wednesday."

"I will be on my way on Saturday morning," I said. "I do not know my destination yet. We will have a good drink before I go."

The last bell rang and sleep was on the menu, so it was goodnight to all and up that wooden hill I went. I was off like a light. I woke up and went to the bathroom to run a bath. It was great and as I came out, there was a noise in the kitchen. I walked in with my towel around me; Lily was there. "Did you enjoy your kip?" she asked.

"Yes, I did," I said. "I needed it as the night before with your friend drained me." I knew the girls had been talking between each other. Off to work I went and the lads were late in but I got on cleaning up the site until they came. I got the last of the rubble loaded as I would be on the phone tomorrow to see where I was going for my next job. Tom, the foreman, turned up. "Well, you have made a good job of the site. Have you made your mind up yet?"

"Yes, I will give you a ring if I get stuck for a job," I replied.

"Well," said Tom, "I will always fit you in." He signed my timesheets and gave me twenty pounds as bonus. It would buy the drinks at the pub tonight. He wished me luck with my travelling and left. I thought I would go to the phone now as it was only 4.30. I walked to the phone box, dialled the operator and gave the number and was put on hold. I told the plant manager that I was off hire from Friday. "Well," he said, "will you go back up north to Whitemare Pool, which is this side of the Tyne tunnel? There is a machine up there standing."

"Yes," I said I had to be up there by Monday. I went back and told the lads I was going tomorrow instead of Saturday. I parked the machine so that the low loader could pick it up. The three of us went to the pub. Tom was behind the bar. I ordered three pints and told him that I was off tomorrow. "Well, it's your last night," he said. "That's it." I shook hands with Tom, then with the lads and went upstairs to take a bath. Lily was in the kitchen. She turned around and I told her that I was off in the morning as I would call on my parents on the way. I could see a tear in her eye. I walked to the bathroom. Lily was determined to have a last shag, so she came in, shut the door and bolted it. Lily undressed in seconds and undressed me. We made love on the bathroom floor. Lily said that she would miss all this next week. We had already put the bath water on, so we got in to wash the sweat off us. We got dry, Lily unbolted the door and the coast was clear, so we went off to our bedrooms to get dressed. I went to the kitchen to see what Lily had made for tea. I got a big smile and a peck on the cheek and a thank you. "Ham, egg and chips all right for you?" Lily asked. It went down well. Lily and I sat and chatted. She asked me if I would be down this way again. "If I am, I will call in; I have your number in my book," I said.

Lily got up from the table. "I will see you downstairs," she said and went. I picked up the paper to read, then came to the kitchen, got my tea and sat down at the table. When I went downstairs, Lily got me a pint of Guinness as I needed all the strength at the moment. Lily said that the pint was on the house. The next thing I knew, John and the Wednesday night team had come to say goodbye, so it was a good night. I had to watch how much I drank as I wanted to get away fairly early in the morning. The night ended and the goodbyes were in hand. Up I went to get some sleep; I slept like a log and it was 6.30 when I woke up. I packed the rest of my gear, went into the kitchen and put the kettle on for tea as I had a mouth like a shithouse. There was a noise behind me; it was Lily. "You are off then," she said.

"Yes," I said, "I will call on my parents on the way up north." I got a big kiss on the lips this time.

"Look after yourself and keep in touch from time to time," she said. I went down, got in my car, and then off I went. The weather was not too good—wet and cold—at this time of the year. It was the end of February 1968. I had looked at the map two days before, so I had a good idea where I was going. The weather got a bit brighter as I got on the AI north. I pulled into a Greasy Spoon Café. The smell coming from the Café was good, so it was breakfast and it went down well. I drove on up the A1 north, then turned off on A19 Middlesbrough, Tees. I reached my parents' house. My friends across the road were out on the street as the snow was going away and the sledges were still out on the street. I said hello to them all. I got to the front door, knocked and my mother opened the door with surprise on her face. She gave me a big cuddle on the doorstep and in I went. Dad was in the front room as his chest was bad and he was off work. I sat down to talk to Dad as Mum put the kettle on. Ronnie, my older brother, came in from the garden. "Hi Billy, what brings you home?" he asked.

I told him and Dad that I was on my way to a job this side of the new Tyne Tunnel—Whitemare Pool. I asked if the rest of the family was all right. Ronnie said he was courting and was still working at Dorman's bridge yard. Malcolm was about to leave school and had got a job on a farm out in Darlington. He still had the allotment with the chickens plus Ronnie had the pigeons out in the loft that Dad had built. Kathy was working at a hotel at Cattrick on the A1. Margaret and Dennis were still at school. Paul was not at home and was living with a girl in a flat at Redcar. He was still not working and still in more trouble. I went to the kitchen and gave Mum some money that I had on me as I had enough petrol and enough to get me out for the night. I went the shop at the bottom of the street to get a paper. The Butcher's was still there and the old school was around the corner. I strolled back to my parents' house and as it was teatime, Mum asked what I wanted to eat but I told her that I had had a big breakfast on the way up. She asked me if I was staying the night and I said I could. I asked Dad if he would like to go out and have a pint. I do not think that I could afford it but I said I would pay. After tea, I got a wash to freshen up; Dad was ready and so was Ronnie. I went next door to my uncle Charlie and aunt Rosy; they were surprised to see me. I asked about their family—Peter, Andy, Maureen and Keith. They all were good, my Aunt said. I asked my uncle Charlie if he would like to go to the club for a pint. Then we went to the club like old times. We sat down in the club and I hoped no one would recognise me from the paper about the Aberfan disaster. The evening was good and I met Dad's old pals. There was Sandy; he was a train driver and I would meet him after school at the railway yard. I asked how his daughter, Sheila, was as she used to go to the same school as me. Sandy told me that she now worked at a bank in the town. It was last orders, so I got the drinks and bought Mum three bottles of Mackeson Stouts as she loved it. We all went back to the house and Mum had a sandwich on the go. I got down on the sofa for the night.

In the morning, the kettle was on as Mum came downstairs. I decided to go to the paper shop for the Sunday papers; Mum always liked the People newspaper. "Do you want breakfast before you go?" Mum asked.

"No," I said, "it is too early; I will get something on the road up north." It was time to say goodbye as Dad came downstairs. Mum gave me my Christmas present—socks as usual. I gave her a big kiss and told Dad not to worry over money problems. I went back towards the A19. I rang up Dennis to see how the land lay for digs. He said, "Well I never! You are back up here."

"Yes," I said, "I am across at Whitemare Pool for a few weeks."

"So am I!" said Dennis.

"Well, that's great! I will call around to see you in about two hours." I replied. I drove back on the A19 and the traffic was getting busier. I went over the Tyne Bridge and on to Wallsend. I reached Dennis' house; it was great to see him and his wife, Sally. "I will call around my old digs to see Gordy," I said.

"You can kip on the sofa for one night. You can find digs near the job and it will save travelling right around as I have to do. I have two more lads in the car from the job." Dennis suggested. I washed up as we were going to the Miner's club; there was a turn on. "We can call at the Penny Wet pub as we go; my brother-in-law and his wife are going there. We rang them up and told them that you are here and they will save seats for us," Dennis said. I told Dennis that I had thought about going around to Mary's but I did not want to get involved with children at this moment and it was only a shag at the end of the day. As we walked into the Penny Wet pub, Tommy was standing at the bar with Patsy. Dennis said, "Look what the cat brought home!" Tommy and Patsy turned around in surprise. Tommy put his arms around me. "Well I never! You look well, Billy boy," he said. I got a big kiss from Winner behind the bar as Tommy was still living with her and marriage was in the air. The crack was good. I told Tommy about where I had been: Aberfan in South Wales, across to Dublin, Ireland, and Oaken Gates in Shropshire and back up here. "Well," said Tommy, "you certainly move around!"

"I will catch up with you next weekend if you are in," I suggested. Tommy and Patsy said yes and all three of us walked down the road to the club. We went across to friends who had saved seats for us. Dennis and I went to the bar for the drinks.

The next morning, it was cold outside when I went for a paper down the road; I remembered where the shop was. The kettle had boiled when I got back and Dennis was up. The job was down to a five-day week as it was winter. Dennis and I sat down and talked about the local gossip and read the paper. Dennis said that there was a bit of work to do on the job at Whitemare Pool; the road had to be averted at the end of the tunnel to the A19. There was a Case shovel machine with a ripper tooth on the back. It looked like it had come from the yard in Birmingham and that's what I would be driving. It was almost dinnertime and the men in the northeast went to the pub or a club on a Sunday. Sally, Dennis' wife, said that dinner would be ready by 3 o'clock. We had the crack for an hour and then went to the club to meet Dennis' friends. We had a good dinnertime session—Yorkshire pudding with gravy, then Sunday roast. Next, it was a lie down on Sunday night as Dennis had to run around in the lorry on the coast road and then come over to the pool job, so it was up early.

On Monday, after tea, Dennis said that he would see me over at the pool job sometime today. Off we went. I drove through Newcastle to the job, found the offices, parked and then went in. The foreman from the coast road job greeted me, "Have you come to drive the Case machine?"

"Yes," I said.

"Have you got digs yet?" he asked me.

I said, "No, I stayed with Dennis Mosley the last two nights."

"Well," he said, "there is a café down the road and it also has a B&B. I will take you down to look at the road job that I have got for you for the next month or so, weather permitting." We stopped at the café, it was open, I went and asked the man behind the counter if there was a room available. I got it, then the foreman, Ron, and I went to look at the job in hand. There was a lot of tarmac of the old road to take up and load. Dennis would join me later with the lorry as one lorry should keep me going for now. I checked the machine over for oil, water and dev and started it up while Ron was there. I spent the first two hours ripping up tarmac. A man named Mick turned up as Ron had sent him down to be the banks man. Dennis turned up with the lorry, which I loaded. It was teatime and we had to pass the café on the way to the tip. I told

Dennis that I got digs in the café and there was a pub down the road which was good. I got a lift on the last load to get my car from the offices. I went the café and looked at the menu, then ordered the steak and chips, which looked good. As I looked around the room, I got a big smile from the lady when she brought it to the table. Then I got my bag out of the car and got a key for my room and went upstairs to number five. It was basic but it was on the job and I did not have to travel far to work. I washed up as there was a pub down the road called The White Horse. It looked a bit quiet for a Monday night. I went to the bar and got a bottle of nuke brown. The lady looked a bit sexy in a low-cut top. The fire was on in the bar. "Nice and warm in here," she remarked.

"Yes," I said, "it's cold out tonight."

"Are you a lorry driver? We get a few of them in here at the start of the week," she asked.

"No," I said, "I am working on the road job outside the tunnel."

"Are you staying at the café?"

"You are very chatty," I remarked.

"Well, there is not much more to do around here in the week. My name is Janet," she replied.

"My name is Billy."

"How long will you be on the job?" she asked.

"Three to four weeks; might be more. It is the second time that I have been up here as I was on the coast road job at Wallsend over a year ago, so I know my way around." I said.

"Do you go to the Jungle Night club at North Shields now and again?" asked Janet. "It is a bit of a dive but you can see how the other half lives."

"Are you married or courting?" I asked Janet.

"I am not in a relationship at the moment," she said.

"If you are doing nothing then one night I will take you out," I offered.

"Yes," said Janet, "I am not working on Friday night. It's a date then. The Landlord and Landlady are away until Wednesday; they are on holiday in Tenerife. Will you be in tomorrow?"

"Yes," I said. There were more people coming into the pub, so the conversation died away for now. It was last orders, so I said goodnight to Janet and walked back to the café for some kip. I thought to myself that you never score on your first night.

It was cold when I got up and I could smell breakfast downstairs as the café opened at 6 o'clock. I washed my face and down I went. I got the tea down but asked the lady if I could please have my breakfast later. She agreed and gave me a ticket. I put on some warm clothes as the machine had a cab on it no heater. Dennis and I got on with the job in hand. The bank man, Mick, looked after the traffic. We got two loads away and it was teatime. Mick went to the cabin for tea and I jumped into the lorry for the café as mine was paid for. I got Dennis his and I told Dennis about the bird in the pub. "You do work fast sometimes," he remarked. I laughed. The job was for five days a week—7.30 to 5.00—as it got dark early. I went to the café and the menu looked good—

lamb chops and mashed potatoes and peas—and it went down well. There were papers on the tables, so I passed my time reading one as I did not want to go out early. I went up to the room and got a shower, which was a shared one, so you had to wait if the doors were locked. I walked to the pub and there were a few more people in as it was games night. Janet smiled as she got me a bottle of nuke brown. "I have to make sandwiches for the games night plus get the chips ready to fry later on," she said. I sat down to watch the domino school which performed not too badly I thought. The home team won darts they lost at crib. So, it was a good night all around. It was time to go but Janet had other ideas. "Will you help me clean up?" Janet asked me.

"Alright," I said. She looked up when the last one had gone and I went around the bar with the glasses. I knew sex was on the cards. "Coffee is upstairs," Janet said and took hold of my hand. I did not need asking a second time. We went into the living room and I sat down while the coffee was being made. Janet sat next to me, the chemistry was good and in no time at all, the clothes started to come off. We were on the floor and going at it like two rabbits and the sex was good. The coffee became cold but we did not care as we were both satisfied. "You will have to go as I don't know what time the Landlord will be back," Janet said. I got dressed, got another kiss, then off I went back to the café. I went up to bed.

It was another cold day when I got up. I washed my face and went down to get tea and a ticket for later on. I glanced at the papers on the table and then off to the job I went. Dennis turned up with some good news as he had heard from Peter Morley that there was a new road bypass going past Morpeth. Dennis had Peter's number that he said he would ring when he got the chance today as there were not many weeks left here. We got on with the job and I had to rip another length of tarmac before I could load Dennis's lorry, so he had an hour. It was a cold and wet day. I got Dennis' loaded and it was teatime, so I went to the café. There was a phone in the café and I said I would try tonight when we were done. We had a good day and the job was moving faster than we thought. Ron, the foreman, came down on the site just to see how we were getting on as we were pretty much ruled by the engineers and how they were setting the job out. The traffic was moved into a single lane as the road was not very busy. I got to the café at night and rang Peter about the job. He said that yes, there was a job starting up at Morpeth at the start of next month, April, when the weather should be better. I told him that I would keep in touch in the next two weeks or so and would ring again. Then I had ham, egg and chips for tea, got changed and walked to the pub. There was a new face behind the bar. It must be the Landlord. I got a Newcastle brown and sat down. There was a lady also behind the bar and both were tanned so I knew that it was the Landlord and his wife. In walked Janet and I went to the bar to talk and get a drink. She said that it was on the house. "Where would you like to go?" I asked her.

"We will go to South Shields as it is just up the road," she replied. Janet went to the bar and ordered a taxi. She said she would leave her car in the car park at the pub. Janet asked about the new tunnel and if I had been in it. I said no but my mate was on the tunnelling machine before he was taken badly. The pub door opened and a man called out, "Taxi!" We drank up and got into the taxi. We had given the name of a pub with music on. I paid the fare. It was seriously lively and we managed to get a seat at the back of the room. We carried on talking after I brought the drinks. "You will have to pay to come through the tunnel but it will save time driving around by Newcastle to go north," I said. "At the moment, I'm taking the old road out and then they will set out a new one. The tunnel opens this year, I have heard."

"Yes," said Janet, "it was on the local news. Where will you go after this job is finished?"

"I don't know at this moment. I have heard that there is a job starting in Morpeth bypass this year. I will plod on here until then. What about you? Have you got any plans in place for the future?" I asked Janet.

"Well," said Janet, "I would like to work in a bank or be a secretary. I will attend night school when it starts again next month."

"Well, I hope you get somewhere," I said. The night was coming to a close, last orders had been called and Janet went to the phone as she knew all the taxi numbers for around here. We got a taxi back to the pub's car park. Janet stated that the taxi will drop her off at her mother's house where she was staying and she would catch a bus to work tomorrow. I got a big kiss before she went. I said that I would call in tomorrow afternoon after work as I was going across to Dennis' for the weekend. I said goodnight and off she went. I walked to the café down the road.

In the morning, we were told that we could work till 1 o'clock. We stuck it and I took the old kerbs out and loaded them up onto Dennis' lorry. We managed to load up four loads as well as having breakfast before it was time to knock off. We called at the café as I was going across to Wallsend for Saturday night with Dennis. He waited as I got a shower and changed. We left my car in the car park of the café. Dennis had his car and the lorry was parked at the offices. We called at the pub and had a pint. Janet was behind the bar. "Are you working all weekend?" I asked her. She said yes and I said that we would catch up with her on Monday night. We both drank up, got in the car and travelled to Wallsend-on-Tyne. The road was busy on the A1 through Newcastle. I had my washbag with me to clean up on Sunday. We arrived at Dennis' house and had a bit to eat, then watched a bit of sports on the TV. Dennis and his wife started to get ready to go to the club. "I will meet you at the Penny Wet pub in about an hour," Dennis said. That was all right with me as I decided to call around at my old digs and see how the old couple were before going to the pub. They were surprised to see me and Gordy was full of himself as usual. Alice was in fine fettle and asked if I wanted a cup of tea. I declined, saying that I was going to the pub shortly. I got up to go and Alice gave a big kiss on the cheek. "Look after yourself, Billy," they both said and off I went to the Penny Wet pub. There was a big cheer from Tommy and Patsy as I walked in. Winner was behind the bar and said hello. "Is it a bottle of Newcastle brown (nuke brown as we called it) for my lad?" Tommy asked me. "Have you got digs across the water?"

"Yes," I said, "in the café near the job."

"Is the job going all right? Where next?" asked Tommy. I said that there was a bypass going to start shortly at Morpeth and a mate was going to start on it as a fitter. Dick Hampton got the earthmoving job on it and was starting at the end of the month, weather permitting. Just then Dennis and Sally walked in. The crack was good, then I bought drinks for Tommy and Pasty as we were going to the Miner's club. "Catch you all tomorrow; dinner is in here. It's a date," I said and then we walked to the club. Dennis' brother-in-law was holding the seats for us. There was a comedian on first. It was Bobby—a well-known comedian around the northeast and was good. He only performed for an hour as he fitted two or three clubs in a night. The group that followed were good and the nuke brown went down well. I noticed Mary in the far corner. She was with a bloke. *So what*, I thought. Dennis had noticed too and smiled. "You are off the hook," he said with a laugh. Mary looked my way and smiled. I smiled back. It was a good night and we got a taxi back to Dennis' house. We had a sandwich, Dennis brought the blanket down and then off to kip.

Next morning, my mouth tasted like a shithouse. I put the kettle on for the first cup of tea was the best of the day. It was cold outside as I walked to the paper shop but at least it was dry. The tea had brewed in the teapot when I got back and was ready. Dennis came down and I said, "You look like I feel." He agreed. Sally came down and the breakfast was on and went down well. I had bought two newspapers—one of the worlds for the sex goings-on and the People paper. We had one each to read before dinnertime session as all northerners do on Sundays—some after church if they were Irish. I washed up first and Dennis followed. Sally said dinner would be ready by 3 o'clock we walked to the Penny Wet pub first to see Tommy and Patsy and Winner was working behind the bar. The crack was good, then we went on to the club to meet Dennis' friends. There was wrestling on as it had started again on Sunday at dinnertime. It was good entertainment as long as it went all right, but in the past, an ambulance had to be called. We both drank up as we were told not to be late home for dinner and off we went. The dinner went down well as Sally was a good cook. We settled down with full stomachs and dozed off. Dennis would not go out on Sunday night, so I freshened up and took a walk outside to leave them to talk on their own. I thought I would call around Mary's but she had another bloke in the club, so I gave that a miss and walked to the Penny Wet pub to see if the lads were in. I could not be too late as I did not have a key to get in and I knew that Dennis would want to go to bed early. When I got to the pub, it was quiet. A man came to serve me and he said that Winner was not on tonight and the Irish lads had been and gone. They said they were going to the Flying Horse on the main road. I said thank you and off I went. There were a few people in as I opened the door. As I walked in, there was a shout from the far end of the bar—it was Tommy and Patsy. "Billy boy, here we are! Is it nuke brown?"

I said yes and told them that I had called at the Penny Wet and the barman told me you may have come up here. "Winner has got the night off and has put her feet up to rest," said Tommy. Tommy introduced me to a couple of friends at the bar and the next couple of hours was good crack. It got around to ten and I got the beer in for the lads as I was going early to let Dennis and his wife go to bed. I said that I would be across next week if all went well. Off I went after saying goodnight to all. I got in and Dennis had gone to bed. Sally was up watching a film. "There is a sandwich in the kitchen for you, Billy," she said.

"Great," I said and I got a cup of tea to swill it down. I sat down for ten minutes and the film finished so Sally went off to bed. I got on the settee and was soon off to sleep.

I woke up as I could hear a noise from upstairs in the bathroom. It was Dennis. He came down and I went up as I was bursting for a pee. With tea down our throats, we set off for work. I told him that I had called at the Flying Horse pub and the lads were in there and the crack was good. The road over the River Tyne was a bit foggy but the traffic was good for a Monday morning. Dennis dropped me off at the café so I could change and he would pick me up in the lorry on the way back. I got another cup of tea as the café was open; then Dennis turned up, so it was another day at the mill. Dennis had to wait as I moved farther up the road so the bank man, Mick, had to control the traffic. I travelled down the road with the machine, then I ripped up some more tarmac to load up on to Dennis' lorry for the tip. We got to the café for breakfast at 11 o'clock and it went down well. It was another good day at work but cold and you had to be well wrapped up. I had my fur-lined flying jacket on. I started my car when Dennis dropped me off at night to give it a run. Then I went in the café to see what was on the menu. There was stew and it looked good, so I had a big plate of that. I had to wait for the shower when I got upstairs. There was a TV in the restroom, so I looked at that for half an hour, then changed and went to the pub. Janet was behind the bar and she smiled at me. "Did you have a good weekend?" she asked. I said that it was great to see old friends and catch up on the crack. I asked her how her weekend went. Janet said, "Not bad, a bit dull. It is not very good living with parents and my mum and dad are not too well at the moment."

"Which night do you have off this week?" I asked.

"Thursday."

"Well, is it a date then?" I asked her.

"Yes," she said, "I will look forward to it."

"We will have a meal first—Indian or Chinese? You must know a good one around here," I suggested.

"There is one of each down the road at South Shields."

"Well, you can sort it out then," I told her. The Landlord came down and we talked about the new tunnel and how it would affect the pub's trade. It would make a difference in the time people took to go to work in Newcastle and over the water. The conversation was good and it was closing time. "I will run you back to the café," Janet said.

"Get off now as it is raining," the Landlord said so in the car we got. The rain was heavy and I got a big kiss when the door shut.

As Janet was like a dog in heat, I knew sex was on the cards but in a Ford Escort, it would be a bit tight as Janet was a big girl but the job had to be done. The sex was great and a good thing there was a wall around the car park, it was a Monday night, the rain was still heavy and the car was all steamed up. Janet dropped me off at the café. I went upstairs and into the shower as I smelt like a whore's handbag and was very sore around the testicles.

The next morning, I was still sore when I walked and Dennis noticed as I climbed into the lorry. "Had a good night then?" he laughed.

"You could say that—a bit tight in a Ford Escort," I replied.

"You never learn, do you, Billy?" Dennis said with a big smile. It was hard to drive the machine for the first couple of hours but I managed and got on with the job in hand. It was a damp and dismal day. Dennis and I talked in the café about the job that Peter was going on; if he had gone, I would give him a ring before the week was out. "Will you come if there is a job going?" I asked Dennis.

"It is a bit far out for me, Billy," said Dennis. "Besides, a friend in the club has a delivery firm so I could drive a van or pickup or lorry, if need be."

"I cannot see this job going on much longer," I said. "Then I will have to go back to the yard in Birmingham so I will see what Peter has got to say first. I have a date with Janet on Thursday night so I will ring Peter then."

The week went by and it was coming up to the end of March. The first of April was the following week when the big earthmoving jobs got on the way in the UK. It was Thursday morning and the soreness between my legs had disappeared; I just knew that it would be back by tomorrow morning as Janet would want sex in the car tonight unless I could find a room for the night. My bed at the café was a bit small but might have to do if I could sneak her in. It was a wet cold day again but the thought of a good ride kept me going. I had never seen a woman with so much hair on her body—armpits and pussy was one big mass. We had to move the machine up the road again as the kerb layers were laying the radius kerbs for a roundabout. Both sides of the road were ready for the topsoil to go on and bring the road up to the level of the kerbs. The foreman, Brian, pulled up in the Land Rover. "Well Billy, it is coming on well," he said. "I will get a machine to load the soil to bring down to you on Dennis' lorry as it's supposed to be dry weather. There is another piece of road to rip up for next week but we will get a low loader to move the machine down the road. There is the tip to sort out and level off before you go," Brian said.

"I will call in to the office and get the timesheets signed tomorrow," I said. Dennis went down the road to park and got the paper out while I got the surplus earth together to load. Mick watched the traffic for me. The rain had eased off but it was still a dull day and I was glad that it was nearly over and a good night was on with Janet in my mind. I got two more loads on the lorry. Dennis dropped me off at the café. "Have a good night," he said with a smile on his face. I went upstairs hoping to get into the shower first as the lorry drivers were in the café having their meals. I got it right for once. I showered, changed, put scent on and went down to the café. Janet was already waiting for me with a smile on her face and had scrubbed up well. I said that I had a phone call to make before we left. I just hoped Peter was at home. I rang and he was. "Hi Billy. I have had a word with Bill Robinson and there is a place for you on the job on a D8 and scraper. There is another one coming at the end of next week from the yard but can you get on the job on Saturday for a test as the job is working until dinner?" he asked.

"Yes," I said, "I will be there."

"Good," said Peter, "see you on Saturday."

"You seem happy with yourself," Janet said.

"Yes, there is another job up north and I have to go and give a test on Saturday," I replied.

"Great," said Janet. "There is a nice Indian restaurant in town. We will get a taxi from here if you like; the car will be all right in the carpark."

We arrived at the restaurant and as I was hungry, we had starters and then a good curry. I just love spicy food but my ass does not, but there you go! It went down well with two bottles of nuke brown. The night went well and Janet was very chatty. "Are you working on Saturday?" I asked Janet.

"I have to work on Saturday at dinnertime," she said.

"I am going over to Morpeth to take a look at this job. If you could swap, it would be nice to have the day out with you," I said. I paid the bill and we waited for the taxi back to the café. As it was still open, we went to the side door and up we went. There was no one near the room and we got down to the real thing. The sex was great, we talked some more and then sex again. I was like a dog on a hot tin roof, then we got dressed and I took Janet back downstairs. We kissed and said goodnight and then I went back up for some kip. I had to get up fairly sharp as the spicy food was starting to come out of me; good thing I did not have to wait for the bathroom.

Friday looked a better day. Dennis came to the café to pick me up. "How did the night of passion go then; was it worth waiting for?" Dennis asked me.

"Sore but satisfied," I said. "I am going across to Morpeth on Saturday morning to give a test."

"You don't need a test," Dennis said.

"Well, there you go. I may have company with me," I said.

"Do I hear wedding bells?" Dennis said laughing. The day went well with the weather being dry and we got the soil levelled off as Dennis brought it down to me. Mick backed off the road and watched the traffic at the same time. I called the office and caught Brian to sign my timesheets for the week. "There is no work for tomorrow, Billy boy," Brian said.

"That's good," I said, "as I have something else on. I will see you on Monday." Dennis dropped me off at the café. I looked at the menu; steak looked good with chips, beans, bread and butter and a big mug of tea. I went upstairs and changed, then down to the pub to see Janet. "I can have dinnertime off tomorrow," she told me.

"Great! 8 o'clock at the café?" I asked.

"Yes," she said. I just hoped that sex was not on the cards tonight as I had to get my energy back somehow. Janet whispered in my ear, "You brought me on." I smiled. *There will be no little Billys running about yet*, I thought.

At closing time, we kissed in the carpark as Janet dropped me off at the café. We kissed and said goodnight and I went in to get a coffee before I went up. "On your own tonight," the man said. I said yes and smiled at him. I sat down, read a bit of a paper, drank the coffee and then went up for some kip.

The breakfast smelled good when I went down to the café. It was 7.15 so I had time to grab some breakfast and it went down a treat. I was reading the morning paper when Janet walked in. "Are you ready for the day out?" I said.

"Yes, will I pass?" Janet asked.

"Great," I said, "no sex for the next few days so I won't have to get the trousers off."

"I have to be back by six to open up the pub as the landlord and his wife have got company for the afternoon," said Janet.

"We had better be off then," I said. The traffic was not too bad on the A1 to Newcastle and over the Tyne Bridge. It was 10.30 when we saw the sign for the roadworks and the site entrance and offices. I parked and went in. I asked to see Bill Robinson and was told to go to the second office on the right. I knocked on the door. I went in and there was a dog beside the desk that growled. It was a Jack Russell. "You must be Billy who Peter the fitter was on about," Bill said.

I said yes.

"Well, the job is long hours with no time off unless it rains but that is a bad word in the muck shifting game. I will go down on the haul road in the jeep and stop a D8 and box and you can jump in the saddle and follow the other two D8s around to the tip and to the cut," he said.

I went across to my car and told Janet that I would be an hour. She said that she had a book to read in her bag. I went with Bill in the jeep down the haul road. Bill stopped a D8 and box, it was loaded. As the man got off it, I got on. "Are you on a test?" the man said. I said yes and he wished me good luck. I was in the seat and off to the smiles of the two men. The D8 was a 22A class and I had driven them on the coast road job. I was in my element in the saddle when I got to the road formation. There was a Ganger (foreman) he would point to where you were supposed to put the load of muck. There was a D8 and blade to level it out, then off I went to get a load again in the cut. I went down the haul road again and met with the two men, stopped the D8 and got off. The man shook my hand and said that his name was Harry. "When can you start," Bill asked me as we got into the jeep. "Peter said that there was another D8 coming next week from the yard. Can you start next Saturday as I do not want to waste the weekend's weather? I will pay the week's lodging and pay you a couple of hours for your time today. You might get digs in Morpeth up the road if you see the lads," Bill explained.

"Great," I said. We got back to the offices.

"See you on the site next Saturday," Bill said.

Then I went across to my car; Janet was reading a book that she had brought with her. "Did you get on?" she asked.

I said that I would start next Saturday. We called at a pub in Morpeth town. It was a couple of miles more to find digs. We drove north again as we approached Morpeth. We had to go over an old stone bridge over a river. There was a pub called the Bridge Inn, then we went down the high street to the pub that I was looking for. It was on the right and was called Earl Grey. Bill, the foreman, had said there could be a vacancy in the B&B. We pulled into the carpark around the back. The time was 11.30. The back entrance was open, so I went in. There were two women at a table. "Can I help you?" one said.

"Yes," I said, "I am going to be working on the new bypass and will start next Saturday so I am looking for a B&B from Friday night."

"How long will it take?"

"A few months, I hope," I replied.

"I am the Landlady," one of them said. "I am called Jean and my man is Stan who is out at the moment. There is a guest in room three but he will be going on Wednesday morning so it will be to let."

"Great," I said, "that will work out just right. Thank you."

I said that I could not have a drink as I had to drive back over the water again. "Not to worry," said Jean, "we will see you Friday night."

I said yes and went back to the car. Janet was still stuck in her book. "How did you get on?" she asked.

"Great. I got booked in for Friday night."

"That was lucky," she said.

"So where would you like to go now? Are you hungry?" I asked her.

"I could do with a bit to eat," said Janet. We called at a café for dinner on the way back through Newcastle and over the River Tyne. I turned down to the River Tyne and on to Scotswood Road and there was a café overlooking the River Tyne. I pulled in and parked. Janet and I went in and looked at the menu. "What do you fancy?" I asked Janet.

"The scampi looks good," she said. I decided to have rump steak as it had just been brought out for another customer. We ordered and then sat down at a window seat overlooking the River Tyne. It was a dry day but overcast and I went to fetch two coffees from the counter. "Well, you keep in touch when you move over to the next job," she said.

"Of course, I will," I said. The meal turned up and we got stuck in. "I will ring the pub when we have a long weekend or when it is raining. You can write the number down when I will be in tonight," I told Janet.

The meal went down well. I asked her if she wanted a dessert but no was the answer. "Well, what would you like to do now?" I asked.

"Shopping. It's difficult getting parking in Newcastle on a Saturday but there is a market down the quayside," said Janet.

"Right," I said, "I will pay the bill and that is where we will go."

So off we went. It was very busy but we got parked along the quayside and we walked back along the market stalls. I bought socks, a work jumper and a woolly scarf. Janet bought towels so I got one too as mine was getting a bit shabby since my mum had given it to me when I left home. We got back to the car with the goodies we bought and headed out on A1 back across the Tyne Bridge and on to White Mare Pool. We got back to the café where Janet got back into her own car after a big kiss. "I will see you in an hour at the pub," I said. I took my clothes up to my room and I noticed the TV on in the next room. It was the 6 o'clock special and it was good show to watch. I must have dozed off as it was nearly 7.30 when I woke up. I went to the bathroom, washed my face, then plenty of Old Spice to smell nice and coat on. Then down to the pub I went and took some washing with me. I knew I was pushing my luck in asking Janet to wash it but Dad always said you will never know if you don't ask. I got at the pub and smiled as I walked in. The landlord said, "You two had a good day today and you have another job to go to."

"Yes," I said. The pub was filling up as lorry drivers parked up at a café and then came in the pub for a pint. The pub was a well-known stopping-off point from Scotland to the South on weekends. I got talking to a couple of them. One said, "I have seen you before somewhere but I can't think at the moment. You were not on TV, were you?" I just smiled as Janet was listening to the conversation as well. I changed the subject and told them about the new bypass I was about to go on at Morpeth, which would make the A1 road better as the traffic would not go through Morpeth and would not be congested as it was now.

"You are like us in a way—all over the country," one of the drivers said.

"Yes," I said, "I love to meet people and the job I do—there are never two days the same. I was in Ireland not many months ago and the people were great to get on with. I was only there on relief but it was great crack."

The night ended as last orders was called. Janet leaned over the bar and whispered in my ear, "One more day. Do you want a lift down to the café?"

"No," I said, "I will walk with the lads. You get off. I will see you tomorrow for dinner in here." We walked outside and I got a kiss on the cheek. The café was still open and the lads got a sandwich and I got a cup of coffee to take the beer taste out of my mouth. The TV was on when I took the coffee upstairs with me. The lads came up and sat down and then one of the lads piped up, "I now know where I have seen you before! On TV and in the papers! You were at the Aberfan disaster with the army digging the children out."

I nodded and said, "It was a job and I do not want to discuss it as it was a bad one." They left it at that. I said goodnight and went into my room.

The next morning, I showered while I could and went down to the café. I got some more coffee down and thought I would go out for a ride for some fresh air as it was a dry day. It would give me an appetite for breakfast. In the car, I drove to South Shields and I went along the quayside to find a place to park, I got out and walked in the fresh morning air which really cleared my head. There were quite a few people about—dog-walking—and the tugs were moving the ships around on the Tyne. There was a paper shop at the corner of a warehouse, so I got the news of the world and then walked on to find somewhere to sit. There was a homemade seat consisting of two five-gallon drums and a piece of wood across it. I sat down to read the scandals in the Country and I did not notice the time. It was just after ten and the breakfast bug was in me, so I got up and walked back to the car. Then I realised how far I had walked but enjoyed it. I got back to the café and the lads had pulled out in their lorries going North or South. I ate breakfast and was set up for the day. It would soon be opening time to see Janet. I took the paper with me to the pub to read with a pint of Guinness for a change as sex would be on the cards today and I would need the energy to keep up. I walked to the pub, it was open and Janet was behind the bar. "Good morning or good afternoon," I said to Janet.

"You are very chirpy this morning," Janet said.

"I had a nice walk this morning in South Shields; got the morning fresh air into my lungs," I said.

"What are you having to drink?"

I looked around the room and saw two people drinking Guinness, so I knew it had been pulled off. I asked for a Guinness. "You might need it before the day is through," Janet smiled.

"You do pull a good head on it," I remarked.

"What am I going to do with you!" she said.

As I took a drink of it, I said, "I will sit down and finish reading the paper since you look like you are going to be busy." I enjoyed my Guinness as it was a while since I had a pint. I went to the bar for another.

"Did you enjoy it, Billy?" Janet asked.

"It was great," I said. "Can I have another?"

"Yes, my love, I will pay for this one as you took me out yesterday," Janet said.

I said thank you and sat back down. Then I heard a voice say my name and when I looked up, it was Mick, my Banksman off the job. "I knew I would catch you in here. Do you want a pint?" he asked.

"No thanks, I just got one here. I will buy you one," I said and gave him the money. "I am having a change as I may need the energy later on," I smiled.

"Are you still servicing the bar?" Mick asked.

"Sort of."

"I came to see you about the job that we are on. The Foreman, Brian, thinks that we will be finished this week," Mick said.

"I don't know about you but I will be moving on next Saturday to Morpeth on that bypass on A1 as Dick Hampton has got the muck shift," I said. "I don't know if there is an opening for you or if you want to travel it, I have got a phone number if you want to see if there is an opening for yourself."

"I will try it tomorrow," Mick said. I went to the bar.

"I see you met someone, Billy," Janet said.

"Yes. It's my Banksman from work."

"One nuke and a Guinness?" asked Janet. "It will be last orders shortly; do you want a lift back to the café?"

"OK," I said. I sat back down with Mick.

"You seem to be getting on all right with the barmaid," Mick remarked. "What is Dennis going to do?"

I replied, "He has got a job lined up with his brother-in-law as a Van Driver locally. I will see Brian in the office in the morning to tell him that I will be leaving on Friday and also ring the yard in Birmingham." The bell rang for last orders but there were not many people left. "How are you getting home?" I asked Mick.

"The bus is in ten minutes," Mick answered.

Janet was ready to go as the landlady was going to finish up. We got the car and went past the café. "Now what are you up to?" I asked.

"My mother and father are away for the day so I thought I would cook a meal for you as a surprise," she answered. Janet lived outside South Shields, so we had to drive through the town to get to her house. We parked outside a nice semi-detached house with a well-set garden. "Make yourself comfortable in the room," said Janet. "I will put some dinner on. I hope you are hungry; it's steak and chips."

I sat on the settee and I could smell the food on the go. I was called into the kitchen and the table was set out. "Get tucked in," Janet said. It went down great. I said that I would wash up for her. She thanked me and I got on with it. Janet dried the dishes. "Come and sit down and relax," said Janet, but I knew there was more than relaxing on Janet's mind. She was going to have her own way before I moved on. I sat down next to Janet and she looked into my eyes. We kissed and then we started to take off each other's clothes, we were on the floor having sex and it was great but I felt uneasy as I did not want to get caught with my pants down. We got up off the floor and dressed. There was a noise at the front door as Janet's parents came in. *That was lucky*, I thought. They smiled as Janet introduced me to them. We explained that we could not stay much longer as Janet had to go back to work to open up the pub since the Landlord and his Wife had gone to see friends. "It was very nice to meet you," said Janet's parents as we left. We got into the car and I said that that was a close one. "Not by half!" said Janet. "I would not have lived that one down if we got caught."

We laughed as we drove to the pub. It was a bit early to open up and Janet had some jobs to do so I got a paper off the bar and sat down to read it. Janet was down in the cellar and she called out to me, "Billy, will you give me a hand down here?" I got down and gave her a hand to move the barrels over and put the right one in place. Janet said thank you and put her arms around me. We kissed and she was getting sexily aroused again and the donkey was rising to the occasion. I lifted Janet onto the barrel and my pants were down in a flash. Janet had no panties on, so we went at it hard and fast and she said, "I am going to get my fill before you go on Friday." I was knackered when I got back to the bar. "Did you enjoy that?" she asked as she went to open the pub.

"Great," I said, "but I am sore now." I also had a damp patch on my trousers where I had pulled out fast; the last thing I wanted was to leave a Baby behind or to pay for one. As it was Sunday night, there was the usual crowd of Lorry Drivers so the conversation and crack was good. You learnt what was happening up and down the country. The Landlord and his Wife came before time and thanked Janet and me for opening up. They let Janet go early and we gave two of the Drivers a lift back to the café. They got out and I kissed Janet goodnight. "Are you still sore?" Janet asked.

"Yes," I said, "I will have a rest tonight, thank you." I smiled and got out of the car. I went in the café, got a cup of coffee and went to the TV room as the lads were in there. We talked some more as I would not be here next week. I went up to my room, got my clothes off and bathed my testicles in warm water as they were red.

The next morning, I was up early. Dennis laughed when I told him what had happened when he picked me up. "How did you get on Saturday?" Dennis asked.

"Great; I passed and I will start on Saturday," I said. "I will call at the office and tell Brian that I am leaving on Friday night. Then I will have to ring up Birmingham yard and tell them. I will do it at teatime." We started and loaded Dennis' lorry up with old tarmac, then carried on ripping some more ready to load up. Mick watched the traffic as it was busy at that time in the morning. I put the next load onto the lorry and then I jumped out as we passed the offices. Dennis carried on to the tip. Brian was in the office. "Hi Billy. You know, you are off hire on Friday."

"Yes," I said, "I will ring up the yard to tell them that I am leaving for another job that I will start next week."

"Where is that, Billy?" Brian asked.

"On the bypass at Morpeth. Dick Hampton gave me the earthmoving job," I explained.

"Good for you, Billy," Brian said. When I got through to the yard on the phone, I told the plant manager that I was off hire and was leaving. He told me that there would always be a job here. I thanked him and then rang off. Dennis was outside so it was into the lorry and to the café for breakfast. Then we carried on with the job as we had to make it last until Friday. We worked through dinner to get the section done so that the kerb layer could set it out on Tuesday morning. It was dark when I parked and Dennis dropped me off at the café. I looked at the menu and ham, egg and chips looked good, so I ordered them and it went down well. Then I went upstairs to get a shower. I took a look at my testicles and they were still red so I bathed them in warm water again before I went to the pub. When I got to the pub, Janet was on. "Had a good day?" she asked.

"Not bad." I whispered in her ear, "My balls are sore." She just laughed.

"Guinness?" Janet asked.

"Yes," I said, "I need all the energy I can get at the moment." A big smile was all I got. The Landlord came to the bar and the conversation changed to the weather and traffic on the roads and when the tunnel would open, which would not be long. At the end of the night, Janet dropped me off at the café. All I wanted was a big kiss and a good night's sleep. I went up to my bed for a good kip.

In the morning, the boss was at the café and I told him that I was leaving on Friday night after work. As I had paid with a week in hand, there was no money to pay this week, so I sat down with a cup of tea. Dennis walked in and he got one to go. "We have to move up the road this morning so you will have plenty of time to read the paper," I said to Dennis. Mick walked in and got a cup of tea. "Have you got a job yet or is there enough work here?" I asked him.

"I spoke to Brian and he said that there is at least two months left here," Mick replied.

"Good," I said. "Well, we will go and look at it." We got into the lorry and got down on the job. The dev lorry was there to fill me up for the last time as the machine would be gone so Mick got that sorted. We got the machine on the road and travelled down. It was the last section to be ripped up, so I got on with it. It was teatime when we got the first load on and then it was to the café. Dennis carried on to the tip. I got a big plate of beans on toast. Dennis walked in as it was brought to the table. "You will be farting all day on that!" he said, laughing.

"I know," I said, "but I needed a change from breakfast."

Only about two loads of tarmac were left and then we would put on the topsoil. We took our time all day as there was no rush. The day came to a close and we left a bit for tomorrow. There was soup on the menu, so I got that down my throat. After I changed, I picked up my washing hoping that I could get Janet to wash it. I put it in a bag and walked down to the pub. The farting got a bit worse and I went straight to the toilet when I got there. Janet just looked at me as I passed the bar. The Guinness was on the bar when I came out. "What have you got in the bag?" Janet asked me.

"My washing," I said.

The Landlady told Janet to take it upstairs and put it in her new washing machine. "You can get it tomorrow when you come," she told me.

"Great," I said. "so, what have you got in mind for tomorrow night?" I asked Janet.

Janet said, "I will be coming in early for dinner, then finish at teatime and we can have the evening out."

"Sounds good," I said. As it was a Wednesday night, which was a games night, the bar started to get full, so Janet was busy. I stood at the bar with a couple of Lorry Drivers I knew from the café. The conversation was about roads up and down the country. As a rule, I would get involved in dominos but the partners were made up. When it ended, the food came out—sausages, onions and chips. I got the leftovers. Janet was ready to go so we gave two Drivers a lift back to the café. The lads got out of the car and Janet said that there was a smell in the car tonight as someone kept farting. She asked if it was me and I said yes. She smiled, I got a big kiss and said goodnight. I went into the café, got a cup of coffee and sat down with the lads. The TV was on; it was the news. I went up to my room and looked at my testicles again. They looked all right and the soreness had gone. I would have to watch in the future not to have sex over barrels in cellars bashing them against the barrels did me no good at all.

I was up the next morning and the first cup of tea was the best. Dennis came in and laughingly asked if the farting had stopped. "I was at it in the pub last night and had to own up when she dropped me off in the car," I replied. Mick walked in and got a cup of tea.

He said, "There is a bit of tidying up and then you can bring the soil down to us."

"OK, we will do that," Dennis said. We got on the job and Dennis went to see if he could get a load with the soil. Brian turned up in the Land Rover and he was pleased with the work. I asked him if he would sign my timesheets as I have made them out. He said OK.

"I can get them in the post early," I said. "I will have to ring the yard with a forward address on Monday next week." Brian went and we got on with the job on hand. It was a while before Dennis turned up with a load as the machine would not start but it was teatime anyway. "On beans this morning?" Dennis said with a laugh. I smiled and said that it was back to breakfast with tomatoes. It went down well and we got a lift back to the job where we levelled the load of soil out, tracked it in, and then had the crack while we waited for the next load. By three or four, we would finish it and we had two more in the afternoon. That just left a bit in the top corner for tomorrow—Friday. I got back to the café to shower and put my Old Spice on as it was my last night this side of the Tyne. "No food tonight?" the man in the café asked. I declined and went out to the town. I posted my timesheets and went down the road to the pub. Janet was dressed up smartly when I got to the pub. She picked up my washing and said that she would put it in the car. "Are we off then?" she said, "Because I am hungry." I gave the Landlady some money for a drink for doing my washing. "Have a good night," she said as we went out the door. I got a big kiss as I got into the car.

"Shall we go to the restaurant that we went to last time?" Janet asked.

"Great, put your car in the café's carpark," I said.

"Am I staying the night with you?" asked Janet.

I said yes and we parked the car at the café. I rang for a taxi and we did not have to wait long. Janet told the driver where we wanted to go. South Shields was busy with shoppers as Thursday night was payday on the docks. We got to the restaurant and we asked for a table for two. We got one overlooking the River Tyne and the nights were starting to darken early so the scenery was great. As it was Chinese, I ordered crispy duck and Janet ordered chicken curry and rice and a bottle of red wine. The meal came and it went down well. We sat and talked for half an hour to let the meal go down. Janet went on about what I was going to do when I moved on tomorrow night. She said she would give me the pub's number and I said that I would ring her when I got settled into the new digs. We got up and I went to pay the bill but Janet insisted that she would pay. We walked down to the pub where there was music so in we went. It was quite lively and we got a seat near the window. I got the drinks and we carried on talking on life in general. The nuke brown and Janet's gin and tonic was going down well. "How are you down below now?" she asked. "Are you still sore? If you aren't, you will be in the morning!" she laughed.

"Great," I said, "it's a good thing I do not have a lot to do at work."

The last orders came and went and we walked to the taxi stand to get a taxi back to the café. We went through the side door and upstairs to my room. The clothes started to come off before the door was shut properly. Janet did not waste any time as she was as horny as hell. The sex was good and my testicles were holding up well. We lay back to get our breath back and we must have dozed off as it was gone six when I woke up and Janet was still cuddled up to me. I thought I had better make a move but when I tried to get out of bed, Janet had other ideas. I was getting sore again but I was satisfied. We got dressed and then Janet went down the side door and into the café. "Good morning," said the man behind the counter. "I hope you both slept well."

"Great," I said. "Two teas." Dennis walked in and I amended the order to three teas. We sat down.

"Had a good night?" Dennis asked.

"Yes," said Janet with a big smile on her face.

"I will call at the pub before I leave tonight," I told Janet. Off she went and Mick came into the café. He got a cup of tea and sat down. "We can't leave the machine where it is."

"When we get there," I said, "we will go up to the compound to load it up next week and so we will clean the tracks out and travel it down the road."

"OK," said Mick.

"How many loads?" Dennis asked.

"Let's get two down, then we will take it from there," I said. We went down to the job. Dennis dropped us off, then went to get loaded with soil. He brought two loads down, which finished it as it was Friday and it was a short day. Dennis and I shook hands to keep in touch as Mick cleaned the tracks out and then travelled the machine down the road to the compound. It took an hour to travel as we had to stop to let traffic past. We got the machine parked, shook Mick's hand and told him to look after himself. Mick said the same and then I walked to the café to get my bags and put them in my car. I called at the pub as Janet was on early. She spotted me coming and came out to meet me. I got a big kiss. "Ring me tonight," she said. I got in the car, waved and then headed for the A1 over the Tyne Bridge going north. The traffic was busy as it was Friday night. I went on to Morpeth, parked the car in the carpark and then went in. "Hello," said the Landlady, "you are here then. There are two more men in here from the job—Jed and Mick. You can freshen up; I will show you your room." It was at the front of the pub. "Next door is the toilet," said the Landlady. *That's good*, I thought, *not far to go after the beer*. I got a shower, changed and went down to the bar. "You clean up well," said the Landlady. "What is your poison?"

"Guinness," I said as I looked around the room and people were drinking it. The Guinness was good. In walked two men and the Landlady piped up that these two men were on the same job as me. They came across to me. "We heard you were coming. You must be Billy," one said, yes was my answer. "I am Jed and this is Mick," they introduced themselves. We shook hands. "Do you want a drink, Billy?" Jed asked.

"No," I said, "I have one here."

"What are you going to drive?" Mick asked.

"I am not too sure," I replied.

"There is a D8 on the job ready to go," said Mick. "I have the D8 with a soiled blade for pushing on the tip. There are three TS 14S motor scrapers, so I have to push them." Jed said that he was on a D8 and 463 box scraper. The crack was good for the evening. I went to the phone in the pub hallway and rang Janet. She was over the moon that I had rung up and asked me if I had settled in. "Yes," I replied, "there are two lads off the job in my digs."

"That's great," she said.

"I will ring you over the weekend," I said and wishing her goodnight, I hung up. I went back to the bar again to the lads and asked them what time they went to work. They said that they usually met up at the fitting shop at half past six, then Billy Robinson would take it from there and decide what machines you would be on for the day. The last bell had gone at the bar, so it was up to my bed, ready to start the new job. I put the old alarm clock on for 5 o'clock and then slept.

I was up before the alarm went off, dressed and went down to the dining room. There was tea and coffee on the table and a packed lunch for all three of us. The two lads followed me down and we got into our cars and drove to the site. All the machines were parked and the dev man was filling them up. Billy Robinson came up to me and said, "Morning, Billy. I will put you on the D8 22A, number 13, with the solid button on the front. As it is a dry day, you can go on the 463 scraper box at breakfast. Until then, go down to the tip and push TS14 scrapers if need be." I checked oil and water and I was ready. The tea man came up to me and asked what I would like for breakfast—a full breakfast or sandwiches. I chose full. He said that it would be one pound ten shillings a week each for seven days. Then I drove off to the tip. I was busy as the ground was wet and it was 11o'clock—teatime—before I knew it. The jeep pulled up and we got in and sat down for breakfast. We lined up, got a plate and the tea man put bacon, eggs and fried tomatoes on. We sat down and it went down well. As I came to the cabin, Billy told me that I had better stay pushing all day as there was a load of wet clay to come down to the tip and the 14S scraper would not get it out. I worked for the next four weeks. The days were long and dusty. I put a sheet up on both sides of the machine where I sat as there was no cab on it. My long weekend was here so I rang up Janet as I usually did twice a week. I asked her what was planned for the weekend as I could finish on Friday by dinnertime. On Thursday night, I put my bag in my car and I was on my way. I had already told the Landlady my plans for the weekend. I thought I would call to see Janet as my balls were full and could do with a good ride but when I talked to Janet on the phone to see how the land lay, she told me that she was working over the weekend. She said she could get Saturday off if I liked. "Great," I answered, "I will pick you up then. I am going across to Dennis if he is in to stay the night if I can." Then I rang up Dennis to see if I could stay there for the night. Sally answered, "Of course you can. Dennis is not home yet but there won't be a problem." I got to Dennis' house and he answered the door. "Hi," he said, "how's the job going?"

"Great," I said.

"Do you want any tea, Billy?" Sally asked.

"No," I said, "I had a big dinner on the site. The tea man looks after us and does the cooking as ordered."

"Sounds like you are well set up on that job," said Dennis.

"How is it going with you, Dennis? Are you still running around with the lorry?"

"There is not much left to do with both the jobs coming to an end," said Dennis. "The tunnel is a month away from opening and that will make a difference to the traffic. Do you want to wash up before we go out?"

"No," I replied. "I had gone to the office's showers before I left."

"Good," said Dennis, "I am ready. We will walk and call at the Penny Wet pub to see if the lads are in." We walked in the door of the pub and Tommy made a fuss as usual. "Is the job all right? And how are you keeping, Dennis and Sally?"

"Great," they said.

"Well, it must be two nuke browns and a gin and tonic," said Tommy. "So, what is new on the western front," asked Tommy. "We were thinking of taking a look at where you are, Billy."

"I will ask," I said, "as the division is in place and could need pipe-laying. I will find out for you," I said.

"We will move on to the club," Dennis said. I asked Winner to put the round for the lads and herself and I paid. "I may catch you on Sunday for dinner on the way back as I am going to see a lady friend across the water tomorrow," I said.

Dennis laughed, "Leg over, more like it!" I just smiled. We got to the club and got a seat. The turn was about to come on; it was a comedian who was not too bad but the group was better and the crack was good. We got a taxi back to Dennis' house. Sally made me a sandwich. "I will have gone by the time you both get up," I said. "I will call on the way back."

In the morning, I was up when it had just gone 7 o'clock. I washed my face, put the kettle on, got the tea down and then out. It was a good morning and the sky was blue as I drove over the Tyne Bridge. I thought, *In a month's time, I will be going through the tunnel and not right around.* The roads were quiet for a Saturday morning and I passed the pub, then on to the café. I went in and the man behind the counter said, "Back again?"

"No, just visiting; but I may want a room for the night if you have one."

"No problem," said the man.

"Can I have a good breakfast?" I asked him.

"Coming up."

I sat down as the papers had come. The breakfast came and went down well. I could not ring Janet up yet as she would not be at work. I had her parents' number; I could give it a try. I carried on reading the paper when Janet walked in to my surprise. "I thought that was your car in the carpark; I was on my way to work early as we are stocking up." I got a big kiss from her. "Well," she said, "are you coming down to the pub to give me a hand?"

I agreed and she told me to leave my car here for now and off we went. The Landlord was surprised to see me. "He has come to give us a hand," Janet said.

"Great," the Landlord said, "you can count the bottles up here and I will sort the cellar out." In an hour, it was all done and the Landlady came downstairs with the coffee and we sat and talked. "You can have the day off if you like," the Landlord said to Janet, who nodded.

"I need to go shopping as the clothes I have to go out in are getting a bit tatty," I explained. She agreed so we went up the town to South Shields, parked and went into the shops. I bought two pairs of jeans and a denim jacket to match, then got myself a good army jumper and four pairs of socks for work. I told Janet that I had lost my suit in Liverpool years earlier but I did not tell her how I lost it. We then went into Binns big store; there were three floors of things to buy for the house if I had one. Janet was picking out things that she liked for her house but I was not ready to settle down yet, so we went out of the store and into the coffee shop with the bags under our arms. "It's hard work shopping," said Janet.

"I don't mind," I said. "It's nice to wear something new now and again." The coffee was good. "Well," I said to Janet, "where would you like to dine tonight? I have to book a room in the café for the night."

"Well," she said, "we will do that now, then I will go and get changed and come back to the café. We can then make up our minds from there." I agreed. I got booked in for the night and then went up to get showered and changed. The room I booked for the night had a big double bed. There was going to be a lot of bouncing about on it tonight, I hoped. I put my new jeans on and the waist was right for a change and the turn-ups were great. I thanked the café owner for the room. "I thought you would like it but don't wear the bed out, will you?" he said with a smile on his face.

I sat down and waited for Janet to turn up as it was teatime and I was getting hungry. "You look smart with the new jumper and jeans," she said when she turned up. I got a taxi and one came right away.

"Where to?" I asked.

"We will go to the usual one," Janet said. There were a few people in for a Saturday night but we got seated where we had sat the last time. I ordered a T-bone steak and chips. "How would you like it?" asked the waiter.

"Medium rare, like my lady friend," I said and Janet started to blush and smiled at me.

"And for you, madam?" the waiter asked Janet.

"I will have chicken and salad." We picked a bottle of red wine. We talked about the job and the lads I met. The meal came and the steak went down well with the help of the red wine. I thought, *I will have to go steady on the drink as I don't want brewers droop tonight especially as I am sure sex will be on the agenda tonight.* "Is it music time at the pub?" I asked Janet.

"Yes, there is a band on in the pub down the road. The customers were on about it in the pub," she replied. So, we paid and walked to the pub down the road. The music was loud at first but someone must have told them to turn it down and then it was good. The night ended and we got a taxi back to the café. "You won't be disappointed tonight, Billy boy," Janet said as she got out of the cab and I knew it was sex on the cards. She was horny as hell; I was just about raped as soon as the bedroom door closed. The sex as always was great and went on for some time, then we talked and slept. When I woke up, there was even more sex and again we went at it long and hard, I was sore again but satisfied. We both had a shower as it was nine o'clock and Janet had to be at work by 11 o'clock. We went down to the café and ordered coffee. Janet had to go and I went outside to her car. "Ring me when you come back; I will thank you for the night out," she said. I got a big kiss, then she left and I got in my car and set off to Wallsend again. When I got to Wallsend, I rang up Dennis to tell him where I was and we arranged to meet at the Penny Wet pub. I could not have a lot to drink but a pint of Guinness was on the cards to get my energy back. Tommy and Patsy were there and asked me how I got on last night. "Great," I said.

"There are no babies on the way?" Tommy laughed.

"I hope not," I said. "Dennis is coming down to meet us shortly." In he walked. I got the round as I was limited to two since I had to drive back to Morpeth. I could have a pint there. I said my goodbyes as Dennis was going on to the club to meet his brother-in-law and I was going to drive back to Morpeth. When I got back, the pub was shut but I had a key for the door. I walked in and I heard the Landlady's voice saying, "You are back. Do you want a pint?"

"Hi," I said, yes please "Guinness."

"Did you have a good weekend?" she asked.

"Yes, but tiring," I answered. "It will make a lot of difference to the Town when the road is finished on the bridge over the river." I drank up and went upstairs and lay on the bed. I must have dropped off as I could hear music when I woke up. I looked at the clock and it was half past seven, so I washed my face and went down to the bar. Mick and Jed were in. "Good weekend, Billy? We saw the car and thought you were around town."

"No," I replied with a smile, "catching up on some kip."

"As it was dusty," Mick said, "the D8 68A has been serviced."

"Is yours a Guinness?" Jed asked as he was going to the bar. I said yes and it went down well. I caught up on the gossip on the site and they told me where they had worked before and the crack was good. As it came to closing time, it was time to go up the wooden hill.

The next morning, the three of us were up and out after coffee. We got on the site and the tea man had the kettle on so I could fill the flasks up with tea as it was going to be a dry day and spring was in the air. The days were long and dusty but life was good on the site and in the pub. I was on the scraper box all week and as it was dry, there was a night shift on only for the mortar scrapers but I did not want anything to do with that. The months were passing me by that year and the job was coming along. With the extra machines on the job, the bulk of the earthmoving was getting done and the weather forecast for the winter was going to a bad one. The job would slow down as August was coming up.

I got a phone call at the pub after work one Friday night from Dennis—he was coming over to see me. So, on Saturday afternoon, I got back to the pub and Dennis and his brother-in-law had come across in a taxi for the night. I changed, got myself something to eat in the pub and we sat down to catch up on the gossip. I told Dennis if he had seen Billy, the lad whom I had bought the Sunbeam Talbot car off. Dennis said he thought he had moved on so it would be no good going around to see him about the money for the car, so that was that. We had a good night around town and as I was working the next day—Sunday—Dennis got a taxi back home. After four weeks, I would have a long weekend so I would go to Wallsend plus see Janet as my balls were getting full. But I was having second thoughts about Janet as she was getting too close and marriage was on her mind. So, I rang her up at the pub to explain that I liked travelling too much and was not ready to settle yet. She agreed to be just friends and keep in touch with one another. So, at the end of the month, I asked Billy Robinson if I could have Sunday off and when he said yes, I set off to Wallsend. I rang Dennis to tell him that I would meet him at the Miner's club at night. I decided to call Mary and see if she still had anybody on and if she wanted to go out. If she did, could she get a babysitter; she was ready to go out. There was a turn on and it turned out to be a good night. We got a taxi back to Mary's for a good ride and a sleep-in but that was not possible as the children were up early for breakfast. I got a paper and, as planned, went to see Dennis at the club for Sunday dinner. I went back to Mary's for dinner and a kip in bed with Mary before I travelled back to Morpeth to work on Monday.

During the week, I got talking to a woman in the bar one night. Her name was Shelly and she was a Staff Nurse at the hospital up the road and lived in the nurses' home. Shelly said that there was a dance at the hospital every two months and there was one on Saturday night. She invited me to go. Shelly was a big girl but you don't look at the mantlepiece while poking the fire. I told the lads that I would not be in the bar as I was looking forward to it. On Saturday, I got back from work, took a bath and put my make-up on. Shelly got a taxi to the pub. I did not eat any food as there was a buffet on. After a couple of drinks and a good talk, we got a taxi up to the hospital. It was in a hall around the back and near to the doctors' and nurses' home. There was a good group on and '60s' music was always good. There were only soft drinks on sale, which was a good job as I already had a couple of nuke browns first. It was 10.30 when the bar shut and it was time to go but Shelly had other ideas. As we went outside, Shelly took me to one side (I knew what was coming!) and asked me to come back to her flat for a drink. I said that I had to go to work on Sunday but she said that it was not a problem as she would drop me off. We had sex and boy was it good, really good, Shelly knew how to use her body in bed.

In the morning, I was up early and looked around to make tea. I took a cup in for her but I had to put it down as I was pulled back to bed for some more. Eventually, Shelly gave me a lift to the pub to get changed, then on to work. I was glad it was a short day. I stayed on that job for six months and kept in touch with Dennis and Janet. I told her what the crack was and she said that she understood and we carried on being friends.

It was October 1968. I was told that there were going to be layoffs on the job. As I was the last one to start, I was going to go first. It was time to talk to Peter about a job as I had heard on the grapevine that there was a pipeline going from Newcastle to Edinburgh. The contractor was PLC from Hitchin in Hertfordshire. The job was a 110-mile 24-inch long pipeline that was being put in. We met at the pub to talk about it as Peter was in the same boat as me with the job. The job that we had heard about was for Wiggles plant on hire to PLC and there was an opening for me as well as Peter with me on a 22RB crane and Peter as a fitter. We had to meet up with the plant manager on Sunday in the pub. He was called Mr David Goudy; he was a paddy. I got the job but I had to put in a week's notice. When I got to work on Monday, I met up with Billy Robinson and told him that I had got another job. He was pleased for me and said that it was OK to leave. On Friday, I had a drink with the lads from the job; I rang Shelly to come but she said she was working nights. I told her what I was up to and told the landlady what was happening as I would have to move back down the line to Ponteland and get digs near the pipeline. On Monday morning, I moved out of the pub and drove down the A1 to Ponteland. I went to the pub to ask for digs. I was told that there was a cottage on the outskirts of the town and was shown the way. I found that they were an old dish couple and very well-spoken and had a beautiful cottage with a spare room. It was one pound ten shillings per night. Anna and Tom were their names. I told Anna that I was not into breakfasts early in the morning but when I got up, the kettle was on and there was a packed lunch—cheese and onion sandwiches. On Tuesday morning, I set off to the road crossing that I was to work at. It was also the place where the 22RB crane was to be delivered. The job was to start at 7 o'clock that evening. The 22RB crane arrived; it was brand new, straight out of the factory. Pete and I got it off the low loader and rigged it up. The foreman for PLC turned up and introduced himself as Chuck O'Brien and he came from York. Chuck's brother Mick, who was also on the job, was the spread boss for the pipeline plus the explosives expert for the job. When Pete and I finished, the crane was ready for work. A lorry tuned up with some steel plates on, so I lifted them off with the crane. The plates were for the road. If we did not get the job finished, there was also a digger—a JCB 6C—to dig the road out. Pete said that I might have to drive as there was no jockey at the moment. Chuck said that he would meet me at 7 o'clock tonight to start work. Pete said he knew where there was a good café for breakfast. I was ready by now. After that, I was going back to my digs but it was opening time so I thought I would have a pint and get myself familiar with the area. It was back to the pub I went in, had two pints and then back to the digs to clean the car as I was not yet tired. I grabbed a couple of hours of rest, then off to work as it was 6 o'clock by now and I like to be early. Chuck turned up as Pete said that I might have to drive the two machines. I got started with the digger. The trench across the road had to be five feet wide as the pipe was 36-sleeve. The main pipe was 24 inches to go inside as a country back lane. I was told that there were no services. I got the trench dug and it was getting dark and the lights were put on. I could hear and see a D7 CAT in front of me. It was a side boom machine; it had its lifting crane on the side. The driver got off and came over to me; he told me his name was Mel and he was Irish. Mel was good crack; he told me his mate was called Shaun and he drove the Cleveland machine which excavated the main trench. Mel was to pick one end of the 24-inch pipe with the D7 CAT side boom and I would pick up the other end. Then we would travel to the 36-inch pipe to thread it through the 36 inches. The 24-inch had spaces on to help it slide through. When we got the pipe through, Mel backed up to lift the 36-inch pipe and got hold of it with the 22RB. When we were both ready, we lifted the completed two pipes in one. We both travelled along the trench. When Chuck got it to where he wanted it, Chuck lowered us both down into the trench and took the straps off the pipe. I parked the 22RB crane and Mel backed off into the field so that I could put sand around the 36-inch with the JCB 6C. Then I backfilled it with clay to compact it to a level and then put the steel plates on until it levelled with the tarmac again. By this time, it was 4 o'clock in the morning and Chuck said that it was time for bed. Back at the digs, I let myself in, made a cup of tea and went to bed.

I got up at teatime. Anna was about and asked how the job had gone. I said OK. I had to go an hour early because I had to move the 22RB crane to another road crossing along the line. I got to the job and there was a low loader on the job. I loaded it up cross-carriage on the trailer. Once the crane was loaded I followed behind in the car. I unloaded the crane, met up with Mel again and Chuck was there. We followed the same procedure as last night and it went well. As I was going home, I drove past a wood. As I come to an opening in the trees, the trees were tipping over. I told the locals in the pub and they said it was here that there is a Ministry of Defence underground storage facility. I thought my eyes were playing up and I did the same for the next three nights. Friday night was the last of the nights for now. On Saturday, I came onto day shift for now, lifting pipes onto four-wheeler trailers to be taken down the line and welded together. I met up with Shaun, Mel's mate. Shaun was good crack as well as Mel and we had a great night. We were on about moving back up to Morpeth and back to the Earl Grey pub as we were moving up to lay the pipes. I rang Shelly to see what shift she was on and told her what I was up to. Shelly was pleased to hear from me. I stayed on for one more week at the digs and told Anna that the night shifts were closing. The job was going down to nine hours a day for the winter. On Saturday, I rang the pub to book a room. I was lucky to get back in. I rang Shelly about Saturday night; I told her about Mel and Shaun and if she could have some of her friends down to meet them. Shelly said that she would sort it out. Mel and Shaun lived in a flat together in Morpeth. I said goodbye to Anna and Tom and told them to look after themselves and then drove to Morpeth. I got myself settled in, then went down to the bar to wait for Shelly. Shelly turned up with two friends, Maria and Joan. The boys seemed to get on well together. It was going to be a good night. At closing time, Shelly suggested that we get a carry-out and go back to the nurses' home for a late one. We ordered a taxi and went to the nurses' home. We went to Shelly's flat as the girls were not working until Monday. Shelly put on some records as the new 45's was out. We kept the noise down so as not to wake the other nurses. Maria got on with Mel and Joan got with Shaun. As we all had the Sunday off, the night was good crack. Time was moving on and the boys paired off into the girls' flats. We decided to meet up in the pub at dinnertime for a pint. Shelly and I finished the night off in bed. I was up early on Sunday morning to clean up. I let Shelly sleep in. I walked down the road to the phone box; I could see a car parked with the driver in it. I said good morning and the driver asked which way I was going. I said I was going to Morpeth and he said he was going the same way, so I got in. The driver of the car was a doctor and was staying in the town with his sister. He said his name was John. I got out of the car and thanked John for the lift and went to the paper shop. The weather was not too bad today. The café next to the taxi stand was open so I decided to have breakfast and sit and read the paper. The girl in the shop was very chatty and asked where I came from and where I was working. I told her it was my second job in the area.

When I finished the breakfast, in walked the man from the taxi stand. He ordered a sandwich and I said good morning. I had met him a couple of times when I wanted a taxi. The man's name was Frank and he asked me if I knew anybody that would be interested in driving a taxi at night. I said I might help him myself at night so Frank asked if I would come tonight. I said that I would give it a try. I went back to the pub to shower and freshen up and to meet the boys for dinner. I knew I could not have a couple of pints as I had to drive. Mel and Shaun turned up at 12 o'clock in the bar and the topic was sex and who was the best in bed. After that, I went for a sleep to get ready for the taxi job at night at 6 o'clock. I went to the taxi office. I was to drive a Vauxhall Cresta My first was an old couple to go to the station; it was good night in all with a couple of tips.

The next morning, I was up to go to the job at the yard at Longhirst village. The 24-inch pipes were stored and then loaded up again to go up the line. Shaun was up at the front line on the Cleveland machine which dug the trench out to put the pipe in. At the front was a pipe-bender machine which was operated by an American called Mack who was full of himself. He also had a big Lincoln car and was always throwing money about. Mack was always getting pulled up by the local police for drinking but when he got pulled up, he would take out a jar of Vicks, put a finger in the jar and then into his mouth. It would take away the smell of the alcohol and he would get away with it. On Wednesday, I went on night shift again at Alnwick to a road crossing. I loaded the crane up again on the low loader on Wednesday morning and then unloaded it on a road outside Alnwick ready for the night. It was back to the pub for dinner and a couple of pints and then to bed.

That evening, I called at the café, which on weekdays was open until 7.30. The girl was on and I asked for a couple of ham sandwiches to take away. The girl was quite chatty, so I asked her name, which was Ann. Her body was fair to middling with the bumps in the right place—tits, I meant. Ann asked if it was me who had been driving the taxi on Sunday night and I said yes, I was helping out John next door. I thought of chatting up Ann but then there was Shelly on the go and words soon got around the village, so I gave it a miss. I said goodbye as I had half an hour to travel up the A1 for work.

We got to work as darkness fell; it was easy as I only had one machine to drive. The Hymac digger was mounted so I could chill out. John O'Brien was in charge as he was the speed boss for the whole job. He was Chuck's brother. We learnt from John that the front end of the line was at a standstill as a Farmer wanted help for the setting out of pegs in a field as one of his horses got lame. In no time at all, Mel turned up with the 36-inch pipe so when the pipe scraper had finished, Mel and I threaded the 24-inch through the 36-inch pipe ready to go in the trench when the digger had finished, which was not long. We had the pipe in by 11 o'clock and started to backfill. John said there was a pub in the village where we could get a late one and asked Mel and me to go with him, which we obliged. Off we went and as it was games night—darts—there was food on. John knew the Landlord and we were in. John told Mel and I that the next crossing was a big river crossing at Berwick-on-Tweed but it would be a daytime one. After a couple of pints, it was time to go. We thanked the Landlord and said goodnight. We headed out back and John said that if we turned up about ten in the morning, he would pay for two shifts. We agreed.

The next morning, I was up and the landlady at the digs was still on breakfast, so I got one. I went back to work. When I got there, I was told by Pete the fitter that the low loader was coming at dinnertime to take me to Berwick-on-Tweed to start work on Friday morning. I loaded the crane up; it was a good thing that it was on basic jib all the time with no rigging to do. I followed the lorry around the back roads to Berwick and we unloaded the crane. John was on the job to blast out rock with dynamite. He had men drilling holes in the trench as the trench had to be six feet deep. I moved the crane as far as I could from the blast so that the windows would stay whole. The whistle would blow, then the bang would come, rock went all over the place and the diggers would move back in to dig it out. A lorry turned up with a load of pipes for me to unload. I placed them for the scrapers to work on. The nights were closing in as it was November and there was already snow in Scotland. According to Pete, the job was through the winter. It was a slow job on this crossing to get the pipes in, what with all the rock in the trench. It took all week. After that, we moved on up the line unloading pipes from lorries. Then the snow came and it was bad. We got a pick-up in Land Rovers from Morpeth to the job. There were ranging rods (surveyor instrument used for marking positions) to follow from the road up to the line as there were peat bogs under the snow. The job was coming to a standstill as the plant on the job was getting stuck in the peat bogs. Two of the pipe carriers, which were D8 CATS, got stuck. We had to wait for a hard frost before we could get it out. A message came around from Pete the plant fitter that we had to meet up at the weekend in the Red Lion in Morpeth as we heard that parts of the job were going to be shut down. We kept going in the yard unloading pipes from lorries as the A1 road was kept clear with snow ploughs. As Christmas was coming up, we would have Christmas up in Morpeth. Then I could see Shelly as she had to work for many days over Christmas. I could also go down and see Dennis at Wallsend. The job was to close down for the holidays and I was all right for work after Christmas according to the meeting with Dave Cody, the plant boss. On Saturday night, I met up with Mel and Shaun at the pub and told them what had been said at the meeting. Mel was going to Ireland for Christmas and Shaun was going to stay with his family in Birmingham. I rang the nurses' home to get hold of Shelly to see what shift she was on. I left a message for her to ring the pub. As there was no work on Sunday, I could do a bit of taxiing. I got a phone call from Shelly saying that she was on night shift and so were the girls, to the disappointment of the boys. So, it was no party or shag tonight. We went for a walk around the town pubs. In the Bridge Tavern pub, there was a party of people on a Christmas do so the boys and I just mingled in with the crowd. There was a group on and the place was lively. As the night wore on, we got talking to a group of girls. They told us that it was the works do. The girls were paired up and we got the drinks on. The girls had come in minibus from outside Newcastle. The one I got on with was a woman in her 40s with no ring on her finger and the way she talked, she was up for anything. As it was a cold night and there was snow on the ground, it was no good for a kneetrembler. As the party broke up and it was time to leave, the woman—her name was Sandra— was a bit wobbly on her feet. She asked me where I was staying and I told her. It did not look like I was in with a chance anyway, not tonight. Sandra gave me a kiss and said she had a good night and then her friends got on the bus. Mel and Shaun came around the corner with the other two girls, which were a bit younger, and got on the bus with them. The boys said that they would catch up with me tomorrow and I walked back to the pub. I let myself from the back as I had a key; the landlord was still serving. He had some friends in and the local police would call in for a drink. One policeman told me about the welders from the job causing a bit of trouble in the area with the women as they were on big money. As Christmas was coming, it might be a bit quieter around town.

In the morning, I went to the paper shop café for a cuppa and a bit of breakfast and as the Landlady had a sleep-in on Sundays, I got my own. My chatty friend was working and asked how I was. The normal conversation. I remembered her name was Ann, and Mel and Shaun were going home for Christmas today and Shelly was working. Ann could pass my time with a little luck. I told Ann that I was driving the taxi that evening and asked her if she wanted to meet up for a drink at dinnertime. She said she would like to. I told her that I would pick her up at 12 o'clock when she finished. Ann's mother and father were going away for Christmas to their aunt's house and she did not want to go. I thought to myself that I was in. As I left, I told Ann to meet me at dinnertime and she said yes with a big smile on her face.

I met up with Ann outside the digs in the carpark. As the main roads were free of snow, we drove down to Cramlington; it was the town where the Charlton's brothers—footballers—came from. Ann and I called in at the Station Hotel for a drink. We sat down next to an old boy who told us that it was the only pub in the village. There were ten clubs as it was a mining village. Ann said we could go back to her mother's and Ann would make a meal for both of us. We bid the old boy goodbye and we went to Ann's mother's place, which was on a council estate and a two-bedroom house. Ann got on with the dinner and I said that I would settle for egg and chips as I loved homemade chips. The meal was good and I settled down on the sofa. Ann sat down next to me and we had sex on the sofa it was good. Then we dropped off for a kip as I could not stop too long since I was on taxi duty by seven. I told Ann that if I finished not too late, I would give her a ring. I got her number and off I went. It was a good night as it was two days to go for Christmas. The pubs were filling up now and I rang up Ann to say that I would see her on Monday.

The next day, I was up early as I had no work to go to and the weather was good. I got on with washing the car first and then cleaned it out. The Landlady came out to the carpark and told me that Frank the taxi man was on the phone. I went to answer it. Frank asked if I could drive the taxi dinnertime onwards. I said that I could. I finished what I was doing, then drove to the café to see Ann. I had a coffee with Ann and we talked some more. I told Ann that she was a good cook as well as good in the bedroom. I got a sandwich down as it could be a long day. I went next door and there was a couple wanting a taxi, so I got on with it. It was after midnight when I got back to the pub; the Landlord was still serving so I got a pint to go to bed on.

In the morning, I was up early and had nowhere to go as it was Christmas Day and the Landlady was cooking Christmas dinner for me as a present. I was hoping Shelly could come if she was not working. I told her to ring me if things changed. I was in the bar with my first bottle of nuke brown when Shelly walked in with a smile on her face. I got up to go to the bar as Shelly only wanted a soft drink. We sat and talked about what life holds for us as I knew I would be moving on in the next couple of weeks. When the customers left, the dinner was served in the bar and I was ready for it. It was good and so was the Christmas pudding. Shelly and I left with two bottles of nuke brown plus a bottle of red wine. We went back to the nurses' home to drink it. Shelly had to work the next day—Boxing Day—so we settled down to drink and have sex for the night.

I was up the next morning, made coffee and took it in to Shelly who had to start at 7 o'clock. I said to Shelly that I would wash up and shower, then ring up a taxi. We got dressed and kissed. Frank picked me up and asked me to help him for a couple of hours as it had been a long night. I said yes as I had nothing else to do. I washed and changed, and Frank took me to the office. Frank went home and I did a few jobs locally. It got busy in the afternoon; Frank came back at teatime and he dropped me off at the pub. I made myself a bowl of soup and bread. I rang up Shelly but she was having an early night so I watched the TV and must have dropped off. When I woke up, it was 9 o'clock and I could hear movement downstairs. I took a quick wash and went down to the bar. There were quite a few people in as it was the only pub open in town tonight. I got myself a nuke brown and stood at the bar at one end. People asked me why I was not on the taxi tonight and I replied that I just helped out Frank to give him a break. Football was the main conversation as they were Newcastle supporters and I was asked who I supported. I said I was not into football. The night was good with the jukebox music playing. For the next two days, I drove the taxi for Frank and called at the café for meals. Ann was pleased to see me and we swapped conversation on life in general. I asked what she was doing tonight and to my surprise, she said she was doing nothing. So, I said that I would pick her up at 6 o'clock. I got to the pub, had a bath, put my best scent on and met Ann at the taxi office. I thought, *I can't drive locally as I might bump into Shelly*. So, we drove up the A1 towards Berwick-on-Tweed, then went around a few villages until we found a good quiet pub. I got Ann a half lager and I had a beer shandy as I had to drive and the police were bad during Christmas time. We had a laugh and Ann was good company. It was a good evening out but it was the wrong week for Ann; you cannot win them all. I took her home and we had a good kiss and cuddle in the car.

The next day, I went to the café to see Ann as it was New Year's Eve and the taxi would be busy. I would carry on helping Frank out so I could not have a drink on New Year's Day. I went back to the taxi office and Frank said that there was a phone call for you and a number to ring back. It was from Shelly at the Hospital, so I dialled the number. Shelly answered and she said that she would be finished at 11 o'clock and if I had no plans, then I could come to the nurses' home to let the New Year in with the girls. I said yes and that I would get Frank to drop me off. I walked around to the nurses' home and when I got to the door, I had to wait for someone to come out or go in as the door lock was numbered. I did not have to wait long as Shelly came to meet me. I had not brought any drinks with me. Shelly said that there was plenty upstairs. We went to her room; there were plenty of people as it was nearly midnight. I was given a bottle of nuke brown. The clock of Big Ben on the TV struck 12 o'clock and we all joined hands in a circle and sang *Auld Lang Syne*. We shook hands and kissed, then put records on. More people joined us and it was a long cold night and it was three in the morning before people drifted away to their own rooms. Shelly and I sat down on the bed, kissed and then lay down with our clothes still on. We went to sleep as we both were knocked out. It was nearly ten when I woke up with a mouth like a shithouse. I put the kettle on, went to the bathroom, undressed to have a shower and there was a noise behind me. It was Shelly getting undressed and she said that I was not getting away that easily. We both washed each other's body and dried each other. She pulled me into the bedroom and the sex was great. It was almost 12 o'clock when we got up again and we needed some fresh air.

"Well," said Shelly, "let's eat breakfast and we will go down the village." So, bacon and egg was on the go in no time and it was good to have a greasy breakfast after a good session. We washed up and walked out like a newlywed couple down the road. I was not back to work until the third and Shelly was on nights tomorrow, so we had a day and a half together. We went to the pub and I went up to my room to put some scent on, then back down to the bar. Shelly had got the drinks. I sat down and the Landlady came across to see what I was doing about dinner as it was at 5 o'clock. We settled down to listen to the music and talk. The dinner was served upstairs as the pub was open all day. It was great, then we went to my room so that the Landlord and Landlady could relax in their front room. Shelly and I started to talk but one thing led to another and it was sex again. We both must have dozed off for an hour as the noise was loud downstairs when I got up. Shelly was awake by this time, so I got a shower first and Shelly followed. We dressed and went downstairs. The Landlady had a smile on her face and I stood at the bar as I got the drinks. Shelly talked about keeping in touch as I was going to move on shortly with the job. Due to bad weather, it was soon time to close and Shelly was on early in the morning. I had one more day to kill before work. I went to the phone and got Frank to pick up Shelly. Frank turned up, I went outside with her and gave her a big kiss. I said I would be in touch and then I went back to the pub and bed.

I was up early and put on the TV. It was too dark to check the car over, so I made a cup of tea and read an old paper. When it was light, I went down to check the car and water and made sure that the antifreeze was all right. I started it up and drove to the café for some breakfast. Ann was on and I ordered breakfast. I went to the paper shop and when I came back, the breakfast was ready. Ann was busy as more people came in, so I paid and went next door to see Frank. Frank said everything was all right, so I drove back to the pub and the Landlady was just opening up, so I got a nuke brown and finished the paper off. To my surprise, Mel walked in. I bought the drinks and the crack was good. Half an hour later, Shaun walked in and *all the best* went right around so it was a good day. Mel and Shaun had another job in hand abroad to go to shortly, so we parted ways.

Next morning, I was up early, had tea and went out as I had to drive to Berwick-on-Tweed. The roads were not bad on the A1 up north. I reached the yard and got a piece of wood to scrape the snow off the catwalk. I checked the engine oil; there was no water to check as it was air-cooled. There was life in the batteries, so I started it up and left it ticking. I went to the cabin and Chuck O'Brien told me and the two banks men that there were two lorries of pipes coming around dinnertime. Chuck asked if the crane was running and I said yes. Alan, one of the banks men, said that he was going to the shops for milk, sugar, teabags, steak and fresh bread. I put the kettle on to wash the pots and clean the frying pan, ready for Alan coming back from the shop. The weather was not too bad; when daylight came, Alan was back from the shop. I cracked on with the cooking of the steak; it was good as it was a piece of rump, so I was set for the day. The lorries turned up and we unloaded them. We talked to the drivers over a cup of tea. There were more coming until spring, so we had an idea that the job was to close down then. Peter turned up in the Land Rover to tell me that there was a meeting in the Bridge Pub tonight to talk about the job. So, I left work and went to the Bridge Pub. Peter was their plus Dave Goudy, the plant manager for Wiggles plant hire. Dave said that there was a meeting today and the job was to close down for all but the Skelton staff and we would be given a week's pay. So, it was time to move on.

1969: New Year

As the winter came on, I moved on. Mel and Shaun got a job abroad. I read the construction newspaper; there was a job at Blyth, which was this side of Newcastle, for Harbour General for a 22RB driver. I rang up the number and got the job, so I set off in bad weather for Blyth, north of Newcastle on the coast. I said my goodbyes to Mel, Shaun and my Landlady. I called at the taxi office to say goodbye to Frank and his wife, Mary, then went to the café to say goodbye to Ann. I also rang up the nurses' home and spoke to Shelly. I told her that I had a job at Blyth and as soon as I got settled, I would give her a ring. As I drove down the A1 towards Newcastle, I saw a signpost, Blyth. The job was at Harbour General on the harbour wall outside Blyth. I pulled up at the offices; the foreman's name was Freddie Green. He told me that the job was working with chippers, lifting shutters at the side of the sea wall, and concrete to be put in to cap the top of the piles. Freddie took me down to the job in a Land Rover to the crane. I checked it over for oil and water, then started it up. He introduced me to the foreman chipper, Mick. The job was for only 10 weeks as the piling was done. Freddie called at dinnertime to see whether I had digs. I said not yet. He said that I could move into the big caravan on the job which was next to the big lighthouse. Freddie brought me the forms that I needed to fill in for lodge money, which was tax-free. After a couple of days, I got in food and the washing up. On Thursday night, we went to the pub after we finished work. Freddie told me that he collects Toby jugs as there were some in the pub. We had left the Land Rover at the end of the site so that we could drive it back from the pub with no bother. On Saturday, Freddie went home to

Bolton and I had the caravan to myself. As we were not working on Sunday, I changed and walked down the Blyth town to the pub. I stood at the bar on my own; a woman came over and stood next to me. She had noticed that I was on my own. We got chatting and I told her that I was working on the wharf. I bought her a drink. As the night went on, I found out that the lady's name was Janet. *Oh no! Not another! But if she rode like the last one, then so what*, I thought. Janet asked me if I would like to go to a nightclub. We walked; it was in the town and was quite packed. I had a job getting to the bar but with a bit of pushing and shoving, I got there in the end. We sat in a corner and talked about her. Janet had been married and had a boy of ten. She told me that she had married at eighteen. The boy was with his dad who had a new partner and she would see him every two weeks. After the drinks, we had a couple of dances before we left. Janet had a flat and with no work tomorrow, I could mellow out. The flat was small and cosy and the coffee pot was on as it was 1.30 in the morning. We sat on the settee but you could see that it was getting out of hand and there was only one place to go. Janet dragged me into the bedroom, as if I needed dragging! Sex was good and I was learning new ways and new positions.

I was up at about 6 o'clock. I looked outside; it was frosty. It was a good thing I had left the heating on in the caravan. I made coffee as I needed some energy to walk back to the caravan. I took Janet a coffee to the bedroom. She was awake. Janet told me to get myself some breakfast but I declined, saying that I would cook when I got back to the caravan. Janet was a barmaid at the pub and was working on Sunday so I said that I would see her later. I left and locked the door behind me. It was a long walk back in the dark and there was an icy wind off the sea. The sand dunes were white and crispy under the feet beside the road. I was glad to get into the caravan; it was warm and I got into bed for a couple of hours as there was no rush to go anywhere.

It was 10.30 when I woke up. I put the kettle on to get hot water for a wash as the shower would be frozen up. We had two five-gallon containers inside the toilet. I put breakfast on and felt better with food inside me. I washed up as I knew Freddie would be coming back tonight. The time was now 12 o'clock so I changed, put scent on, got the kettle with warm water for the windscreen so that I could take the car to the end of the road and then a short walk to the pub. Janet was behind the bar and smiled and got a nuke brown. She asked me about dinner and the landlady said that she would plate me up before I left. The convention was football—Newcastle United. I was asked which team I supported; I said myself and that was that. I got a couple more nuke browns down, picked up the dinner, paid for it and went back to the caravan to watch TV. I warmed up the dinner in the oven later, watched TV and dropped off as it was dark when I woke up and I heard an engine outside. I knew it was Freddie back and in he walked with his bag. He asked me if I had a good weekend and I said yes. I lit the oven to warm the dinner up. He asked if I was going down to the pub after dinner and I said yes. I ate my dinner and then put the plate in the sink. I would wash up tomorrow. I put my big coat on and I went in Freddie's car to the road's end. We went into the pub and Janet was serving behind the bar. Freddie was well in with Rose, the Landlady, as she ran the pub on her own and both were interested in Toby jugs and collected them. I had other interests on my mind—sex with Janet. We both got nice beef sandwiches that went down well with the beer. Janet got me to one side and told me that she would have to go the doctor's and get some pills if I kept having sex with her; otherwise, I would be pram-pushing. We made a date for Thursday as Wednesday was games night in the pub and she had to work. Rose had a taxi to go home, so tonight sex was out.

The next morning, I was up at six, got a cup of tea down, and then went out to see the lads in the canteen. The lads were on about the Lady on a camass bike and had I been with her on the weekend. "No," I said, "but tell me more." Big Mick the chipper said that a woman on a bike would ride down the road to the lighthouse where I had the caravan, then the piling men would shag her ass off on the beach. The weather was bad and it was a bit rough on the ass this time of the year. I said that I would look out for her. I went and got the crane ready for work. They were cold days as the wind blew off the sea and the crane had no heater in it. There was also a 360 digger on the job with one jockey driver. The machine was a 580 HYMAC digging out roads and drainage. Freddie asked me if I could drive it when there was no work for the crane. The weather started to get better as it was April and the nights were getting shorter. The job was coming together and the roads were ready for tarmac. On Thursday night, Freddie and I went down to the pub together as usual and I met up with Janet. We then walked up the town to the Swan's Head as a group was playing. The music was good—'60s'. It was packed but we got a seat. I only had two bottles of nuke brown as I had work the next morning and Janet was saying that I could stay the night so she would want servicing. When the night was over, Janet and I walked back to her flat. The kettle was on but no drinks were made. I walked back into the room and Janet stripped me and we were in bed. The sex was good again and the talk was to become an item. I thought, *the job had only a few weeks to run and it would be time to move on so play it cool for now.*

I walked back to the caravan as it was a good morning and getting light. Freddie was up and the kettle was on. I went to start the crane up. There was talk around the job about layoff s. I was asked if I had heard anything yet from Freddie and I declined. Freddie was going home again at dinnertime and the lads were knocking off at 4 o'clock so I had the weekend to myself.

On Saturday, I told Freddie that I would do the shopping if he left me a list. I was showered and changed by six. I would eat out at the pub and I drove to the end of the road and parked the car. I walked to the pub; Janet was on and I got a smile and I asked for a menu. The steak sounded nice, so I ordered that and washed it down with a bottle of nuke brown. I asked Janet if she would like to come back to the caravan tonight and she said yes. I asked if she would do the washing and I told her that I would pay in kind. I got a big smile. When the evening was over, we both got into the car back to the caravan. It was good that

I had left the heating on low. I put the TV on but Janet had other ideas. Janet was like a ferry—roll on and roll off. I got up at 6 o'clock and put the kettle on. Janet was still sleeping like a new-born baby. It was too early for breakfast. I picked up the construction newspaper. it was called Jackers Journal Construction news for the building site workers. I noticed a job for a 19RB crane driver in Manchester; the firm was called Connell Finnegan's. I wrote the number down on a piece of paper and thought I would ring the number on Monday as the job was coming to an end for me since the 22RB crane was going away on Wednesday, Freddie had said. Janet was up by now and we talked about what might happen this week. "Are you going shopping today?" Janet asked.

"Yes," I said. There was a list on the worktop that Freddie had left. We got ready as it was coming up to 10 o'clock. We drove up the town; Janet got what she wanted and I got what was on the list. I dropped Janet off at her flat with the washing and told her that I would see her tonight at the pub. I took the food back to the caravan and checked the car over, ready for the move. I washed it and then washed the caravan out as it was a nice day. It was soup for dinner with bread. I had bought the construction newspaper as well as the morning paper. At the back, there was the same job as last week for a crawler crane driver in Manchester for O'Connell and Finnigan's in Droylsden. It was a demolitions as well as an earthmoving firm.

I put on the TV to watch sports but I must have dropped off to sleep as it was 6.15 when I woke up. I got myself tidied up with a bit of a wash and shave, got into the car and drove it to the end of the road and went to the pub. Janet passed me my washing with a smile on her face so I took it back to the car and thanked her. I bought her and the Landlady, Rose, a drink. I told Janet that there was a job in the paper and I was going to ring about it on Monday during break time as it was time to move on. Janet asked if I would fancy going to the nightclub after work and I agreed. So, I went steady on the nuke browns. We ordered a taxi for us as well as a customer to make a careful. After last orders at 10.30, we got in the cab with the customer, dropped him off in town and went around to the nightclub. There was a queue to get in and it took ten minutes to get inside. It was packed but we managed to get a drink and we both found a corner to stand in. The group was live and had a lot of followers and the music was good to dance to. It was a good night. We could not get a taxi back to Janet's flat, so we walked as it was a good evening. The usual happened: the kettle went on but never got used as Janet was randy as a dog on heat, so it was to bed and sex was good I learnt new positions and was very pleased with myself and extremely satisfied.

I was up the next morning at daylight. It was nice to have a cup of tea as the first one was always the best. Janet was still asleep when I left. I called at the paper shop for the paper and then walked back to my car on the quay. I went to the caravan for breakfast and a read of the paper. As it was a nice day, I decided that I would go for a walk along the shore. It was on my side as the docks were on the other. The things on my mind were this next job and if I got

116

it and what was involved. It was another challenge to move and meet more people. The fresh air was good. The oil tanks were offshore and one was coming in with tugs around it as it was high tide. I must have walked a couple of miles before I decided to turn back as it was time for the pub and I was getting a bit dry in the mouth with the salty air. I walked in at the pub and Janet came across to serve me. "I did not hear you go out this morning," she whispered in my ear.

"No," I said, "you looked just like sleeping beauty." I told Janet that I had been for a walk down the coast and had enjoyed it and was ready for a drink. I asked Rose what was on for dinner and she said lamb. "We will have two of them," said Janet. "I hope you get the job."

The door opened and in walked Freddie. "Hi," I said, "you are back early."

"Yes," said Freddie, "I called in to see a friend on the way back but he was called out at the last minute, so it was just as easy to carry on here." Rose was pleased so it was another dinner on the go. When it was quiet in the bar, Rose brought the dinner out to the bar and the four of us sat down to eat it. The food was good—no cooking or pot-washing. Freddie was going to be engaged for the rest of the afternoon, so Janet and I disappeared for a few hours until opening time again. Janet and I went for a nice walk but I could see where we were heading—her flat and the bed. Janet had to be back at work by 7 o'clock so we had a bath together to save water. We had sex again over the bath and then walked back to the pub. Freddie was down the cellar sorting out the barrels. Rose had a big smile on her face and I knew that she had been serviced. Freddie and I sat down and talked about work. I told him that there was a job opening in Manchester in the paper and I was going to ring about it in break time tomorrow. "You do that," said Freddie. "I hope you get it as I will have to lay you off next week anyway as I have told from the office." The crack was good in conversation and music and it was time to go. Rose had got Janet a cab, so it was a goodnight kiss for a change and back to the caravan and bed.

In the morning, I was out on the job and got the crane up the road to be derigged ready for the low loader for Wednesday. I got on with the job in hand on the 580 HYMAC before it went away. At dinnertime, I got into my car and went to the phone down the road to ring about the job in the paper. The girl on the other end of the phone put me through to an Irishman. He said he was asking people to come and give a test. I told the man that I was a travelling plant operator. He asked me if I could go down there next Saturday and I agreed. I went back to the site to carry on with the job for the rest of the day. Freddie and I talked at teatime in the caravan. We dished out the stew that Freddie had made; it was good. I showered first and then Freddie. Then it was off to the pub to wash the stew down with nuke browns. I knew from the tone of Janet's voice that she did not want me to go but she kept smiling.

On Wednesday morning, the low loader turned up and so did a fitter to strip the jib down ready to load up and take it away back to the yard. There was no more work for the crane at this time. The HYMAC would go on Thursday. I should be done with it by then, just a bit of topsoil to level off. The other lads were local and were looking around for jobs. Freddie was taking the caravan home before he went to the yard for an office job. Wednesday night was as usual. We had dinner—Freddie had prepared two nice big lambs chops with mashed potatoes and mushy peas and gravy. It went down well and we went down to the pub as usual. It was darts and dominos night and that was always a good night. Janet looked lovely as usual with a low-cut top and tits stuck out. It always made my prick twitch when I saw them. Rose came across to talk to us. I did not know until then that Freddie and Rose had set up a going-away party on Thursday at teatime for all the lads on the job with food as well. I managed to get into the dominos game as the pub was one short. I had to put a different name on the sheet to play. We did not win as the other pub's team was good but the supper that Rose had put on finished the night off. Rose had got Janet a taxi, so I got a big kiss outside before she left. Freddie and I went back to the caravan.

In the morning, I was up and went to the canteen to tell the lads that there was a party at the pub tonight and they were pleased with that. I worked with the lads for the rest of the day, cleaning up the site. We knocked off early to get ready for the party. Freddie was ready when I got to the caravan. I washed, changed, put on my smellies and we both went to the pub. There was office staff there too—two engineers, Neil and Andy. They were also lodging in the town and were good to get on with. The food layout looked good; Rose had done us proud. The '60s' music was always good to hear. It was a very good night all around and I did not want to drink a lot as I had to drive tomorrow and Janet would want a good old servicing tonight. I said my goodbyes to all. Rose had got a taxi for both of us as I knew Freddie would be servicing Rose. As soon as we both got into Janet's flat, we were like two rabbits on the floor and then the bedroom. My testicles were empty and I did not know when I would get more sex.

I was up early to get a good start to drive to Manchester. I put the kettle on and took one cup to the bedroom for Janet. She turned over and smiled, "Will you ring me tonight at the pub?" I said yes and got a big kiss. I drank my tea and went down the road for a taxi to the caravan. Freddie was back as well. I got a shower to wash my dick as I did not want to catch anything. I packed my bag and went into the office to say my goodbyes to Freddie. He said, "I hope we will meet again one day."

"Yes," I said and got into the car and set off for Newcastle on the A1. The traffic was busy at this time of the morning. I drove down as far as Durham and then pulled into a Greasy Spoon café where I got a good breakfast. I did not know when I would be eating again. I arrived in the area and followed the signs for Droylsden and found the yard. I parked and went to the office. The girl was Irish and spoke with a good accent. I told her that I had come about the job in the paper for a crane driver. She got up, went to the next office, then came out again and told me to go in. There was a big Irishman who shook my hand to welcome me and said that he would give me a test in the morning. He asked me where I came from and then asked if I had somewhere to stay. I said not yet.

He said that his receptionist would sort it out. He told me to report at 8 o'clock in the yard. I thanked him and went back to reception. The girl rang around the B&Bs and pubs. The pub was called The Three Legs Of A Man and the girl give me directions and off I went to find it. After asking a few people, I found it and parked in the carpark. I went into the pub and the man behind the counter asked me what I wanted. I told him that I was booked in an hour ago. "You must be Mr Billy Rennison," he said. "Yes," I replied and then he showed me up to the rooms. He said, "My name is also Billy and my wife's name is Tina." The room was clean and a single. It was two pounds per night. I accepted and went back down to the bar. There were two Irishmen at the bar and they were drinking Guinness, which looked OK. I asked Tina for a pint. The Irishmen asked if I had just pulled in and I said that I had a job at a plant hire firm and had a test on a 22RB crane in the morning. "We wish you luck," one man said. He said his name was John and his mate was Paul. As usual, I got along with Irish people and the crack was good you could always have a laugh with them. John told me that he was on for McCalpine's, who was building the M62 motorway, and if the test did not turn out well, they would get me a start on the job. It turned out to be a good night. I turned in on last orders and had a good night's kip for a change—no sex!

I was up the next morning and followed the way I had come to the yard. The big man was already in and came across the yard to meet me. "Good morning," he said. "Jump into my Rover and I will take you to the crane and see how you perform. You will get a lift from the yard each day. Are the digs all right?"

"Yes," I said. We got to a big demolition site. It was an old steelworks.

"There is a mountain of soil at the back of the works and I will remove it on the motorway job as fill. It will take three weeks, then you can knock down the steelworks for me," he said. I checked the crane over for oil and water, then started it up. I was a bit slow at first with the drag bucket. After a few tries, I got better. He watched me, then walked away and let me get on with it. I got the feel of the machine after a bit. I must have been at it for an hour. He came back and told me that I had the job starting from Monday. I thanked him and he took me back to the yard. "Can you be at the yard by 7 o'clock?" he said. "I will pay you from then."

"I will be there," I replied. "Have a nice weekend. Thank you." I went back to the pub, parked the car in the carpark and then went for a walk around the town to get myself some breakfast at a café. I was feeling quite pleased with myself on passing the test. I found a café fairly full; then you know that it is not bad to eat in. I went to the counter to order off the board. *A full breakfast*, I thought, *as it could be a long day and it was almost dinnertime*. I got coffee and sat down. The food was quickly served by a plump-ish lady with a big smile. "There you are, my lad," she said, "enjoy your meal." It went down a treat. There was a paper on the counter, so I got it and sat and read it as there was no rush to go anywhere. The lady came over to take the plate and said, "You are new here."

"Yes," I said, "I pulled into town last night."

"What have you got planned for tonight?" she asked.

"Nothing yet."

"My name is Valerie," she said. "And you are?"

"Billy. I fancied going out as I have not been anywhere for a long time."

Valerie said that we could meet outside the shop at around 8 o'clock. I agreed. "So, it's a date," she said. I got up and thought to myself, *Well, chatted up on the first day in town!* I walked back to the pub and the two Irishmen, John and Paul, were at the bar. "How did you get on with the test?" they asked.

"Great," I said, "I passed. I start on Monday at 7 o'clock. I also got chatted up in a café for a date tonight."

"Well," said John, "you have had a good morning. Three pints of Guinness, Tina, and put one in for yourself." I thought I better pace myself; otherwise, I would be pissed for my date tonight and with the twinkle in Valerie's eye, she could have raped me there and then. At closing time, I went up to lie down but put the alarm on for six to get a bath. The next thing I knew, the alarm had gone off and I had not heard it. The time was five to seven, so it was a bit of a rush to get a quick bath and put my scent on. It was a half-hour walk so I had to get a move on. I did not want Valerie to think that I had stood her up. When I got near the shop, there was a woman standing outside; it was Valerie. She looked a picture and had scrubbed up well. There was a big smile on her face when she saw me coming. "Hello," I said, "you look well. You know the town so where do we start?"

"Well," said Valerie, "there is a group at the Railway Tavern on Old Field Road; the group is called the Dubliners. It's an Irish band."

"Right, we will go there."

It was a 15-minute walk and when we got there, it was packed but the music was very good. There was a break in the music and we could talk. Valerie told me a bit about herself: her husband went off with another woman and there were no children in her life. You could tell by her talk that she was hoping for one with her marriage but it wasn't to be. Then I told Valerie that I came from a big family and I loved travelling at the moment and hoped to get a job abroad. I had filled out a form in the Daily Mirror paper for a job in Western Australia but had no replies yet. I had put my parents' address on the form and I had not rung home for three weeks. I reminded myself this coming week. "I have just started a new job in Manchester—a demolition job for a local firm—and I passed the test this morning," I told Valerie.

"Good for you," Valerie said. The music started again and Irish music was great to listen to. I managed to get to the bar again for drinks. Valerie was on gin and tonic. Valerie smiled when she took a snipe, "I do not like to have sex on the first date because you never know what you might catch." I had learnt from the lads I had met on jobs so far. The night was coming to a close and Valerie was well up front. I walked her to a taxi stand at the end of the road. "I will see you on Monday in the café," Val said, "and as I am working all next week since the boss is off, we will sort out a dinner date for next week."

We said good night and Val gave me a peck on the cheek and got into the taxi. I set off back to the pub; the lights were on and the Landlady told me to use the side door if the pub was closed. I had a key. Tina was having a lock in with some friends and asked if I wanted a nightcap before I turned in. She said that I could have a Guinness before she turned it off to clean the pipes. I stood at the bar as Tina turned the beer off and cleaned up. "My barmaid has got the night off," Tina said. I was introduced to Tina's friends and we talked for a while. They drank up, said goodnight and left by the side door. Tina asked me to help her move some barrels in the cellar and she led the way. I got them moved and Tina thanked me with a kiss on the lips. I put my hands around her waist and pulled her in to me. The passion was good and we both looked at one another, put the lights out and went upstairs. We both undressed each other and the sex was good as I found out later that Tina had not made love for some time. I was complimented on how good a lover I was. I fell asleep thinking that it was an end to a perfect day.

I woke up early on Sunday morning. I had a cup of tea, then went to find a paper shop and have a read. I came back and had breakfast. It was a dull day but dry. I asked a man in the street where the shop was and he told me that it was a 10-minute walk. I got the paper and went back to the pub. As I walked in, I could hear a movement upstairs. Tina was in the kitchen. "Good morning," I said and she smiled.

"You were great last night," she said.

"You were not bad yourself."

"Do you want bacon and eggs as I am getting it for myself?" she asked.

"Yes please," I said and it went down well. I got stuck into the paper when Tina called me upstairs. She asked me if I would give her a hand doing some cellar work. I went down to the bar and Tina showed me what she wanted and I got on with it. When I was done, I sat at the bar to carry on with the paper as it was opening time by then. John and Paul came in and I bought the drinks. John asked me how I got on with the date. I said that it went good; I did not let on that I had sex with Tina. When I got back, the subject had changed and it was back to work again, which was a good topic. I learnt a lot from the lads and the conversation was good until dinnertime. Tina shouted last orders, then John and Paul said that they would see me in a week. I went upstairs and Tina followed me, asking, "Are you hungry?" No was my reply. I thought I would grab an hour's kip and then have a bath tonight. Tina had other ideas. As I got into bed, the bedroom door opened and Tina walked in with no clothes on and smiled as she got into bed. My reaction to her warmth of her body was sensational and we were at it like two animals on heat. We both just lay there to get our breaths back and talked about her Husband and why he left. His mother was an invalid and she did not approve of Tina as she was four years older than him. I lay back and just listened as I was good at that. I must have dropped off. When I woke up, Tina was in the kitchen. I got up, put my clothes on as I was going to have a bath and went into the kitchen. Tina said there was a chicken in the oven if I wanted it. "Food is in the fridge; help yourself," she said. "I will have to open up now and I will see you when you come down."

I took a bath—the water was hot and a good soak was what I needed at this moment. My mind went into overdrive thinking where to move on next. There was the M62 job or look for a job somewhere else. I decided to ring up my Aunt Rosy who lived next door to my parents to see if there was any reply to the advertisement I had written weeks earlier. I got dressed and went downstairs to the bar. Tina smiled and asked if I had enjoyed my bath. "Is it Guinness or nuke brown?" Tina asked. I needed the energy so it would be Guinness. "How long have you got left on this job?" Tina asked.

"I am not sure," I said. "Maybe a week, two weeks. The firm told me that they had work for me but who knows."

There were not many drinkers in, tonight being Sunday night. I had two more pints, then went up as it would be closing time shortly and I needed a good night's sleep. So, I said good night to Tina and I went up.

Next morning, I called at the café. Valerie was in early, so it was bacon and tea. The lads were in. One said, "I think you are going to drive the rubber tyre shovel and load us up with brick rubble. We have to run to the McAlpines on the M62 at the Withamshaw job so it will be a two-hour round trip for three lorries."

There was a fair amount of brick rubble around the site with all the buildings that I had knocked down over the last few weeks on the job. I guessed there were two weeks left. I got to the rubber tyre loading shovel, checked it for oil and water plus dev and then got the three lorries away. Big Pat turned up in his Land Rover and we walked around the job. Pat said that there was plenty to keep going for a while as he had another job for me after this. I got into my car and drove to a phone box to ring home to see if my mother and father were all right. I had my Aunt Rosy's number as she lived next door. My Uncle Charlie answered the phone and he asked where I was. I asked him how my mum and dad were and he said that he would fetch my mother to the phone. Andy came on the phone and he told me that Dad was not too good with his chest and was off work at the moment. My mother came on the phone and asked where I was and if I was all right. She then told me about Dad and I said that I would put some money in the post this morning to help them. "There is a letter for you," my mother said. "I will send it to you if you give me the address." Mum got a pencil and paper and I gave her the address of the firm I was working for. Then she told me about my Brothers and Sisters, and I said that I would come home when this job was finished so it was goodbye for now and I rung off.

When I got back on site, the first lorry was back and I wondered what the letter would say. But I could just dream on and get on with the job in hand. At the end of the day, I called at the café for tea. Valerie was on and pork chops was on offer. I ordered and sat down with a pot of tea and the grub was good. "I will be finished early tomorrow night; do you want to call around to the house for tea after work if I give you the address?" Valerie asked.

"Yes, I will look forward to it," I replied. I got a peck on the cheek and a big smile as I could see where Valerie was coming from. I got back to the digs and was ready for a pint after the big feed. Tina was behind the bar and the Guinness went down well. The lads walked in, so it was two more pints. The crack was good. I mentioned that my dad was not too good at the moment. It was last orders but I had enough for one night and I went up for a wash and some sleep. I heard Tina come up after locking up and the bedroom door shut so it was going to be a quiet night.

Next morning, after a cup of tea, I went to the café. Valerie was on. I ordered my breakfast, then sat down. Valerie brought my breakfast and also an address to get to her house this evening. "I will be there," I said, "with a bottle of wine—red or white?"

"Red," Valerie said so I finished the food and went off to work. I went with a smile on my face. All day, I wondered what I was going in for but it was another night of sex. It was a long day but, in the end, I asked the lads about the address and an easy way to get to it. It was in the Salford part of the city. I reached it, parked the car and went to the door. Valerie came. "You are on time, I see."

"I have not had a wash yet," I said and I went in.

"You can have a shower; I will get you a clean towel. The dinner is nearly ready," she said.

I went off to the bathroom and into a posh shower, grabbed a towel and got dry. There was a dressing gown hung up, so I put it on and put my skids on— underpants, I mean. I went into the room; the dinner smelled good and I hoped that the taste was just as good. "You smell nice," Valerie said, "like a whore's handbag."

The dinner went down well and I was as full as a butcher's dog. The wine that followed was also good. The TV was on and we sat and watched it. It was getting late. Valerie said, "You are not going back tonight; you are staying."

"I will wash the pots, I offered. Valerie dried them and we sat down again. I got a peck on the cheek; that was the calling card. She caught hold of my hand and it was bedtime. The sex was the best. If ever a man had been raped, I was! She did all the work and My testicles were sore by the morning. I had a job getting in the loading shovel but I did not let on to the lads that I was sore. At the end of the day, I went to my digs and got a pint of Guinness off Tina, who said, "You were not home last night, were you?"

"No," I said, "a friend from work took me out on the town for a drink and I slept on the sofa for the night." I just hoped that Tina did not want sex tonight as my balls were empty. The Guinness went down nicely and *I would have my strength back tomorrow*, I thought. At closing time, I told Tina that I was going up to catch up on my sleep as I had a night of drinking last night. She wished me goodnight and up I went.

I woke up at 5 o'clock in the morning, had a cup of tea and off to work. I called at the café and the lads were in. Valerie asked, "Same as usual?" I accepted. The coffee came, then breakfast, which went down well after the

Guinness and my body seemed to perk up. I got to work and got the three lorries away, then had a minute to myself to think where I was going from here. If there was no job, I would get the Jacket's Journal, the construction newspaper, and see what's about. I decided to nip out after loading the next lorries. I got the paper and sat down on a piece of wood; there was a job at Thomas Ward's at Sheffield. I would ring them up on the next load as a pay phone was down the road. I got the lorries away again and walked to the phone box with the paper in hand, rang the number and was put through to the plant yard. The plant manager's name was Eddy Berk; I told him that I was a crawler crane driver and a travelling man. "You know, we only have Smith's cranes," Eddy said. "Are you familiar with them?"

"Yes," I said, "I will come to the yard on Saturday morning."

"It is on Rotherham Road on the left-hand side near the 600 group yard; say, 10 o'clock?" Eddy said.

"I will be there," I told Eddy. "I will have to give a week's notice here."

"That will be all right as the job we want you for is a week or so away yet," Eddy said. I rang off and went back to the job as one lorry was back and the driver was having his dinner in the cab. I asked Patrick, the driver, about the work situation and he said that it was not so good at the moment. *Well,* I thought, *it is Friday tomorrow and I will ride to Sheffield in the morning. I will keep it to myself until then.* The afternoon went by fast and it was nearly 6 o'clock. I was feeling a bit peckish and so I went to the café. Valerie was on with a smile on her face. "How are you? She asked. "You were up and gone the other day."

"Still sore," I said. Valerie just laughed and asked what I would like to eat. I saw that the lamb chops looked good. She told me to sit down and she would bring it. I told her that I would have a pint of milk to wash it down. The food was good and Valerie sat down for minute. I told her that I was going for a ride on Saturday morning to Sheffield to see someone about a job and I could be late back if she wanted to go out at night. "Why not come around when you come back? I will have a meal on for you," she offered. "Please let me know what you are doing by dinnertime. I will give you the café number now." Valerie got the number and sat back down with a serious look on her face. I knew then that the relationship was getting out of hand as I just wanted a friend. I promised Valerie that I would ring her and come around on Saturday night. I got a peck on the cheek and said goodnight and then went back to my digs. Tina was behind the bar and I told her that I was going for a ride out in the morning and may not be back until Sunday. I got the pint of Guinness down and she told me about the problem she had in the cellar and said that she could do with a man around the place. This was major hint-dropping. They say that if you are riding the horse, you have to shoe it, but not a double. Tina pulled me another pint because I knew there was not going to be a lot of sleep tonight. Tina called last orders and I gave her a hand to collect the glasses and wash them. I finished my drink and then I told Tina that I was going up now. "I will be up in a minute," was the reply. I went into the kitchen, put the kettle on as I wanted a cup of tea to take the taste of drink out of my mouth. There was a noise behind me; Tina had walked in. "Tea?" she said. "I will have one too." We sat down at the table. "What have you got on tomorrow?" Tina asked me. I told her that I was going to see somebody in Sheffield. I did not mention a job to her yet in case it backfired on me as the digs were good and there was sex with them. I went to my room; Tina was not far behind me. The sex was great but it was sleep that I wanted most of all. Tina was still in my bed when I got up, dressed and got a cup of coffee. I set off over Woodshead, which was a road of beauty in the summer but in winter, you could get stuck in the snow for days.

September 1969 was coming up and I remembered that it would soon be my 24th birthday. The drive was good and I stopped at a café for breakfast. The taste was good as it was freshly cooked. I carried on until I came to the outskirts of Sheffield. The plant yard was on Rotherham Road opposite the 600 group yard. I drove into the plant yard and parked. There were men near the big workshops, so I asked where the plant manager's office was. I was directed to a big office in the middle of the building. It was upstairs. I knocked on the door and a voice told me to come in. I told the man that I was Billy Rennison and had come about the job. He said that his name was Len and we shook hands. The job required travelling away from home a lot which was what I wanted. "What are you like on Smith's cranes?" he asked.

"Well," I said, "I am into RBs."

"Well, you should get the hang of it as the levers are long but the cab is on the opposite side of the crane. I will take you downstairs to meet my foreman fitter, Frank."

Frank took me across to a Smith's 21 that was in for repair. I got in and he showed me what the levers were for. He left me to get on with it for half an hour. When he came back, the crane was on blocks and the tracks were off. He must have had an eye on me as when he came back over to me, he said, "I see you got the hang of it. I will take you back up to see Len and tell him that you will be all right."

We went to the office. "How did he get on?" Len asked Frank, who said that he would pass, no problems. "When can you start?" Len asked me.

"Well," I said, "I will put in a week's notice if that's all right."

"Great," he said, "there is a job to start in Ellesmere port in Cheshire in a week's time; I will give you the details now before you go."

"Great," I said.

"The job is for MH Tunnelling," Len explained.

By the time I left, it was dinnertime, so I called at the Moulder Arms pub for a pint and to see what the crack was over Pauline and the so-called baby of mine. I went in and the Landlord, Roy, was pleased to see me. As I was driving, it was one pint or two shandies. Roy said that Pauline had been in a month ago but that was only a flying visit. I had to say goodbye for now. I worked my way back over Woodshead. A mist came down and I had to go slowly. When I was coming back down towards Manchester, the mist cleared out again. It was teatime when I got back to the café and Valerie was on. "Hi," she said, "did you enjoy your day out?"

"Yes," I said, "I got the job. I will give a week's notice on Monday as it's only right to do so. You never know when you might need a job again. What have you got to eat?"

"Ham, egg and chips," Valerie said.

"OK, that will do," I said and sat down and stuck my head in a paper with a mug of tea in my hand. The food was on the table with a smile from Valerie. She came and sat down as it was quiet. "What have you got on tonight?" Valerie asked me.

"Not a lot," I said. "We could have a quiet drink somewhere if you like. I will take the car back to the digs and freshen up and meet you at the Railway Tavern."

"It's a date then."

I thought as I drove to the pub, *I just hope Tina does not want sex before I go out*. As it was Saturday, the pub was open all day. The lads were in. "Well Billy. What sort of a day have you had?"

"Good up to now," I replied. "I went to Sheffield to Thomas Ward's plant hire and got a job in Ellesmere Port on hire to MH Tunnelling with a Smith's 21 crane."

"Great! When do you start?" Mick asked.

"A week from Monday," I said. "I will give a week's notice where I am." Tina was there with a pint of Guinness and a smile. She had been listening to the conversation. "Good for you," Tina said. I got the round in and put myself for one but I said that I would have it when I came back down after freshening up. The water was hot, so a bath and a good soak were in order. I forgot to lock the door and Tina popped her head in. "I hope you smell nice when you get out," she said and laughed. I was out and dry, then went into my room. Tina was in my bed. "Who is at the bar then?" I asked her.

"The new barmaid I settled on in the week; Ann is her name," she said. The sex was good; Tina was horny as hell and I could not wait until tonight. I had to go to the bathroom again to wash myself as Valerie would want sex also. I hoped it was the wrong week for her. I got downstairs to the bar. The barmaid asked what I wanted. "Guinness," I said. *To get my strength back*, I thought. I told her that it was already paid for. Then Tina came in and stood at the bar and smiled. Tina asked where I was off to and I said that I was going to meet the lads from work. I drank up and went out. I walked to the Railway Tavern pub and went in but could not see Valerie anywhere. I went to the bar and got a pint of Guinness; the music was about to start. I stood near the door so as not to miss her if she came in. I waited an hour but then thought, *Billy boy, you have been stood up*. It was just as well. The music was good as I was well into Irish tunes. I stayed a bit longer, had another pint and walked back to the pub just as last orders were called. Tina pulled me a pint. "Can I have a Jameson's whisky as well?" I said.

Tina looked up and said, "You are pushing the boat out tonight, Billy boy!"

"I just fancied one for a change." I sat down and Tina joined me. "Did you meet the lads?" she asked.

"Yes," I said, "but they had the girls with them and were going out on the town and I did not want to play gooseberry." Tina laughed. The pub closed down and the three of us—Tina, Ann and myself—just talked for an hour with another drink. I could feel myself getting pissed so I called it a night and left the two girls talking and went up for a good night's kip.

Sunday mornings, people lie in but not me. I put the kettle on, had tea and went out to the paper shop. There was quite a bit of building going on in Salford and the surrounding area and new machinery on the jobs was coming out all the time. The labour man was getting done away with as machines were taking over. I enjoyed the walk out. Tina was up when I got back. "Would you like some breakfast, Billy?" she asked.

"Yes please," was my answer as I sat down to read the paper.

"I have got a job for you before you disappear," Tina said. "There are some barrels in the cellar that want moving, if you would please."

The food was put on the table and it went down well. "Have a minute before we go down there; let your food go down first," she said. "I will miss you when you go. It is good to have a man about the place to do jobs as well as for sex and you are different—you go with the flow."

I smiled and said, "Come, let's see what needs moving." We got down to the cellar and Tina showed me what to move to set up the barrels for the coming week and finish cleaning the pipes out for the beer. "What are you doing for dinner as I will cook if it's for two, "she offered.

"Great," I said.

"Ann is on today. It will give me a break from cooking and cleaning."

I turned around and Ann was coming in through the door. I emptied the slops out in the sink as Tina pulled the fresh beer through the pipes, then went upstairs. Ann pulled me a Guinness with a shamrock on the top. "You are a dab hand at that," I said.

"Practice makes perfect," she said. I laughed. "Tina really likes you," Ann added, "as we had a talk last night."

I said, "She is great to get on with but I am not ready to settle down yet; there is a big wide world out there to explore. But I will keep in touch."

The lads came in, so the Guinness flowed and the crack was good. Then it was time to close up. The lads said that they would see me in a week before I left. I locked up after Ann had gone; the dinner smelled good—beef with Yorkshire pudding and gravy. It went down well and I was as full as a butcher's dog. We both sat on the sofa and went to sleep. I woke up to find Tina cuddling up to me and it was time to open up to let Ann in but when I got downstairs, Ann was in the bar as Tina had given her a key for the side door. I went back to freshen up with Tina already in the bathroom. I got a big kiss on the lips as she came out.

It was a quiet night; there were a few people in. At the end of the night, Tina and I went up to bed. It was the best sex ever as there was no rush it was slow and sensual.

I was up next morning, had tea and called at the café. The lorry drivers were in. "How did you get on Saturday, Billy?" one asked.

"Great," I said. "I am going to a job in Ellesmere Port for MH Tunnelling with a Smith's 21 crane next week. I will tell Big Pat when he comes around this morning."

The conversation was overheard by Valerie as she came out from the back and to the table. "Sorry about Saturday," she said. "I will tell you later tonight. Are you in for tea?"

I got on the job as there was not a lot to do but there was some steel to load up on one lorry and that would keep us going until dinner. We were about to go for breakfast when Big Pat drove up in his Land Rover. I got out of the machine to talk to him. I asked him how the land lay.

"Not good, he replied. "I tried to get you on hire for the M62 job but the job is not ready for a crane yet so I will have to lay you off for a while."

"Well," I said, "I had an inkling this would happen, so I got another job and I was going to put in a week's notice."

"You have made me feel better as I don't like to lay off good machine operators. They are so hard to find," Pat said and shook my hand. "Good luck with your travels. You can pick up your cards and wages on Friday by dinnertime if you like. I will make sure you get a good bonus for this job."

I thanked him and then he left. We carried on with what we were doing, then went to the café. Valerie was not on yet so that was good as I did not have to explain what I was up to at the end of the week. I had enough with Tina as I would be on my knees. I could do with three days free of sex and recoup myself with pints of Guinness. I got back on the job as there was some brick to be tidied up, so I started the wheel shovel up, then loaded the lorry for the tip as it had steel reinforcements in it. This kept us going for the next day or two. I missed going to the café on Monday night as Tina was making a meal for me. Then I bathed and went down to the bar with the lads and a couple of pints of Guinness. Tina came over to me and whispered in my ear, "You can rest for a few days as I have come on." I looked disappointed but was glad. I got a big kiss before bed and sleep was in order.

The week went fast. I bumped into Valerie on Wednesday at dinner time and she came and sat down next to me as I ate my ham, eggs and chips. She told me that her ex was back on the scene and the relationship was back on track. "Good for you," I said as I left the café. What a relief for me! Only one to worry about—Tina. I got back to the pub. "Do you want any tea, Billy?" Ann asked me. I said that I would get my own. The barmaid, Ann, got me a pint of Guinness. "Are you ready for the move to another job?" she asked.

"As ready as I will ever be. I will go upstairs in a minute to ask if Tina will wash my clothes," I said but when I got up there, they were all done. Tina said, "I hope you do not mind me going into your room and getting them out."

"Great," I said, "I meant to ask you last night."

It is a woman's intuition," Tina said. I got a big kiss. I got back down to the bar and Mick and John were in. "How was your day?" Mick asked.

"Good, as there was not a lot to do and Big Pat said I could leave by Friday dinner and go to the yard and pick up my wages and cards," I replied. "I will travel to Ellesmere Port on Saturday to find digs." The Guinness went down well and the night ended with Tina in my bed but just to cuddle up.

On Friday with plenty of coffee down me, I went to the café. Valerie was on and I got an early breakfast. I had one lorry on today and the driver, Tom, was in the café so there was no rush to load it. Valerie put the food on the table and wished me luck on my travels and I said the same to Valerie. I got a peck on the cheek as I left. The morning passed quickly and I parked the machine and went to the yard. I went into the office and the girl asked me if I had come for my wages. I said yes and she said that there were two wage packets—one was a big bonus. As I turned to go out, Big Pat came out of his office to say goodbye and shake my hand. "Ring me from time to time in case you get stuck," he said.

I agreed and I left, got into my car and drove back to the pub to pack, bathe and change. As I was running the bath, the door shut behind me. Tina was in her dressing grown, my clothes were off and the sex was great over the bath. We both washed and dried each other, then got dressed and went down to the bar. Ann pulled me a pint and smiled, "You look as if you need it." The Guinness went down well. Tina was whispering behind me that there was more to come. Sex or Guinness? The lads came in and there were a lot of Tina's friends. It was a good night and to my surprise, there was a buffet on as it was a going-away party for me. I got a few drams of whisky down me and was a bit pissed when Tina put me to bed. The head was banging a bit when I got up, put the kettle on and sat in the kitchen. Tina walked in as bad as me and got a cup of coffee. We sat down and talked. "Will you come back at weekends?" she asked.

"I will, and I will ring you when I get settled in." I said. I got my bag and we kissed. When I left, Tina had tears in her eyes and I was just as bad. I drove down the east road towards Ellesmere Port. I stopped at a café, got some food and felt better as I drove into Ellesmere Port. I came to the station, parked and thought that I could find my bearings on foot. The job was on Oil Sites road and I was directed to it, so I got back into the car. I went over the railway bridge, turned left—it was a long road with chemicals works on it—and the job was on the left. The crane was there; it was locked up but I would sort it out on Monday. The offices for the job were on a different road. I drove back to town and found the road plus offices but they were all locked up as it was almost dinnertime. The pubs were open and you could find digs in a pub. I parked in a street and the pub on the corner was called Thatcher's Arms. I went in; there were a few people in. I asked the man behind the bar for a pint of shandy and did he know where there were any digs around. "I am full at the moment," he replied, "but I have an address of a woman who does. It's down the road; you can walk from here." I thanked him, drank up and then walked down the road. The house was an end terrace. I knocked on the door and a lady opened the door. She spoke Irish and I asked her about digs. "I have one single left; how long are you here for?" she asked.

"Two months," I answered.

"Come in and I will show you the room."

I went upstairs; it was a back room and the bathroom was shared. "Great, I will get my car and bag; how much is the rent?" I asked her.

"Five pounds per week."

I went back to get my car and parked it. I went in. The lady's name was Bridey Shannon and she stood well in a low-cut top with tits stuck out. Bridey asked me where I was working and I told her that it was a tunnel job down the road. "There is another man on that job but he is out at the moment. He is Irish as well; Pat is his name," she said. "He will probably be in the pub down the road as a lot of Irish people go there and there is the Shell club on the edge of town with bingo and good turns on; especially on weekends."

"Good," I said, "at least I won't be bored then." I decided to go for a walk. Bridey asked if I wanted food—it was pork chops, peas plus mash for dinner. I said OK and then off I went. It was the first of September 1969 and it would be my birthday again. I had a nosey around the shops in the high street. There was a nightclub down by the Railway pub. I walked past the club and into the Railway pub. I looked around; there were a few people in and a lot were on Guinness, so it looked like a good pint. I asked for one. The barmaid looked well; her tits were well jacked up and worth a good scalping and she could definitely give a good head. I got lucky. I stood at the bar as the tits were reeling me in and the lady gave me a big smile. I picked up the pint and she said, "You are new in here."

"Yes," was my reply, "I have just pulled into town an hour ago to work on a job in town." A group of men were also standing at the bar. One of them asked me, "What is the job?"

I turned to talk to them, "It is a main waterpipe going through the town."

"We are on it," one man said. "What have you come to do?"

I replied that I was to drive a crane. The Irishman introduced himself as Patrick—Pat for short. "Have you got somewhere to stop?"

"Yes," I said, "a house up the road—Mrs Shannon's."

"Great! I stay there too; it's a great grub spot. Your name?" asked Pat.

"I am Billy."

"Welcome to the gang. We are here to do the digging as miners," Pat said. Patsy was his mate. The Guinness flowed and the crack was good. Last time was called so it was back to the house for dinner. As we walked in, Bridey said, "You two boys have met up then." The dinner was good and a lie down was on the cards. I must have slept well because the house was empty and quiet when I woke up. I washed my face to freshen up and got a shave, then walked to the pub. It was packed. I got a pint of Guinness. I could see Pat in the far corner of the room, so I went across. "Hi, you made it," he said with a laugh.

I said that the meal was good and filling. Pat said, "Bridey is a good cook. She will pack you up as she does me if you don't like breakfast too early. I think the job is best on a five-day week as we will be working in the streets as well as the main road. Are you coming to the nightclub when the pub shuts as all this crowd will be going and you get a lot of girls from New Brighton? They come on the train and then get a taxi back so there is no shortage of talent."

I smiled and said that I would give it an hour. When last time was called, we went outside. We got inside the club; the music was loud. The three of us got one end of the bar. There was fanny galore and we got served but Pat went on gin and tonic. I stayed on Guinness but it was warm. Pat spotted a girl he knew and went off to dance. Patsy and I talked for a while, then he said goodnight. I looked around to see what was free but the tiredness was creeping up on me; it had been a long day. I walked back to my digs; the key was under the plant pot as Bridey had told me. I opened the door and then put it back.

The next morning on Sunday, I got up and dressed. The breakfast smelled good. I went down and Bridey was in the kitchen. "Did you have a good night last night?" she asked.

"Yes, we finished up in the nightclub but I left Pat to it and came back."

The breakfast went down well. "Pat's not home yet and I am going to the church now," Bridey said. I walked out; the morning was fresh. I had noticed a paper shop the day before. I got a paper and decided to walk the food down. I got to the bridge where there were seats to sit on. I read the paper and watched the world go by. Then I walked up to where the job was to start in the town. It was time to go to the pub as there was nothing else to do on Sundays. I got to the pub; Pat and Patsy were at the bar. "How did you get on, Billy?" Pat asked.

The sleep got the better of me," I laughed. "You must have done all right as Bridey noticed that your bed had not been slept in."

"I had a good night," said Pat. "What about you, Patsy, how did you get on?"

"I was like you, Billy. I had plenty to drink so I called it a night," Patsy said. "Will you be going to the Shell club tonight? I will sign you or Bridey will; there is a good turn on plus bingo with big money at stake."

Pat said, "We better not be late for Sunday dinner; Bridey likes us all around the table for the big meal."

We drank up and told Patsy that we would see him at the club tonight. Pat and I reached just in time as Bridey was dishing out the food. We sat at the table and had to say grace before we started. I was so full that I could not move. Pat went up to bed to catch up on some sleep. I must have dropped off in the chair as when I woke up, Bridey was getting ready for the club and Shamus, Bridey's partner, was ready and told me that the bathroom was free to wash up. I went up and knocked on Pat's bedroom door as I went to the bathroom. He shouted that he was ready and we went out with Bridey and Shamus. It was a good evening for a walk. When we got to the club, I had to sign in. Bridey did me the honour and I had to put some money in the box. The bar was downstairs for men only. It was a big club; we went upstairs and it was nearly full. It was just 7 o'clock. We got seated as Bridey's friends had saved seats. I went to get up to go for the drinks but Bridey insisted that she would buy the first round. I was introduced as the new lodger. The turn came on; it was a group and they were good. Then it was bingo; the women played that as the four of us went downstairs to the bar to talk. Pat and Shamus were into horses and galleria football, so the crack was good. Then we went back upstairs; the bingo had finished and Bridey had won ten pounds on a house, so it was drinks all around again. The evening finished with dancing, which I did with Bridey, and she complimented me on what a good mover I was. "Are you as good in bed?" she said.

I smiled and laughed, "You will have to find out!" As we walked home, I remembered to ring Tina up but it would have to wait until tomorrow. It was a cup of tea, then bed as it was a 7 o'clock start to the job.

The alarm went off at 6 o'clock. I washed and dressed in my working clothes. The tea was on the table as Bridey was up. Pat followed me downstairs and we got tea down. We walked down the town to the offices. The contractor manager was called Glen and came from Rotherham, South Yorkshire, which was not far from the yard in Sheffield. He told me that the job was a five-day week with the odd weekend off because of the public as the job was a main sewer. It would go up and down streets and safety had to be maintained at all times. The start was where the crane was and would join up with the one from the Shell refinery and come across the Manchester canal into Ellesmere Port. "Sounds like a long job," I said to Glen.

Glen said that it should be finished by January 1970 if all went all right. I turned around and there were two men in the doorway. Glen said that they were the two foremen that I would be working with—Tony and Stan. Glen said that Tony was the shaft foreman. I shook hands with them both. Stan was the site agent for the job. Tony and I got into a Land Rover. "So, you are our crane driver for the job, Billy," he said. "There is a 360 HYMAC getting delivered today from your company, Thomas Ward's. We have hired it with no driver as we were told that you or my brother, Stan, could drive it."

"Oh," I said, "you are brothers."

"Yes," said Tony, "we are used to mining as we were down in the pits in the Rotherham area for years." We reached the crane, opened the gate and there was a lorry to be unloaded with big timbers on. "You sort out the crane first, Billy," Tony said.

I checked the oil and water first, then diesel. It had come from the yard with a full tank so it would be all right this week. I got it started up and played with it to get the feel of the levers as Smith's cranes are the wrong way around compared to Ruston's. Pat and Patsy came and said hi. "You have met," said Tony.

I said that Pat and I were in the same digs. The chains were put on the hook and we got the lorry unloaded. The shaft we were about to sink was 42 by 42 feet wide and long and 20 feet deep and was all marked out for us to start digging. I put the crane out of the road for now and used the Hymac digger as it had arrived. I checked it over for oil and water and then started to dig. I put the earth to one side near the road so that it could be loaded onto a lorry. Later on, we dug out two feet square all around and then used the crane to put the big timbers in for the first frame. By this time, it was breakfast time and the four of us jumped into the Land Rover and went to the station café. There were a few people in. It was teas all around. "We will be getting a cabin on the job and a tea boy so it will be better for you to cook your own," Tony said. We all agreed. The breakfast went down well. There was no break at dinnertime as Bridey did a meal for us. When we got back to the job, there were sheet piles to put around the timbers. We knocked them in with an air hammer hung from the crane and used a compressor to drive them down. Then we dug more earth out of the middle of the shaft to put more timbers in to hold the sheet piles. It was getting dark on us so we put into place two lighting sets that had turned up so that we could see down the shaft. We were on 12-hour shifts—seven to seven. The first day was good and busy. "Pat and Patsy, are you ready for a pint of Guinness?" I asked. I was ready for one, so it was lock up and then walking to the Railway Tavern and the first one did not even touch the sides. We had to be home by 8.30 as Bridey would have dinner on the table unless we told her any different. So, it was three pints and then digs. The boiled bacon and cabbage went down great and after that, it was a wash and bed. Pat and I, then Tom followed a bit later, went out as he had to write a letter to someone.

We did not go to the office the next morning as we had the key for the compound. There was a lorry waiting outside with large diameter pipes on. This was the first of many to come. The pipes we were about to lay were four feet in diameter and the main sewage line for Ellesmere Port. We had to put them in a way that we could reach them at all times when we started to dig out. I got the crane started up and put it into place to unload the pipes. There were four to a lorry and weighed two tons. We got on with the shaft; Tony and Stan turned up and the next load of pipes would come on Monday. We should have the shaft sunk and the back wall in and concreted to jack off by Monday. We might have to work on Saturday so we would have to be ready for it. "There is a cabin and drying room all in one set up for you," Stan said. We had a late breakfast at the café; it was good as you got served straight away and it went down well. It was raining when we got out of the café but it was expected for this time of the year. It was a long afternoon. The cabin came and I got it unloaded. I put the gas bottle in the drying room as the clothes were wet. When we finished, it was pub time. We had a bucket on low gas to wash hands and swill faces to look the part. Then we went off to the pub; the Guinness went down well, then it was back to the digs. Bridey had pork chops on the menu with mashed spuds and peas. We sat down to watch an hour of television. Then it was bed and we were ready for it.

The next morning, I washed my face and went downstairs. The tea was in the pot and the three of us walked to work. I started the HYMAC and lowered it down the shaft as the top frame was in. We had to dig the muck out for the next frame but the lads had to fill the bucket by hand using an air tool to loosen the muck. Then shovelled it into the bucket of the HYMAC. It was breakfast time and I got the timber ready. When we got back, in went the second frame. Then the HYMAC was no good after that so it was the crane with the kettle bucket on to fill up. The reformed steel was on the site, cut to size, then the timber shutter was put in ready for the concrete to be poured the next day. It would have to stand for three days before we could jack it. The next day, the concrete was delivered to the site and I skipped it in to form the back wall. The job was going well. We got a diesel tank, so we had fuel for the plant. On Wednesday evening, Stan came to tell us to go to the road where the offices were and travel the HYMAC around on the road to start another shaft while the concrete set. There were going to be three shafts in that road. The first one would be at the end of the road. The road was called Oil Sites road and the Shell refinery was at the end. Stan had the drawing out on the canteen table. It showed the old sewer and the new one to be laid through the town on Oil Sites road. There were factories that turned out soap and powder and needed a new sewer to get on top of the job. At the end of the road was the Manchester ship canal and the pipes had to go under the canal on the next stage of the job. The next morning on Thursday, the three of us got on the job. I checked the HYMAC for oil, water and dev and got it ready for the road tracks to be cleaned out as Pat was on with them. Patsy had the kettle on as we had to wait for daylight. We pulled onto the road as the traffic had started to ease off as people were at work. Pat walked in front of me and Patsy walked behind. We thought we could cut down the side streets but there were too many cars parked in the street. So, we went to the top of the road, then turned right onto the main road and over the bridge in the traffic. There, on the other side of the bridge, was the lollipop lady getting the children across the road, so we had to wait until we were instructed to carry on. I got a big smile as I passed her. Her body looked in good shape for a middle-aged woman and I got a twinge between my legs. We travelled on down the road to the next turning on the left, which was Oil Sites road. The plant yard of McAlpines was on the right and had a lot of plants in it as the firm did a lot of business abroad. Time was rolling on when we got to the compound that had been set up at the end of the road on the left. Stan was there in the jeep, so it was decided that it was breakfast time. Off we went to the café and Stan went to the office and would pick us up on our way back. The food went down well. Stan picked us up and the shaft was already marked out. There was a lorry parked to take the spoils away, so I started to dig. I got down to five feet right around the shaft as the top service ground was made up. We got down to the clay before we cut the top frame consisting of 12 by 12 timbers and 10 feet of steel sheet piles. Pat and Patsy trimmed the sides up with a jigger pick run off a compressor. I lowered the 12 by 12 timbers cut to size into the 10 feet steel sheet piles around the outside of the timber. I pressed them down with the bucket of the HYMAC. I loaded the lorry with the spoils again and dug out the middle of the shaft. This shaft had to be 20 feet deep to allow the fall of the pipes when they were installed. After four loads of spoils, we were ready when Pat and Patsy had gone into the shaft and trimmed the sides with the jigger pick. I lowered the 12 by12 timbers and then some more steel sheet piles around the timbers, but this time, I had to use an air hammer from the compressor to drive the steel piles down. It was getting dark as we had no lighting set on the job yet, so it was an early finish. The three of us had a good day and Stan was pleased with the progress of the job and asked us to keep it up in order to get it ready for the concrete on Monday. Even if it meant working on Saturday, which we did. On Saturday night, we knew we had done it and the Guinness went down and sleep set in. It was Sunday and we relaxed. Pat and Patsy liked Gaelic football (Irish team sport played between two teams of 15 players on a rectangular grass pitch) and it was on in the Railway pub on TV. After breakfast and mass at church with Bridey and husband, Shamus, I went for a long walk as it was a nice October morning. I got the paper on the way. I walked down Oil Sites road to the Manchester ship canal. There was a big oil tanker going down so I sat on a wall and watched it go by. I read the paper at the same time. By the time I got back, the Railway pub was open and the landlord wished me good morning and said, "Is it a pint of the black stuff?"

"Yes," I said. Pat walked in so it was two pints.

"After we have watched the football, do you fancy a ride down to New Brighton on the train? Pat asked. "There is an Irish club there where some friends go from back home in Ireland. The club is open all day." So, when the football finished, we went to the railway station, got on the train to New Brighton and walked to the club as it was not far from the station. We had to get signed in, which was ten shillings. There was a group of Irishmen at the bar and were over the moon to see Pat. I shook hands with two of them; the others did not shake hands due to the troubles in Northern Ireland but were friendly enough and the crack was good. The drink went down well. It was night-time when we got back to the Port on the train. We did not make the Shell club but it was a good day all around.

It was Monday again and the second shaft was going down well. Stan turned up to tell us that it would be all systems go on Wednesday morning in the first shaft, which pleased the lads. There was another load of pipes to unload before breakfast, so Stan gave a lift around to get them done in the first shaft. The tea-man they had set on, Peter, went to the shops to buy the grub—bacon and eggs—while we unloaded the pipes. The cabin was now set up and Peter was not a bad cook. The breakfast went down well after the drink on Sunday. The diesel tanker had come so I topped up the crane and the generators with diesel and then jumped into the cab of the tanker and took him around to the HYMAC. The lads went with Stan in the jeep and we carried on with the second shaft. We should not be far away from finishing it by Tuesday night, if all went well. It was a long day and with the lights on, it was well past 7 o'clock when we knocked off. Stan had come around to see how long we would be and he took us to the first shaft to clean up and get changed, then dropped us off at the pub. It was a full round of thee pints of the black stuff, then home. The dinner was in the oven; then it was a wash and the bed.

Tuesday was a long day as well and we got the shaft ready for the shuttering to go in for the back wall; the chippers would do that. The day had been a wet one with heavy rain at times so the clothes had to go in the dry cabin at the end of the shift. It was a big day tomorrow as we had to start the first drive on the job. The lads were up before me and the kettle was on as it was the first day of big money. No more daywork for now anyway. The plant was all filled so when we got there, I checked for oil and water, then it was all work. I lowered the hydraulic jacking station down the shaft and then the shield. The miners worked in the tunnel, I got the jacking ring down, then the miners started to dig out into a skip. I lowered down when we got the shield. Peter shouted that breakfast was on the table in the cabin and it went down well. Pat and Patsy rushed the food down and were down the ladder into the shaft to tunnel away. After an hour, they were ready for the first pipe. Stan and the site agent were on the site plus the engineer to take photos of the first pipe. They used laser light for the line. There was no dinnertime as such and I put tea in the kettle plus two cups in the skip. It was a long day and after 7 o'clock when we knocked off and we were ready for the Guinness. The two miners, Pat and Tom, were pleased with the first day. Two pipes in plus a shield for every pipe was a good start and the target of four pipes a day would make good money as the shield was the same length as the pipes. The miners had already told me that they would look after me, bonus wise, so it was in my interest to look after them. The stretch that we were doing would take 55 pipes to the next shaft we had just sunk down the road. We should breakthrough in three weeks at four pipes a day and five days a week, accounting for the weather. It was 9.30 when we got back to the digs; the dinner smelled nice and the taste was even better as it was boiled bacon and cabbage. The earth out of the shaft was heaping up. Stan came over to me and asked if I would work on Saturday with the HYMAC and load up two lorries for the tip if he got two on hire. I agreed and he was pleased. The day went well and so did Friday. The lads were going home to Manchester for the weekend and I had keys for the compound. Peter and I went to the second shaft to travel the HYMAC. After I cleaned the tracks out, there were two lorries outside the shaft. I portioned the earth to load them in. Peter put on the kettle while I got them away. I could smell the breakfast as I got the second one away. There was no rush as the tip would take an hour to turn around. I cleaned the area around the shaft while Peter washed the pots. We managed to get five loads each so that there was plenty of room for next week. It was dark when Peter and I locked up and he gave me a lift to the digs. When I got in, Bridey was in the kitchen and said, "Hi, Billy. What time do you want your tea?"

I said that I was hoping to have a good long bath. I got into the hot water. I missed Tina in the bath with me; the donkey had had a rest the last few weeks but it was club night tonight and there had to be an old granny that wanted servicing. I thought I would ask Bridey to sign me into the club. Then I would go to the nightclub if there was no spare at the Shell club. I got out of the bath and went down; Bridey had tea on. "Did you have a good bath?" she asked.

"Yes," I said, "and the water was hot."

"It is ham and chips for tea; is that all right?"

"Great," I said and it went down a treat.

"What is your plan for tonight?" asked Bridey.

"Will you sign me into the club?"

"Of course, I will," she replied. She said she and Shamus would get ready in an hour, so I watched TV and then all three of us walked to the club. It was a cold night. "Are you at work tomorrow?" Shamus asked as we walked along.

"No," I said with a laugh. We got to the club, signed in and went upstairs. It was quite full but Bridey's friends had saved some seats as Bridey had rung up her friends first. The turn was on first and was not too bad. Then it was bingo and Bridey's friend won so it was drinks all around. Then there was dancing so I asked one of Bridey's friends to dance. Alice was her name with a good figure all around she had all the right bits in all the right places. During the last waltz, Alice pulled me in really close to dance and as we walked back to our seats, Alice asked me what I was doing now. I told her that I was going down to the nightclub for an hour or so.

"Do you mind if I tag along with you?" Alice asked.

"By all means do," I said. The four of us got a taxi as it was raining; we dropped Bridey and Shamus at the house and then went to the nightclub. Alice and I were lucky to get in as it was quite full. Alice found a corner to stand in while I went to the bar to get the Guinness. It did not look too good, so I got a nuke brown and Alice was on gin and tonic—a double. I got two bottles of tonic as I was horny as hell; I did not like having sex on the first night but the donkey had been in the stable long enough. The noise was too loud to talk so we danced for a while. Then a table became free in the far corner, so we made a beeline for it and sat down to talk about one another. Alice had a job at the Shell refinery in the office; it was five days a week and the sound of it was good money. The time was moving on and it was 1 o'clock in the morning. The club did not shut until 2 o'clock. Alice was ready to go so I asked if she wanted a taxi or, if the rain had stopped, she would walk. We both got up and walked outside; the rain had stopped. It was a good mile to Alice's estate, so we set off holding hands. We got to Alice's road, stopped and kissed. I could feel that Alice wanted more. She told me to wait there and she would go in to see how the land lay. I stood for five minutes and then Alice waved me down the road. Alice's parents were away for the weekend and Alice's Brother was staying at his girlfriend's for the night. The house was upmarket as Alice's parents also worked at the Shell refinery. I walked into the room and she put the kettle on. But the donkey in my trousers was more interested in pussy. I kissed Alice again and pulled her in close. Alice said hang on and she went back into the kitchen. She came back with the coffee, put it down on the table and we both sat on the couch. Then we kissed again and the clothes started to come off; the sex was good and it was worth waiting for. Alice wanted more on the floor. The time was now 2.30 in the morning but with no work on Sunday, it was great. My energy had run out as we rolled over. I got up and dressed. I said that

I would go in case her parents came home early so we kissed again. I asked her if I could meet her again tonight, with it being Sunday. "Yes," she answered, "we can go for a drive if you like. You can pick me up at 12 o'clock?"

I agreed and set off back to the digs. The key was out so it was up to bed. It was gone nine when I woke up and washed and went down. Bridey was in the kitchen. "Breakfast, Billy?" she asked. "You must have had a good night with Alice."

"Yes," I said, "she is a very nice person." The breakfast went down well; I went to the paper shop and came back to the house to read it until 11.45. Then I went out to the car and checked it for oil plus water. I went back into the house to put my scent on, then drove around to Alice's house. I knocked on the door and a lady opened the door and smiled and told me to come in. She said that Alice was upstairs getting ready. "I am Alice's mother," she explained.

"I see where your daughter gets the good looks from," I said and I got a big smile. Then Alice was down in front of me.

"Well, have a nice day," her mum said. We went to the car.

"Where would you like to go, Alice?" I asked. "County or seaside?"

"Seaside," she answered. "Southport."

So off we went. The roads were not too busy for this time of the year as it was late October. We reached Southport and looked for a carpark along the sea front. We found one, parked and looked out at the sea. It was cosy to sit and talk with no noise. Alice held my hand and we kissed. I asked her about her past. She had had a steady relationship for three years and then she found out that he was two-timing her with younger women. It took her a long time to get over him as they were engaged and had been saving up for a house before getting married. "What about you, Billy?" she asked.

"Well," I said, "I love travelling at the moment and meeting people like you." She smiled. "Would you like to walk along the seafront?" I asked her. She agreed and we went off arm in arm. There were ships going up and down the Mersey, large and small. We came across a café. "Would you like a cuppa?" I asked. Yes, was the answer and we went in. I asked her what she would like—tea or coffee. Coffee was the reply. I walked to the counter and asked the lady for two coffees. There was a fruit cake on the counter. I turned to Alice and asked if she would have that.

"Yes please. It will tide us over until this evening," she said. I walked back to the table and sat down. "Would you like to go for a meal this evening?" I asked.

"Great," Alice said. We got the coffee down and then a trip to the toilet before we left. We carried on walking down the seafront arm in arm. The sun was going down so we turned around and walked all the way back and to the car, which took more than an hour. We had not noticed how far we had walked. It was nearly dark when we got back to the car. We started it up and warmed it, then put the heater on. The car that I had was a Ford Consul 375 with a bench seat in the front and collar shift gears, so there was plenty of room for sex with the seat back and for cuddling up. We kissed again, then started to go back to

Ellesmere Port. I dropped Alice off at her house to get changed and was asked in to wait. Alice's mother started to make a fuss. While Alice was upstairs, I got the third degree from her mother such as where I was from and the job I was doing in the Port. She looked at me with distrust and then Alice walked into the room to my relief. "We are going for a meal," Alice said to her mother.

"Well," said her mother, "enjoy your meal and evening out.""

"I won't be late," said Alice as we got out of the house and into the car. I parked the car outside my digs and we both walked to the high street. "Indian or Chinese?" I asked Alice. Alice chose Indian so we walked down to high street. A girl asked us, "A table for two?" I said yes and we were seated next to the window. We were asked what we would like to drink. I requested for a bottle of beer—Carlsberg. Alice asked for a gin and tonic. "This is a good restaurant," Alice said. "Me and the girls came here a few months ago for a night out." I ordered a beef curry with poppadums and Alice got a chicken curry with poppadums.

"Do you want to walk up to the Shell club for an hour or the Railway pub?" I asked.

"The Railway pub."

The meal came and tasted well; I was pleased and full as a butcher's dog. I paid the bill and the walk was good to get it to go down. The evening had turned cold and the coal fire was on in the Railway pub. We both stood around it. The landlord asked me, "Guinness?" I said yes and he asked what the lady will have. Alice chose gin and tonic. We sat down in the corner. Alice said, "Thank you for a lovely day."

I replied, "Let's hope there are more like them."

Alice said with a smile, "You never know what's around the corner. How long will you be on this job?"

"March plus, going on weather and things that might go wrong in the tunnel work."

"It will be Christmas," Alice said. "What will happen to you; where will you go?"

"I'm not too sure," I said. "I may go up north to my parents as I have not called at home for a long time. I do keep in touch as my Aunt Rosy has got a phone and lives next door to my mum and dad. I'm not sure which of my brothers and sisters are still at home at the moment."

I got the drinks again; then the bell went for last orders. I sat back down. "Will I get a date for next weekend?" I asked.

"Yes," said Alice with a smile.

"The week is all work for me, seven to seven. Long days of work and then bed and sleep."

"There is a good turn at the Shell club next Saturday; it is a ticket do. I will get two tickets for us," Alice said.

"That will be great," I replied. "I will be looking forward to your company." The second bell went so we drank up. It was a good night to walk Alice home. We stopped at the top of the road, kissed and said goodnight. I watched Alice walk down the street and she waved before going inside. I went back to the digs, to bed and sleep.

The clock went off at 5.30 Monday morning. The tea was made when I got downstairs as Pat was up. "The smile on your face says that you had a good weekend, Billy boy," he said.

"Yes," I said.

"Patsy will be late this morning as he went home to Manchester for the weekend so, Billy, we will fill up all the plants and get the gear down the shaft," Pat said. Peter turned up and Pat said that we would have a late breakfast this morning to wait for Patsy to come off the train. Peter asked for the tea money for the week and then got on with the cabin work. I got everything ready. The skips were lowered down the shaft. The day was dry but the forecast for later was rain. There was a shout of good morning as Patsy arrived on the job, so we had breakfast and then it was all systems go. We got five down the shaft and four in the drive as the rain started mid-afternoon, but it was a good day all around and two pints of the Guinness went down well in the pub. We had boiled bacon for tea, then bath and bed it was. It was a good feeling when Mondays were over and I earned a bit of a bonus as I got five pounds per pipe. Tuesday was a wet day and we only got three pipes down the shaft and mucked out two. We had to stop back in the dark to unload pipes, so it was 8.30 when we were done and in the pub for our two pints of Guinness before dinner. Wednesday was another wet day and another lorry was waiting to be unloaded so it was a slow start. We all decided to have an early breakfast before Patsy and Pat went down the shaft. Breakfast was on the table in the cabin. Peter was not a bad cook.

We got three pipes in and one down a shaft so only four today. The foreman, Tony, came on the site as we knocked off and were getting changed. "Billy, will you and Peter work this weekend to load up the surplus muck on two lorries if I get two on hire?" We agreed. "Great," he said, "I will get it organised."

On Thursday, we got six pipes in the drive and one down the shaft. Friday was an early finish for the lads to go home on the train to Manchester for a long weekend. It would be forty pounds to pick up when I got the timesheets signed on Monday. I was on my own tonight (Friday) so I could have a good bath and soak my body in nice hot water, ready for the weekend. When I got home, Bridey said, "You are early, Billy. There is a stew on the stove; help yourself. I am going out." I heard the front door close. I was in the bathroom and the bath water was on. There were some bubble bath salts on the side so in they went. It was great not to rush. I must have dropped off as the water was nearly cold when I woke up. I got dressed and went downstairs. I must have been in the bathroom for nearly an hour but I felt great. I decided to give the stew a miss as it was gone nine. I went off to the pub. The landlady said, "The usual, Billy?"

"Yes," I said and sat down. The pub door opened and Alice walked in. I got up and asked Alice, "Gin and tonic?"

"Yes please," she said. "It's great to see you. God, you smell great, Billy!"

"Just had a good soak in the bath."

"Well, what sort of a week have you had?" Alice asked me.

I said, "Good, not too busy. The lads have gone home to Manchester for the weekend and I am working in the morning, loading spoils onto two lorries to get a good start on Monday."

"My parents have gone away for the weekend," Alice said with a smile. "Your eyes have lit up, Billy!"

"You bet," I said. Even the donkey was twitching in my trousers. I was glad when the last bell went as my balls were full. We drank up and walked back to Alice's house. The kettle went on as I got myself settled in the front room. "Tea or coffee?" was the voice from the kitchen. Coffee was my answer. We cuddled up on the sofa and it was not long before the clothes came off and we were on the floor. Alice had only a single bed in her bedroom and did not want to go into her parents' bedroom, so it was a matter of putting cushions under my knees to stop the soreness and carpet burns. We were ready for sleep as I had to be up early for work. Alice got me a blanket to cover me on the sofa and an alarm clock. I put it on for six so that I could go back to the digs to change. We kissed and my eyes closed. The next thing I knew was the clock going off. It was a cold morning as I walked back to the digs. I got the kettle on while I changed. I drank the coffee and walked down to the compound. There were two lorries waiting for me. I got the gates open. I knew the HYMAC was full of diesel and checked it over for oil and water. One of the lorries backed in and I got it loaded and the other one too. All in all, there was an hour's turnaround, so I tidied up and got ready for the next load. I walked to the shop for milk and the paper and sat down to read it, but one lorry was back. I decided to go to the café when I got the next one loaded. I told Jim, the driver, that we would have our break on the tip as the last load was to be at the tip by 3 o'clock. Jerry was the other lorry's driver and he told me the same. The lorry dropped me at the top of the road and I walked into the café. There were not many people in. The lady behind the counter said, "You have not been in for weeks."

I said, "We have a tea man on the site who cooks breakfast for us to save time."

"Well, what are you going to eat?" she asked.

"A fry up with black pudding and fried bread with coffee," I ordered and sat down to read the paper. The breakfast came and it went down great. I walked back and Jim picked me up on the way back. I got him away again and then Jerry went. I went to the cabin to finish the paper. I thought it would be two more loads each and it would be 2 o'clock or more. That would be all for the day. I got the area cleaned up ready for Monday, signed the timesheets and locked up. I fancied a pint, so I walked to the Railway pub, got a pint of Guinness and sat down to watch sports on TV. Horse racing was on. I was not a gambling man and had no interest in it. I drank up, went back to my digs and Bridey was in the kitchen. "Hi Billy. How long before you want your dinner?" she asked.

"I will get a shower first. Half an hour OK?"

"Yes," Bridey replied. "Are you coming to the club tonight?"

"Yes, if Alice will go too. Her parents are away for the weekend and she might have other ideas."

Bridey laughed. The shower was good and I put my scent on and went down for dinner. Sausage and mash was on the go and went down well. "I may see you at the club," I said to Bridey as I walked out the door. I checked whether my car was all right. I walked around to Alice's and knocked on the door. Alice came to the door with her bathrobe on. She was pleased to see me. We kissed as the door shut. "You smell nice," Alice said. "I am just getting ready."

I went into the room and sat on the sofa. I got hold of Alice and sat her down. We kissed and the bathrobe came off. Alice undressed me and the sex was good on the mat. We lay back to get back to normal. I went upstairs to wash the donkey in the sink as Alice got into the shower. When Alice was ready, we walked to the club. We were lucky to get a seat; Bridey had saved us two. I got the drinks and bingo was about to start but with no luck on my part. The turn was a group and were not too bad. They were better in the second half when the drink got to work and the dancing was on the go. During the last waltz, Alice got really close. "Are we going to the club or not?" I asked.

"No," she said, "we are going back to the house for supper." I could manage the supper, which would include sex again. We got back to the house, put the kettle on and I put the TV on although I was not interested in the TV. Alice shouted out, "Do you want a cup of cocoa?"

I said that would be great and she brought it in. We sat down on the sofa and cuddled up. "It will soon be Christmas," Alice said. "What are your plans?"

"I have not really thought about it yet," I replied. "I usually call back at home to Middlesbrough to see my parents and family. What are your plans, Alice?"

"I just stay at home and all the family get together," she said. "I am not sure I want to do that this year."

I was getting tired, so the blanket came out and Alice covered me up on the sofa and kissed me goodnight. In the morning, I put the kettle on and read a local paper that was on the table. There was a piece about the work going on in the Port and the inconveniences we were causing. I heard a movement upstairs and I went up to ask Alice for a cup of tea, but I got a bit more sex, which was great. Alice said, "You did not think that I was going to let you go that easy, did you? My parents will be back today so it will be no sex tonight. I will cook you breakfast now."

We had a shower together; the donkey had to go in again and we both had another orgasm as the hot water ran over her body. I had always wanted to do that; it was a fantasy of mine. I sat on the sofa to get my energy back. Alice came in with the bacon and egg and it went down well. "So, what would you like to do today?" I asked Alice.

"Not a lot; maybe go to the pub if you want, then a meal in the Port," she replied.

"OK," I said, "you're on." We washed up and then it was time to go. Alice's parents came in as we were going out and I talked a little with them. I got the feeling that I got on with them but I was not ready to settle down yet. We reached the pub as I needed a Guinness to get my energy back. My testicles were sore but I was satisfied for a week at least. We sat down and the small talk carried on with Alice holding my hand. Christmas was three weeks away as it was the first of December 1970 today. I told her that we should reach the next shaft this week, so it was going to be a busy week ahead. I told Alice that there would be a bottle of whisky lowered down the shaft. "The lads can celebrate with a drink so long as they don't burst it," I said with a smile.

Where will you go from there?" asked Alice.

"We will move on to the streets. We will sink two shafts at the top and bottom of the street, then drive from one of them."

Alice said that it was an interesting job.

The next job could be totally different," I remarked.

"Where next?" she asked.

"I don't have a clue," I said. I got another drink before last time. We talked some more and then it was time to go. I walked Alice to her home and we kissed at the end of her road. I went back to my digs and to bed.

I was on my own the next morning as the lads would not be back until 8 o'clock off the train I walked down to the site and opened up. Peter, the tea man, turned up as the plant was ready to go. We had the kettle on. The pipes were in place and we had only six pipes to go for this drive, then strip out and load up to go around to the next road. The lads turned up, we had tea and then went to work. We got three pipes in and it was a good day for all. We went to the pub and talked about the weekend.

"How was your weekend, Billy boy?"

"Sore," I told Pat and Patsy.

"Good for you, Billy," was the reply.

"How was your weekend?" I asked Pat and Patsy.

"Partying and pissed up!"

I laughed and said, "I think this Spinster is getting too close with marriage on her mind."

"We should be done by February so hold on until then," Pat said with a smile, "and keep shagging the goods."

The next day at 3.30, we were near the end of the drive and the lads were at the other shaft. The agent and office staff were down to see the lads come through. The bottle of whisky was put down the shaft. I went to the other shaft to lift sheet piles with the HYMAC to a round of applause from the staff. They had a good swig of the whisky and then came up the shaft with the bottle. We all went back to the other shaft to strip out the gear. Then we celebrated in the pub. The Guinness and whiskeys went down well. The three of us got to the digs. Bridey had plated the dinner up as it was 11 o'clock. I slept like a log. If it was not for getting up for a piss, I would have slept in. I warmed the dinner and ate it. Then I woke the lads up at 6.30. I was hungry; the dinner had a bit of skin on the gravy but went down well. The lads had eyes like piss holes in the snow but the coffee went down well. It was all day work so there was no rush. I just had to be there when the lorry was there to load up the gear to take to the next road, which was a long road. There were going to be three shafts in it. I drove the HYMAC on the road to unload the lorry at the next shaft. We had four loads and we were at it all day. We had more pipes coming the next day so next morning, I had to travel the crane around on the road again but we set off early to beat the traffic. We were working on the road where the lollipop lady lived. She would walk down the road to eye me up. *Well*, I thought, *I can see you getting a good scalping*. We had heard that she was game. We were careful not to be late home from the pub on Wednesday night so as to not get in the doghouse with Bridey again. We knew that we would not be driving in the shaft this week but just getting set up for Monday. Pat and Patsy were bringing their mates back on Monday to start on the shafts on Oil Sites road. This road went down to the Manchester ship canal past the soap factory and the McAlpines yard. Bridey was sorting the digs out with some neighbours, Frank and Willy. It was Friday again and the lads went home on the train as there was no work on Saturday. I went to the digs, got fed and watered, washed up and changed and then walked around to Alice's house to see if she wanted to go Christmas shopping on Saturday. She was over the moon when I asked her. We walked to the club; the same old faces were there. "Club or not?" I asked Alice. "Great," was the reply. There was no luck in bingo and the turn was not very good. The donkey was not going to get any sex this weekend as Alice's Mum and Dad were at home. It was not a cold night to walk to the club and stand in the queue to get in. When we got in, Alice sat while I went to the bar to get served. I sat down and we talked about where we were going to shop. "Chester is a nice place to shop," Alice suggested.

"Right," I said, "that's settled then. It will be good for the car to get a run out."

The night came to an end and I walked Alice home. We kissed on the road's end. "Ten in the morning?" she said.

"OK."

In the morning, I was up early as I could not sleep in. I had tea, went to the paper shop, came back for breakfast and sat down to read the paper. I went outside, checked the car for oil and water and started it up. I drove around to Alice's house. She came out as I pulled up and had a smile on her face. "My mother was asking questions on our relationship; she was asking when the engagement is."

I just smiled. The traffic was not too bad and Alice showed me the way around the back roads. We reached the town and looked for a carpark in the high street. We managed to get parked. As we walked down high street, Alice asked, "What would you like for Christmas, Billy?"

"I never gave it a thought," I said.

"It is nice to surprise each other with presents," Alice said.

"OK," I said with a smile. We walked around browsing. I got more working socks plus a good shirt which Alice chose. Alice picked up a tie to match but I told her that I don't wear them.

"OK," she said, "can I pay for the shirt?"

"OK, if you insist," I said. There was a nice dress. Alice picked it up and from the expression on her face, she liked it. She tried it on and came out of the changing room looking a picture. "I will take it," she said.

"That is one of your Christmas presents," I said. She was over the moon. "Can I wear it before Christmas?" she asked.

"Of course, you can," I said and got a big kiss on my cheek. I was ready for something to eat as I was hungry and Alice agreed so we found a pub that served food. We went in and I got a pint of beer shandy and Alice wanted a coke. I got the menu and sat down in a window seat. "What do you fancy?" I asked Alice "We could have a light meal now and go for a proper meal tonight."

She agreed so it was ham sandwiches for now. We left the pub and walked past a jewellery shop and stopped to look at rings. I could see what was on her mind. She said, "Doesn't that look lovely, Billy, that big sparkling ring?"

I said that it did and smiled as we walked on. We got back to the car and sat for five minutes before we pulled out, kissing and cuddling. I could feel myself getting horny and Alice was really going for it. I said that we had better move to a better place than this. Alice said that we could go a different way back. I pulled out of the car park with the donkey still hard as hell in my trousers. Alice must have been this way before because there was a big layby and it was hidden from the road with trees on both sides. The donkey was a bit soft but Alice soon rectified it as she got it out. I pressed the seat lever and the seat went back. Alice was screaming with delight as she orgasmed and the windows were all steamed up when we finished. My balls were sore getting rubbed on the leather seat. I got my breath back and opened the car door. There was another car pulled up behind us and they were still at it as we drove off. We stopped outside another layby and got out to put our clothes right. I parked the car at the digs as we did not need it any more today. I went in and Bridey was in the kitchen. "Are you going to the club, Billy?" she asked. I said yes and went upstairs to wash the donkey. I showered and put on more aftershave. We called at Alice's house as she wanted to freshen up and change her clothes before we went to the club. Alice's mother was in the hallway. "Did you both enjoy your day out?" she asked.

"It was great," we both said. Alice went upstairs and her mother asked me where I was spending Christmas. "I am not too sure yet as I might go up north to see my parents as my dad is not too good," I replied.

"You can spend Christmas with us, if you like," she offered.

"Thank you," I said. Alice came down in the nick of time and there were no more questions.

There were the same old faces at the club with Bridey and her friends. The turn was not bad but no luck in bingo. It was cold as we walked back to Alice's house. We kissed goodnight for we had an exhausting day and I was knocked out. Bridey was still up when I got in, so the kettle was on and I took a cup of tea up to my room.

Sunday morning was a bit damp as I walked to the paper shop, then back to the digs to read before Bridey got up to make breakfast. It was going to be a quiet day: a walk to the pub at dinnertime and back for dinner and sleep. I knew Alice was staying in tonight to wash her hair and all that and the donkey had his fill for one weekend.

Monday morning came around again and it was back to the job as we were on the second shaft in the street and outside the lollipop lady's house. The lads had just turned up as she came out of the house with a smile on her face. I knew she was game for some donkey. "I will make you tea when I get back," she said to me. The lads had gone down the shaft and a lorry turned up to empty the muck. At 9.30, the lady was back with a smile on her face. The lorry had just gone so I got out of the crane to talk to her and she told me that her name was Mary. I told her that my name was Billy. "Is it tea with sugar?" she asked. I agreed and she went in. The lads came out of the shaft at breakfast time. "I will miss this one this morning," I said. "I have a job to do."

I went down the street; Mary brought the tea out and I got on with the bullshit to chat her up. Her tits looked fair to middling and a good handful to play with. "Would you like a sandwich as I am about to make one for myself?" she asked. "Go around the back because of the neighbours watching across the road."

So around I went and the donkey was getting a twitch in my trousers. I went into the kitchen; the frying pan went on. "Bacon all right?"

"Great," I said.

"There is more tea in the pot if you want some," she offered. She moved her body next to mine. Mary gave me a peck on the cheek and I turned with one on her lips and put my hand around her back to pull her in. The donkey was throbbing in my jeans and Mary could feel it. Off went the gas under the frying pan. We went into the front room and down on the sofa. I was like a rat up a drainpipe and, by God, she was tight! Mary squealed as the donkey went in. Mary knew how to move her body. "You can leave it in," she said, "I have been sterilised. We both orgasmed. It was good that it was an easy day because I was absolutely shagged after that. We both dressed and went back to the kitchen. I went to see if Pat and Patsy had come back; they were just coming down the street. Mary brought the bacon sandwich out to me plus another cup of tea.

"Thank you," I said.

"Any time," Mary said with a smile on her face.

Pat said, "You have got it made." If they only knew! I quickly got the bacon and tea down and got back on the crane. The lads went down the shaft to dig into the skip. I was glad to have a pint of Guinness that night to get the energy back. I thought to myself in the pub that I could not stand it every day, what with Mary and Alice on the go and all. I decided to talk to Mary in the morning. There had to be some breathing space. All the Guinness in the world would not give me the energy to keep it up but I loved sex.

The next day, Mary came out of the house smiling. Peter, the Banksman, was in the lorry to tip the skips so I called Mary to the side of the crane. The lads were in the shaft. "We will have to go steady on the sex," I said. Mary nodded her head and said, "OK. Is it four bacon sandwiches and four teas when you come back?"

I put my hand in my pocket and pulled out a five-pound note. "Will this cover it?" I asked.

"Yes," she said and then went off up the street. The lads came out of the shaft to cut some more timber. "How are you getting on with the lollipop lady, Billy?" they asked.

"OK," I said. "There will be bacon sandwiches in an hour."

"Good for you, Billy," Pat said. "No sex today?"

"No," I said, "I would be on my knees to keep that up." I got a big smile from both of them. The foreman, Tony, turned up. "We have got to cover this shaft up when you get it down to depth as there will be no drive until after Christmas," he said. "You can move down the street and start at the end. Make sure the services will be supported before you cover it up with sheet piles."

Mary was back and the bacon sandwiches were out. A good job that Tony had just gone. It was a late dinner in the pub. We finished the shaft and went to the yard and loaded the lorry up with sheet piles. We covered the shaft. It was gone 4 o'clock so it was an early finish as we walked up the street. Mary was coming down. She called me over, "Can you move the box in my kitchen into the shed?"

"OK, can do. I will catch up with you in the pub shortly," I told the lads. We went down the passage into the kitchen. She kissed me on the lips and the donkey rose to the action. We went into the front room. "I cannot get over yesterday; I want more," Mary said. I thought to myself, *I hope Alice did not want it tonight as Mary was about to empty my balls.* The sex was great and Mary knew all the moves but the carpet was rough under my knees, which were getting sore. Mary cried out during her orgasm and I rolled over to get my breath back. I got dressed. Mary had a big smile on her face as we kissed. "I will catch up with you in the morning," I said as I walked out the back door and down the passage. There was a flicker of a curtain across the road. I smiled as I walked past. I got to the pub; Pat and Patsy looked at me and said that I looked knackered. They said that they would get me a pint of Guinness to pull me around. The donkey and my testicles were sore. "You are burning the candle at both ends," Pat said.

"You are right," I said. Down went the Guinness and it was my round. Pat said that we could not be late as Bridey was going out and dinner would be in the oven.

"OK; one more," I said.

Pat said, "When we get the down the next shaft, we will make it right for Christmas. There is a low loader to take machines into McAlpine's yard. As Christmas is in two weeks, it's daywork for the next two weeks."

"What are you two doing over Christmas?" I asked.

"Manchester," Pat said, "with family."

The same for me," said Patsy. "What about you?"

"I was going up north to see my parents, if the weather lets me, but Alice wants me to stay down here."

"You will get these women," said Patsy.

"Sex isn't all that important in life, Patsy," I said with a smile. We drank up and got to the digs just as Bridey was going out. "The dinners are in the oven," she said. "They are all the same."

"Have a good evening," we said as the door closed. The dinner went down well and I sat down to read the paper. The lads went to their rooms. It was 10 o'clock when I woke up from the chair I must have dropped off in. I had a quick wash and went to bed. Pat was down first; tea was on the table. Then Patsy followed us down. It was just breaking dawn when we got to the job. As we could not start until 8 o'clock, it was paper time in the cabin. Peter had the kettle on. We had a good day and Mary was all smiles as she walked past us. As my balls were still sore, I told her that it would be a day or two for me to come around; she laughed and walked on down the street. She brought tea as the lads were about to come up the shaft. Pat made a comment to me, "What are you buying Mary for Christmas, Billy?"

"The arch in my balls; I think she took it," I said. Mary smiled as she picked up the cups and teapot to take back.

"On Thursday we break up," Patsy said. "Are you staying down here or jibing out, Billy?"

"Out," I said. "Alice's parents are not in my league to spend Christmas with so I will tell her tonight and go north. Thursday morning, I will ring the next-door neighbours to let my parents know that I am coming. Dad is not too good."

"Good for you," said Pat. We spent the next two hours tidying up around the shaft, then brought the scaffolding around the shaft after covering it with sheets. We went back to the first shaft on Oil Sites road and did the same for the afternoon. Then it was pub time. I got the round in as I was not staying long because I had to meet Alice after work. I went to the digs; Bridey had dinner. I told her I was leaving on Thursday morning and would be back in the New Year. I sat down to eat. "The lads will be along shortly," I said.

"I will put the dinners in the oven as always," Bridey replied. I got a shower, put on the scent and walked out to meet Alice down the road. She was waiting at the end of Oil Sites road as her dad had dropped her off. We kissed and then we walked to the pub on Sutton road. The Travers Rest was quite packed with people leaving work. Alice found a seat and I got the drinks. "What are you doing for Christmas, Billy?" Alice asked.

"I am going up north to see my parents and friends," I said. "Dad is not too good."

"OK. Are you coming back?" she asked.

"Of course; after Christmas. I will spend New Year with you, if you like."

"Great," Alice said and that put a smile on her face and she cuddled right up to me. I gave Alice the Christmas card I had brought with me. She opened it and read it and said thank you. We drank up and I walked Alice home. To my surprise, Alice's parents were out and her Brother was staying with friends, so sex was on Alice's mind and the donkey did not take a no. It had to be a quickie so as not to get caught with my trousers down. The sex was good and the kettle went on. I got dressed in the nick of time as lights turned on in the drive. Alice's mum greeted me as she walked into the room. I was presentable again. Alice walked in with coffee and then her dad came in. "Had a good evening, both of you, I hope?" he asked.

"Yes, great," I said. "I am going up to Middlesbrough tomorrow to spend Christmas with my parents. My dad is bad with his chest and off work. I should be back in the New Year, if all goes well. I will get off now as I have an early start," I continued, "so have a good Christmas."

Alice's mum got up and kissed me on the cheek and I shook hands with her dad I went to the door with Alice; we kissed on the doorstep, then I said my goodbyes and walked home. I was glad to be out of it as her mum and dad wanted to get to know more about me. I got to the digs.

The next morning, I was up at 6 o'clock. The kettle was on as Bridey was up. "Do you want any breakfast before you go, Billy?" she asked.

"No," I said, "it's a bit early for that. I will stop on the way up north."

I went out the door. I had checked the car over the day before and headed out towards the M62 and north. The dawn was breaking and the weather was good for this time of the year. I got on the A1 going north. It was time for breakfast, so I was on the lookout for a Greasy Spoon café. There was a café on the right-hand side, so I pulled in. It was quite busy but I got served with a buck some lady with tits down to her navel and the cleavage on show. She was very polite when I asked for a full breakfast. "With toast?" she asked.

"Yes," I said as I stared down at her tits with a smile.

"Drink, sir?"

"Yes," I said, "coffee please."

"That will be two pounds," she said. "I will be over in 10 to 15 minutes."

I said OK and picked up a paper. I went to a table and sat down to read; my breakfast was not long in coming and as she put the breakfast down on the table, she asked me, "You have not been in here before."

"No," I said, "just passing through to go up north for Christmas to see my parents and friends. I might stop for the New Year."

"Well, it's nice to meet you. Enjoy your meal and Happy Christmas to you."

"Likewise," I said. The breakfast went down well and I was full as a butcher's dog. I said goodbye to her as she looked across from the counter. I went out the door; I could have pulled her with a bit more time on my hands.

I carried on up A19 towards Teesside; the time was coming up to 9.30 in the morning and traffic was starting to build up as I got near Middlesbrough. Mum would be up by now as I pulled off the road into town. I turned left onto the bottom street, which was Archibald Street. I pulled up outside house number 21. Mum was surprised when she opened the door and I got a big hug. The kettle went straight on and then the questions began: where have I come from and where I am working at the moment. We sat down to talk as dad was still in bed but I could hear him getting up to come down. "His cough was still bad," I said to Mum.

"Yes," she replied, "some days are worse than others. He has not been to work for weeks; he is still on sick leave."

Dad came downstairs followed by Ronnie, my eldest brother. We shook hands and he said, "You do come home sometimes then."

"When I get the chance," I said. "I am working at Ellesmere Port in Cheshire near Liverpool. The job is good with good grub at digs with an Irish family. It will go on into the New Year," I explained. "The firm I am working for is Thomas Ward's plant hire. I am on a crawler crane."

The next to come down was Paul, one year younger to me. He was still at home. I asked him what he was up to these days. Paul said, "We both still have the pigeons. I am going to let them out." Paul went outside.

"How long are you here for?" Dad asked me.

"A couple of days," I said. "It depends on the weather as it was bad in the south for a couple of weeks." I went back to the car to get the Christmas card and my bag. I put my bag in the front room and gave Mum the card. "Have you had breakfast?" Mum asked.

"Yes," was my answer, "I called at a café on the way up here." I sat down to talk to Dad and Ronnie when Margaret peered in. "Stranger, aren't you?"

"Well," I replied, "travelling is my life; it is no good hanging around here. You have to learn to move on." I went on, "I was in Ireland last year for two weeks and it was great. I was working over there, then came back to North Wales on a campsite in Holyhead. The job was for a British cable factory. It was living on a campsite and the crack with the lads was great."

"It's Christmas Eve tonight," I asked Dad, "are we going to the club?"

"Yes," Dad said. "I could do with a pint. I have not been out for three weeks."

Mum smiled. "We will have to go early to get a seat, with it being Christmas Eve and all," said Ronnie.

"Are you courting?" I asked.

"Yes," said Ronnie, "Margaret is her name and she lives near the club.

"Good for you," I said as Mum brought me a cup of tea. Dad and I went out to the garden to look at the vegetables that Dad had grown. "The potatoes look well," I said. "The sprouts too."

"It's a good crop for both this year," Dad said.

"Are we going for a pint at dinner time? I will ask next door if Uncle Charlie is coming."

Yes, was the answer from over the fence so I had a wash and shaved and changed my clothes. We all met at the front door. Uncle Charlie had put on weight since I last saw him. Dad had to sign me in as my card had run out. Uncle Charlie got the drinks and Dad found out where his mates were. Sandy, the train driver, was at the next table and they both wanted to talk about health and in general. Sandy asked me if I was still travelling. I told him that I had been working in Holyhead and across Ireland and had just travelled up from Ellesmere Port, where we were putting a new sewer through the town. I told him that I was working with a load of Irishmen and the crack was good and I had got four to five weeks left there. Then I would move on to drive another crane or plant somewhere else. I said that I was working for a Sheffield firm called Thomas Ward's and they were in demolition as well as plant hire.

The talk turned to Ronnie and Margaret getting married and where he was going to live as he still worked in Dorman Long's Steelworks yard with Stan, another mate of Dad's. They both drove overhead cranes. After another pint it was time to go home and talk with Mum after giving her a hand to wash up. Then I got ready for the club and as tonight was Christmas Eve, we had to be early to get in. The dinner went down well as Mum's cooking was good and it had been a while since I had it this good. By the time I had a seat and talked to Mum and helped her wash the pots, it was time to get ready for the club. Dad, Mum, Ronnie, Margaret and I were going to the club. We got a seat at the back with two tables and five chairs. I sorted the bingo tickets out and brought the drinks. The club was nearly full and it had just turned 7 o'clock. There was a group on as well. Mum won full house on bingo as I was watching her card and I shouted for her. 10 pounds went into the kitty for drinks but I told Mum to put it in her purse and she did so with a smile. So, it was a good night with Ronnie and Margaret dancing. We went home, had a cup of tea and I went to sleep on the sofa in the front room.

I was up early next morning and went for a walk to rekindle my old hornets. It was cold and wet for Christmas Day. I walked around my old school and up Acklem Road and around the cemetery where I used to have my paper round. An hour or so passed and I enjoyed the walk. When I got back, Mum was up and the kettle was on. Bacon and eggs were on the go. As it was Christmas Day, there were no papers and nothing to read. Breakfast went down well; Dad came downstairs still coughing. Ronnie had slept at Margaret's house. Paul was at some girlfriend's. There were only Dennis, and Margaret and Malcolm at home at the moment. Kathy had a job at a hotel on the A1 and was living there. Dennis and Margaret were still at school. Irene had married Dennis, so he was my brother-in-law. Irene had been living with Nanny in Middlesbrough before she got married to Dennis. He too had a speech problem and stuttered like Irene. That is where they had met—at a special school. Dad started to cough again. Mum said that he should go to the doctor's after the

New Year to get tests done on his chest. Dad put on his cap and scarf, drank his tea and we both went to the garden. I had a look into my old garage to see what junk had been put there and Dad and I talked about old times. Ronnie appeared in the garden and came up the path to let his pigeons out. He had 25 in all and he said that he was breeding from them. "Are you coming to the club shortly for a pint?" he asked.

I said, "OK I will. What about you, Dad?"

"Well," he said, "the pennies are a bit short at the moment."

"You don't need any money," I said. "I have your Christmas present on me." I gave him 100 pounds. "Christmas present for you and Mum." Dad looked at me in amazement and thanked me. I went into the kitchen and gave it to Mum in front of Dad. I told them I thought they needed it more than presents. I got a big hug from Mum and that said it all for me. We were all ready and Uncle Charlie was in the street waiting for us. When we got to the club, I got the beer. There was cheese and biscuits on the bar plus tripe in vinegar and pigs' trotters. It all went down with the beer. It was a good conversation at dinner time to find out what had gone on since I had been away. The TV was still black and white, there was a football match on and the street was full of cars, just as it was when I was young. I told Mum that I would get back to the digs to be with Alice and her parents for the New Year. Ronnie and I went out at night and he was a bit short so I stood his corner as well as my own but that was life.

The next morning, I went down the street for the paper and back for breakfast as Mum insisted on it before I left. I had already said my goodbyes to Ronnie the night before as he had slept around at Margaret's. Mum and Dad saw me off at the front door and so did Uncle Charlie and Aunt Rosy. Then I was on my way back south on the A19, then A1, then east towards Liverpool and Ellesmere Port. I got back just after tea and walked into my digs. Bridey was getting ready for the club. "Are you coming to the bingo?" Bridey asked.

I said that I was not too sure until I went around to Alice's.

"If you are, ask the doorman to come and fetch me to sign you in," Bridey said. I put my bag in my room and freshened up, then walked around to Alice's. Her mother answered the door and said, "Am I glad to see you! Alice has had such a face on since you left." Her mother shouted up to her that I was here and down Alice came with a big smile on her face. "Hi," I said, "I said I would be back."

"How are your parents?" she asked.

"Mum's OK but Dad's got chest problems," I replied. "Are you ready to go out?"

Alice said two minutes and went upstairs again. Her mother said from the kitchen, "Alice thought you were not coming back." Alice came down and said, "I am ready now."

"Club if you like?" I asked.

Alice agreed and we got out of the door. Alice turned around and kissed me. "What's that for?" I asked.

Alice said, "For coming back." We reached the club and the doorman recognised me and fetched Bridey to sign us in, which she did so with a big smile on her face. We went upstairs; Bridey said she had saved seats for us if we came in. We had missed the first session, so I got tickets for the second part, then went to the bar and got a pint of Guinness and a double gin and tonic for Alice. I was full as a butcher's dog plus no sex for a fortnight and the glint in Alice's eye said it all. But Alice's Mum and Dad were at home so that was out. We were having some luck on the bingo. Bridey asked, "Are you two coming back for supper?"

"Yes," was my answer.

"I have a taxi ordered for 11.30," Bridey said. We got back to the digs and Bridey got the kettle on while I paid for the taxi. "Are you hungry?" she asked me. I refused with a smile on my face. We sat down and talked about how Christmas was and what Bridey had got, then she went up to bed. Alice and I sat on the sofa and finished our coffee. Then we went up to the bedroom. As soon as we shut the door, the clothes were coming off and the sex was great. I just hoped that Alice was still on the pill; if not, she might get pregnant as it was too good to pull out. We rolled over as it was sleep time with Alice in my arms. When I woke up to go to the toilet, it was daylight. I had a shower as Alice was still asleep and got dressed. I went downstairs, put the kettle on, had a cup of coffee and then went to the paper shop and for a walk. It was a cold and wet morning and the New Year was two days away and work was four days away with five weeks to go. Then I would move on but what would I tell Alice, should I keep in touch or what? I was not ready to settle down yet.

When I got back to the digs, Bridey was up as I could smell the bacon on the go. I could hear movement upstairs and water running. Breakfast was on the table for me. "Does Alice want breakfast?" Bridey asked me but before I could answer, Alice walked in and said, "Yes please." Alice sat down at the table as Bridey brought the toast in and asked what we were doing today. "I am going out for the day visiting some friends," Bridey explained. "You have got the key, Billy."

Alice looked at me and said, "The sales are on in Liverpool; we could get the train now."

"That's an idea," I replied. "The train runs every half hour so it's a day out."

Alice asked, "Can I phone my mum and tell her, Bridey?"

"Of course, you can," Bridey said.

"I will do the washing up," I offered. "You get yourself ready and get off."

Bridey left and Alice and I sat and talked. Alice asked the question that I had been dreading, "What will you do when the job is finished?"

"Move on, I suppose," I said. "Not thought about it yet but I will come back whenever, or you can come to me."

"Great," Alice said. "I love you, Billy."

We kissed and I said, "I have feelings for you too, Alice. You get yourself ready; I will wash the pots." I got another kiss. The station was busy when we got there but we got on the 10.30 to Liverpool Central and got a seat. The weather was cold but we were both covered up well. The shops were busy with the sales on as we walked around and discussed what to buy. Mum had brought me socks as usual for Christmas so that was out. The jeans looked good but the waist and length did not match; the length would have to be taken up. "No problem," said Alice, "I will do it good." So, I bought a pair.

"What do you fancy?" I asked Alice.

"A dress would look well if I can find my size," she replied.

I said, "Well, it is coffee time." So, we found a café, ordered and sat down.

"I am glad you are back, Billy," Alice said.

I held her hand and smiled, "What's next on the agenda?"

Alice shrugged her shoulders and smiled, "The coffee was good."

"You are not hungry yet?" I asked.

"No," was the reply, "the breakfast was good. It's a great grub house, Bridey's." We walked around more to look at what was on offer but nothing came to mind apart from toiletries like aftershave. Alice bought make-up. "A good pint of Guinness will go down well in the Irish bar, O'Malley's," I suggested. We went in. "Gin and tonic?" I asked.

"Yes please," was the reply. It was busy but I smiled at the barmaid and got served quickly. Alice was still quizzing me on my next move. "It will work out, you'll see," I said. The Guinness went down well as it was brewed with Irish water and the head was great and white. We headed out and were back on the train with the shopping. We went into Alice's house and her mother was in the kitchen.

"Had a good day, you two?" she asked.

"Yes," Alice said, "I got a dress."

"And you, Billy?" her mother asked.

"I got some toiletries like aftershave and scent."

"Are you two hungry?" her mother asked.

"I think we will go out for a meal to finish the day off," I said. Alice went upstairs to freshen up and was down in a flash.

"Where would you like to eat?" I asked.

"Surprise me," Alice said.

"There is a Harvester outside town; we will jump into a taxi and go," I said. I spotted one coming down the road, put my hand up and he pulled up. It was busy when we got there but we got a table. We looked at the menu.

"I will have steak," I said, "and you?"

"Scampi," Alice said and that's what we ordered when the girl came across.

"Drinks?" the girl asked.

"Shall we have wine for a change?" Alice said. I agreed.

"White or red?"

"I'll leave it to you," I said. Red it was.

"Where will you go when this job is finished?" she asked again.

"I don't know. Probably back to the yard in Sheffield; then who knows where I will be. We will keep in touch weekly by phone." The meal turned up and we poured the wine.

"Where are we going for New Year?" I asked. "Bridey's said that she can get tickets for the club on New Year's Eve—five pounds each. We can go to the club when we leave here, if you like."

"OK," said Alice. "We will get a taxi as it is raining."

The meal went down well; I was full as a butcher's dog. We reached the club; I gave the doorman a drink and went upstairs. It was bingo so we both sat at one end of the bar, waiting to be served. We got served when the bingo was over. I looked across to where Bridey was sitting and she waved us over to get two chairs from the back of the room. Bridey moved around to fit us in. I got up to buy some bingo tickets for Alice and me, one book each. We had missed the first house but there were three to go so we were in with a chance. I waited for one number but someone called before me and Bridey won the next house and bought a round of drinks. The night ended good and I walked Alice home and we decided to meet up tomorrow for a walk down the Manchester canal. When I got back to the digs, Bridey had left a sandwich out to eat so I made a cup of coffee to wash it down.

The next morning, I was up early. I had a cup of tea and walked out to the paper shop. It was a cold, wet winter's day and New Year's Eve too. I walked the long way back to the digs to get some fresh air as it would be a long day. I got back and Bridey was up and into the breakfast. Shamus was sorting the fire out as it was a Saturday. "What's on the agenda today?" Bridey asked as she dished the breakfast out.

"Well," I said, "I will go around to Alice's to see if she wants to go for a walk, then call in at a pub along the canal bank for a pint."

"Dinner is at 3 o'clock. I will get it on when Shamus and I get back from church."

The breakfast went down well—the last breakfast of 1970! The next one would be in 1971. I took a slow walk around Alice's; she came to the door as she saw me walk up the drive and gave me a nice kiss on the doorstep.

"I am full as a butcher's dog with breakfast inside me so I thought we would walk it off as it's a nice winter morning," I suggested.

"OK," Alice said, "I will put on my boots and big coat." We set off down to the Manchester canal. The skies were grey but dry. The sun was trying to get through.

"It's the last day of this year," I said to Alice. "We will make the most of it."

There were plenty of people about, wishing all the best for the New Year. We reached the Canal Tavern pub. It was 12.30 and the seats were a little damp. I had a newspaper in my pocket to put down on the seat to sit on. Alice asked me if I would like to come for dinner on New Year's Day as her mother had asked her. I agreed and said, "Bridey is having a party at her house tonight and you can sleep over with me, if that's all right with you."

We went into the pub for a drink; there was nobody drinking Guinness, so I left it alone and had a beer shandy. Alice had the same as it was going to be a long day. We sat and talked about next year but I knew that with the way my life was right now, I was not ready to settle down yet. We drank up and walked back the way we had come. I had enjoyed the walk and the fresh air. "Pick you up at 7 o'clock," I said to Alice as we got to her front door. "It will be full tonight."

"OK," she said.

I thought I would have a lie down for an hour as it was only 2.45 and I had a long night ahead. I was up at around 6 o'clock. I showered and went off to pick up Alice. She looked a picture when she came to the door; even the donkey in my trousers twitched.

"Am I OK for you?" Alice asked.

"You would bring the ducks off the water," I said with a big smile. There was a queue at the door to get in. Bridey and Shamus were in the front, so it was not a problem. Bridey got us all seated and I went to the bar and bought the drinks and got myself seated next to Alice. There was a group on and they were good. The crack around the table was good in Irish terms and the night was full of laugher and dancing. At 12 o'clock, *Auld Lang Syne* rang out, then the kissing and wishing commenced. There were two taxis to take us back to Bridey's house for supper, which was all laid out. There was a chimney sweep outside the door with a black face; he had to go into the house first for luck. I was handed a bottle of Guinness and Alice was on gin and tonic and the night wore on and friends started to leave. Alice looked tired so up we went to bed. Sex looked a bit bleak as the drinks had taken over so a cuddle and sleep and then it was daylight.

I was up and left Alice sleeping as it was gone 7.30. Bridey was up and had the kettle on. "We had a good New Year's Eve," Bridey said. I agreed. "Is Alice still in bed?"

"Yes," was my answer. There were no papers today so after breakfast, I went for a short walk. I thought, *What will this year bring and where will I be at the end of it?* There were four or five weeks left on this job. *What will I do about Alice as I didn't feel ready to settle down even if I have feelings for her?* I had a lot to think about. I got back to the digs; the breakfast smelled good as I opened the door. Alice was up so it was good mornings all around. Bridey asked, "What's on the agenda for today?"

"Well," I said, "the weather is not too bad for a walk."

"I will have to go home and get changed first," Alice said. I was full of Breakfast. The time was 10.30. Alice said her parents would be up when we go around. We went in and her mother wished us, "Happy New Year, the two of you. Have you eaten yet?" We said yes and Alice went upstairs to change. Her dad walked in.

"Happy New Year, Billy," he said.

"Same to you," I replied. He asked me what we were going to do today. I replied, "It looks like a good morning for a long walk along the canal towpath."

"How long have you got left on this job, Billy?" her dad asked.

"Four or five weeks left, but there is a small job just up the road, I heard. MH Tunnelling had got it before we broke up. I don't know where yet and the crane is going there so we will see."

"How are your parents going on?" Alice's mother asked.

"Mum's great. Dad still has a bad chest and is off work to go to the doctor." Alice came into the room and said that she was ready.

"Well, dinner is at 2 o'clock, if that's all right with you," her mother said.

We went down the road and I turned to Alice and said that I did not know I was invited for dinner.

"Well, you are now."

"We will call and let Bridey know."

We called around to the house to tell Bridey not to put out dinner for us. Then we set off down towards the towpath on the canal. The weather wasn't too bad for walking and there were plenty of people doing the same and wishing us a happy new year. We walked for a couple of miles and the pub we passed—the Canal Tavern—was open. When we walked back, I turned to Alice and asked her if she was ready for the hair of the dog. She agreed and we went in. The fire was roaring in the fireplace. I asked Alice what she wanted.

"Just Britvic orange," she said. I got an Underberg to settle the stomach and a pint of Guinness to follow it. We sat down and talked; it was the same topic: what I was going to do when the job got over. Well, all I could say was that we would keep in touch as I did not know where I would be working. I knew in my heart that I loved travelling at the moment. We drank up as time was rolling along and we just got back in time as Alice's mum was dishing out the dinner. We washed our hands and sat at the table. Alice's mum asked, "Were there plenty of people about?"

"Yes," we said.

Then her dad turned the talk to work as there were a lot more houses to be built outside Ellesmere Port. A new sewer had been put in plus a new shopping centre to go with it. "Do you want a pudding now?" her mum asked.

"No, thank you," was my answer as I was full. Her dad and I got up from the table and went into the front room where her dad asked me if I would like a whisky. He said that he liked one now and again and it went down as we all watched TV as the day went on. Alice took me to one side with a gleam in her eye and said, "I will show you that record I bought upstairs in my bedroom. Is that OK with you, Mum?"

No sooner had we got into the room than the clothes started to come off. The sex was good and it was late when we woke up as we must have gone to sleep when we finished. Alice went downstairs. "Mum and Dad have gone to bed."

We had a cup of tea in bed and cuddled up again. It was morning when we woke up again and we got up and dressed and went down. We had breakfast on the go and it went down well. Her mum came down and said good morning with a smile on her face. "What's on the agenda today?" her mother asked.

"I don't know," said Alice.

I said that sales were on in Southport so we probably would go there for a ride in the car. It could do with a run for the day. Plus, it's back to work on Monday."

We were out of the house and walked to the digs. Bridey was up and asked if we had breakfast.

I answered, "Yes. We are going for a ride out to the sales at Southport. It will give the car a good run.

"OK," Bridey said, "see you later."

I checked oil and water before I started it up and it was OK after the run up to my mum and dad. It was mid-morning when I stopped at a phone box to ring Aunt Rosy to wish a happy new year to all. "Everything OK at home?" Alice asked as I got back into the car.

We drove to the town and started to look out for a carpark space. We found one just out of town as there were plenty of people about. It was more of window-shopping as we had got almost everything before Christmas. We went in the big shops like Woolworth and Binns as both had sales on. Next, we called at a café for tea and sat down and talked about work for a change. "Well," I said, "I will be here to do the other job at Sutton on the railway bank. I am taking only the HYMAC with me as the crane is going back to the yard in Sheffield. I am not sure how long the job will last."

Alice smiled. "Well," I added, "as I said to you before, we will keep in touch." Alice held my hand as we sipped our tea. We left the café and walked back to the car and drove back to the digs. I parked the car and went in. Bridey said, "There is some tea for you two to eat as we are going to the club. Are you coming? I will save your seats."

"OK," I said and off went Bridey and Shamus. Alice said that she was going upstairs to freshen up with a twinkle in her eye, so I followed. The sex was great, then we both freshened up together and went off to the club. It was a good evening to walk to the club. We got in and went upstairs just as bingo was about to start. I asked Alice if she was interested and she shook her head. Nobody on the table won and the group was a bit loud but not bad. "Well," Bridey said, "back to work for everybody and up early." Bridey and Shamus got a taxi home and Alice and I walked to her home. We kissed on the doorstep and then I walked to the digs and had a cup of tea before turning in.

Next morning, the kettle was on, then a walk to the job. I got on the site at the office and Mick and Tommy were there with a shake of hands right around to wish a happy new year. Glen said to Stan and Tony that we would be on the move with the HYMAC this week up to the Sutton railway as we had to put a 24-inch pipe under the railway line. "Stan, Tony and Billy, go get the machine ready first as the crane is off hire and Thomas Wards is coming for it this week," he said. So off I went down the street to the last shaft where the HYMAC was parked and boarded up to protect the windows. I checked oil, water and dev to top up, then grease. I then had to wait for the low loader to come. Stan was all for going for breakfast as the lorry was going to be an hour yet. As we got to the café, it was happy new year all around and the order went out. It went down well for the start of the new year. I got back to the machine; the lorry was just setting up. The driver said, "Can you put your machine side by side?"

"OK," I said and it was chained down. Then Stan and I went in the front to show the driver where to go. The traffic had calmed down and it was not that far. The road was not very wide but there was a passing point, so it was good to off-load and go into a field though a gate. We went down a track to the railway embankment. A lorry turned up with sheet piles and timbers for the shaft that we were going to dig. It was already marked out and after getting the lorry away, it was down to digging the shaft out. The first timbers went in and then sheet piles all around. They went down with an air hammer from a compressor. We had a good day. It was becoming dark at 4 o'clock and I met up with Pat and Mick in the pub. They had been finishing off the manholes in the streets in the Port and the Guinness went down well. Then it was back to the digs and Bridey was dishing the grub out. I showered and went to bed.

Next morning, Bridey had got breakfast on as I had to drive to Sutton in the car and meet up with Tony and Stan on the job. It was another good day as we got down to the depths before the lads started to tunnel under the railway line. Then it was to the concrete bottom of the shaft and putting the wooden shutters onto the concrete back wall to jack off. Considering that it was day three of a two-week job, it was going well. It may well be the end of the job for me and I would have to say my goodbyes to the lads plus Alice, which was going to be hard. The lads started to tunnel on the fifth day. It was only 50 metres long and six feet in height and so it would not take too long as long as there were no obstructions. I took the bucket off the HYMAC to lift the small skips out of the clay and tip them on top of the ground to be loaded onto the lorry later. I called around to see Alice to keep her informed as to how long I would be on the job and promised to keep in touch. However, it was not going down very well as she thought that I would change my mind and stay around. It was a quick kiss on the doorstep and goodbye. *Well*, I thought to myself, *that's it and hello, New Year*, as I walked away.

The next day, Stan asked if Alice was worried about me leaving. I said that I was not ready to settle down yet as there was a big world out there to see and conquer. As the job was underway, I put Alice to the back of my mind for now. The crack in the pub was good as usual and the Guinness went down great before dinner.

Bridey asked me the next morning where the next job was. I said, "I will go back to the yard in Sheffield and work it out from there."

"What about your girlfriend?" Bridey asked.

"Well, we all have to move on at some time," I said. "It's not over yet as I will keep in touch for now and see how we get on." So, it was back to work and we were digging in the shield and the clay was coming out fast. Four pipes went down today and there were 10 more to go. The end was in sight. Tony came on the site and told me that another week was left to load the clay up when the drive was finished. Then I would be off hire, so it was time to ring up the office in Sheffield. Mr Billy Butler, the plant manager, came on the phone and said it was back to the yard for now and see where to go from there. I came off the phone and went back on the job. The lads were in the portable cabin that we were using and I told them what happening. "Well, Billy boy, it will soon be goodbyes all around."

It was time to go back down the shaft. Six pipes to go until Friday. At the end of the day, two more pipes went down. Tony turned up as I was leaving and asked if I would work on Saturday as he had got two lorries on hire to load the clay away. I said that it was no problem and then it was off to the pub. The Guinness went down great as usual and I went back to the digs for the big feed of the day.

Wednesday was a slow start as it had been raining most of the night and the shaft had water in it. It had to be pumped out first. It was breakfast time before the lads got digging into the pipe. I got the next pipe ready to go down the shaft and the lads got three pipes in. We had put out on the other side of the railway and put a shaft in with sheet piles but it was only 10 feet down. At the end of the day, the pipes would have only electric cables going through them, so the angle of the pipes was uphill and not too deep. I took the HYMAC around on the road when the drive was nearly through and lifted the sheet piles up so that the pipe could be jacked through. It was a custom to put a bottle of whisky down the shaft as the lads broke through to celebrate the drive's end. On Friday morning, Tony the foreman went in front of me with the Land Rover as I took the HYMAC around on the road early before the traffic got busy. We were in place with the HYMAC. Tony and Peter hooked the sheet piles with a chain and shackle onto the bucket of the machine. I lifted each one out and laid them down on the ground to make a stack of them to be loaded up, It was only the front ones to let Pat and Tom come through as they were in the pipe's drive. They were in the shaft now to a cheer from us on the top of the shaft and Tony lowered the bottle of whisky down the shaft so that the lads could open it and drink up. We locked up on the site as it was going to be a long weekend and the lads were going home. We went back to the yard to finish the whisky off and get the timesheets signed and in the post. I was told that it was going to be my last week. I asked to use the phone to ring the plant manager, Billy Butler, at Thomas Ward's. I asked him what the crack was, workwise. "Well," he said, "load the HYMAC up and I will see you in the yard a week from Monday unless I ring you next week."

"OK," I said. "Well," I turned to Tony, "it's my last week."

He said that all good jobs came to an end. Pat said that it would be party night next week as he knew that there was a good comedian coming to the club. The tickets were ten shillings each with a ploughman's lunch with the ticket. I said that I would work on it over the weekend. We left the office as it was 4.30. I fancied a pint in the Railway tavern and Peter said that he would join me for a change. The Guinness was good. "What will you do at the end of this job?" Peter asked.

I said that I was looking around at the moment with no joy. We parted after two pints and I said that I would see him on Monday. The tea was on the table when I got in. "No warm-ups tonight?" Bridey asked. I smiled.

"What's it like at the Working Men's club?" I asked Bridey.

Shamus spoke up, "Not that good."

"Well," I said, "there is a comedian on next week; a ticket does plus a ploughman's meal as well. I will call tonight to see if I can get tickets."

The tea went down well—homemade steak pie, chips and beans. I went up, changed and walked down to the high street to the club. As it was early, I thought I would get the tickets I needed. There was a doorman and asked me if I was a member. I said that I had a member affiliated card from up north. I took it out to show him. I told him that I was just working down in the Port and I heard there was going to be a good night this week with Bernard Manning plus supper to follow. He said yes. So, I asked him if there were any tickets left for me and the lads to come. He got them out from a cupboard and counted them out. "Twenty in all," he said.

"Can I buy 10 of them?" I asked.

"Yes," said the doorman, "at five pounds each." I paid the man and asked if I could go in to have a pint. Yes, was the answer so in I went. There were not so many men in as it was early yet. The barman seemed to be friendly as I asked for a pint of Guinness and it was pulled right and tasted good. The man asked if I was working and I said yes. "I just finished the new drainage pipes through the town."

"So, it was you causing the congestion," he said.

I said, "It's finished now and the night out is like a going-away party for us all." I drank up and said to the man, "I will see you next Wednesday if you are on."

"I will be here," the man said. I went back to the Railway pub, got my drink and sat down. To my delight, Alice walked in. "I thought I would find you in here and surprise you."

"Yes," I said with a smile. I told Alice that I been to the Social club and got tickets for Wednesday night for the lads as the firm was paying for them and it was an all-out evening—men only."

"Oh well," Alice said with a smile and then went quiet. At the end of the evening, I took Alice home. I was leaving on Friday morning and heading back to Sheffield.

Wednesday night went well and the crack was good with the lads. The lads and I went for a drink for the last time at the Station Hotel. In walked Alice with a smile on her face. We sat down in a corner and talked about keeping in touch for the future. We said our goodbyes then and there; I walked her home. She had tears in her eyes at the front door. I went back to the digs and said goodbye to Bridey. The next morning, I had breakfast, then checked the car over ready to travel onto Sheffield. As it was Friday, the traffic was busy and I stopped at a café and used the phone to call the Moulder's Arms at Rotherham to see if they still did B&B. Roy came on the phone. He said, "Hi Billy; yes, we do."

"I will be in within an hour," I said. I arrived at the Moulder's Arms and took my bag up to the room. The Landlady greeted me. I went downstairs for a pint to see Roy who was behind the bar. We got talking and he told me that Pauline was looking for me. Apparently, she had my baby girl; she hadn't lost it. She moved away with a bloke called George who brought the baby up. The baby was called Ann-Marie. She was looking for me as George had passed away in 1970 because of cancer, Roy explained. Pauline was back, living on her own with Ann-Marie. I left it at that for now. I told Roy to call in if he saw her. On Saturday morning, I had to go to the yard, which was on Rotherham Road. I met up with the plant manager, Billy Robinson. We went into the office and had a conversation about work. It was a bit slack at the moment, so he was going to lay me off. We left it at that and he told me to ring him at a later date. On Saturday afternoon, I went back to the Moulder's Arms for a pint and a talk with Roy. He told me that there was a job going on at Rotherham power station. The main contractor on the job was a demolition firm called Ogdens of Otley. I decided to call on the job on Monday to see what the crack was and left it at that. On Sunday morning, I went for a walk up Rotherham Road to see where this job was. When I returned to the pub, I got a surprise as Pauline was there. She started to tell me about the baby and that George had offered them a home at the time. Ann-Marie was eight years of age but Pauline had not told her that I was her dad yet. She was going to bring her down later in the week to meet me if I was going to stay in the pub. On Monday morning, I got up and went to the power station to see about the job and what it entailed. I met the foreman named Frank and he told me that he wanted a driver for a 22RB crane, which I told him I was used to. There were three buildings made of concrete and were three stories high. They were going to be knocked down and loaded. I asked Frank when I could start. He said straight away if I could. The crane was coming on Tuesday. I said that I would be here in the morning to start. I went to the pub to tell Roy. "Good for you," he said over a pint. I went out up the town to where the old job was and it was now a block of flats. It was teatime when I got back and to my surprise, Pauline was waiting for me with her daughter, Ann-Marie, in her school uniform. She looked smart. Pauline took me to one side with Ann-Marie and introduced me to her as her real father. "I did not want to hurt your feelings as you were too young to understand," Pauline explained. "That's why I told you that George was your dad. Now you are getting older and can understand. Billy is your biological father"

I said I would meet up with them both and take them both out for a meal at the weekend and both agreed. When they finished their drinks, they left and I went to the bar. Roy asked me how I got on and I said that it looked like I was the dad and Pauline told Ann-Marie that I was her dad.

On Tuesday, I went down to the job at the power station. The low loader was there with the crane on its back. Frank the foreman said, "Billy, there is the crane and get on with it. I will show you where to start in the next hour."

The day went well. Frank told me there were only six weeks of work and I would have to move on to somewhere else. I accepted. On the Friday of that week, Pauline turned up at the pub as I got in from work and we arranged to go to the Chinese restaurant for a meal on Saturday night. I went to work on Saturday morning. After dinner, I went to the Rotherham swimming baths. There was also a sauna. I went to Burton's, the tailor, and bought a suit off the peg for Saturday night. I had to go back later because it had to be altered. I had a bath, put on my new suit, went down to the bar and got a compliment from Roy. Then Pauline and Ann-Marie turned up and we went for Chinese, which went down well. At the end of the evening, she asked me to come back to her house but I refused. I got them a taxi to town and went back to the pub. The following week on Saturday, Ann-Marie and I went shopping to Sheffield where I bought her a three-quarter leather coat, which she loved. On Sunday, we went to the Crich Tramway Museum in Derbyshire, which was a good day out for all of us. On Monday, it was back to work at the power station; this was my third week as the job was going well. I did not see any more of Pauline that week. In the fourth week, Pauline called at the pub to see me. She asked me to move in with them to save my money for digs. I declined and left well alone. During the fifth week, Pauline contacted me at the pub and took me to one side to tell me about the money, which was George's redundancy money and had been in her bank account. After George passed away, she spent it. His ex-wife went to the solicitors to claim it back. I was a bit taken aback by all this as I was still unsure whether Ann-Marie was my daughter or not. I left it at that. In the sixth week, it all kicked off when Pauline threatened me that if I did not come up with any money, I would not be able to see her again and that was the end of me seeing Pauline and Ann-Marie again. The job was coming to an end and it was time to move on again. Time to get away from Rotherham for a while and let Pauline cool down.

The next job on offer with Ogden's demolition firm was outside Otley and near the yard. During the weekend, they were going to blow up a chimney, so I went to the yard and the lady in the offices got me digs for a week or so as it was her friend and they were all right. The man on the job was called Fred Dibner and he was a steeplejack by trade and heights were no problem for him. He used long ladders joined together and tied them to the stack on the old bolts that were for the steel ladders but had broken off over the years. The canal ran down the side of the job and any brick rubble that went in there would be cleaned out at the end of the job. On the opposite side of the canal was the Singer sewing machine factory and it had scaffolding right around plus over the roof to protect it. Fred Dibner used tyres to burn after he had patched a hole at the side where it was supposed to fall on the site. The hole was choked up with sleepers that would burn along with the tyres. There was a brand new 22RB on the site, so I drove that to knock down the outbuildings. The job was good and Fred was good to work with. He knew his job in the Power Station North Wales, so I said yes to the job. I went back to the pub and told Roy that I was moving out on Sunday morning and would drive down to North Wales and find digs. I went to work on Saturday morning to load the crane and I would catch up to it again on the next job. I left and went back to the pub to shower and change and went out for a walk around Rotherham. I called in at a pub and there was steak on the menu, which went down well. I walked back to the digs. Roy was on and we had a good talk about Pauline. I did not believe Pauline's stories as I had inquired years earlier about the baby that she was to have. I was told by her friend, Ann, that she had had a miscarriage, so I left things at that.

On Sunday morning, I was up and left early and set off to North Wales. The drive down was M1 first, then M62 to M51 to North Wales. I found out where the job was at the power station and then I drove to Queens Ferry to look for the digs. I looked in at a paper shop in the town, got the address of the widow and asked the shopkeeper where it was. As it was gone dinnertime, the lady of the house was in and I got booked in for approximately four weeks as I was told by Fred. The job was for McAlpine's and it was to build two new cooling towers and we were to take the two old ones down by blowing them up using explosives they called it blaster baits in the trade a nickname of an English demolition expert and it was going to be something different for me. I asked the landlady where the nearest pub was and took a walk around town. Two pints and something to eat was on my menu. The pub was called the Black Swan and the menu looked good for Sunday lunch. I looked around the pub to see if anybody was drinking Guinness but no one was so I left it alone and got a pint of lager instead. I ordered the lamb dinner that went down well with the lager. I walked back to the digs and had a lie down for a couple of hours. I showered and went back to the pub. There was a quiz on so there were plenty of people in but I did not want to get involved as my school days had been few and far between. I got to the digs at bedtime, was up and gone next morning to the power station. I had to wait at the gatehouse for the lads to turn up with the passes. The lads turned up and so did the low loader with the crane on. The next step was the introduction in the offices and we met Mr Bates himself and he explained what the job was. We had to first help him drill holes in the concrete legs to place the jelly and detonators. For the next three days, the four of us spent the days drilling and it made our arms ache. They moved into the digs down the road, so I had company in the pub at night and the crack was good with Fred and the lads. On the fourth day, we helped Mr Bates by putting the jelly in the holes we had drilled. On Saturday, it was to be blown up, so it was an early finish and back to the digs to wash, change and go down to the pub for a meal. Steak was on the menu and it went down great with the lager.

On Saturday morning, large crowds turned up to watch the towers come down and me and the lads had to marshal to keep the crowds back. I had a whistle to blow if anything went wrong as I was standing on the main road. The time was 12 o'clock and the explosion went with a bang as the first tower went down and dust went up in the sky. Then there was a second explosion and the second tower went down to a cheer from the crowd. I started to walk back to the site to meet Fred and the lads. We walked around the towers. The concrete had all gone in, which was good. The job was for me with the crane and the one-ton ball and bomb it down so that it could be landscaped with topsoil. This was my job from Monday. Fred and the lads set off for home in the van and I went back to the digs in Queens Ferry to get showered. I went for a look around and something to eat. I thought about going to see Alice at Ellesmere Port but then, I did not want to set things off again, so I gave it a miss. I had a nosey around here. Food was on my mind, so I found a transport café where the meals looked good. The steak looked well on another man's plate, so I ordered it and it went down well. As I was not driving, it was to the pub next. The Black Swan had not looked too bad the night before, so I went in for a pint. I stuck to lager as I could not see anybody drinking Guinness but the lager went down well. I looked around to see if there was any talent going spare. There were a few grannies going spare. So, I tried my hand. I started about the weather and the lady said that I was not from North Wales. I said that I came from Middlesbrough. I said that I was working down at the INS power station. "It blew up the big towers yesterday," said the lady.

"Yes," I said, "I was there and my job is to flatten it all down to topsoil it over."

"Well," said the ladies, "we are impressed with your job." Then they introduced themselves, "I am Jane and this is Mandy."

"I am Billy. I travel with my job anywhere. I am lodging down the road. The lads have gone home to their wives and girlfriends."

I got up to get another drink and asked if they wanted one.

"Yes please," Mandy said. "It's two gin and tonics." I got another pint of lager and sat back down. "Where is your next job?" Mandy asked. I said that I did not know. I would find out in two weeks' time when the job was finished.

"Have you no home at all?" Jane asked.

"No, not really," I said. "I have roamed around England since I left school, from job to job with no help from anybody. There is plenty of work if you want and the money can be good. What about you two?" Mandy said that she was divorced and Jane said that she was a widow. We got on well together.

"What are you doing tomorrow?" I asked. "I have Sunday free. Dinner out?"

"Well, that's a good idea," one said to the other.

"Is 12.30 OK?" I asked.

They agreed and then it was time to find something to eat so I went to the café I had gone to a few days before. The steak and chips and beans were on offer and they went down well. I went back to the digs to lay down for a while; I must have dropped off to sleep as it was nearly dark when I woke up. I got up, washed my face and went out to the pub. I got a pint of lager and looked around. Mandy sat on her own, so I went across to her. "Hi Billy," she said.

"On your own?" I asked.

"Yes. I had a date but it looks like I was stood up," she laughed.

"Well, if he turns up while I am here, I will just move on," I offered.

"Good of you, Billy," she said. "Jane wanted to come but did not want to play gooseberry."

As the night wore on, the banter got better and we got to know one another. The gin and tonic got to work and by 10.30, Mandy was ready for home and sex, I thought.

"Are you coming around, Billy?" she asked.

"I could as I am not in a rush to go anywhere," I replied.

It was not that far to Mandy's house and it looked smart from the outside with a garden and flowers. I went in and Mandy put the kettle on. I sat down in the lounge and made myself at home. Mandy sat next to me and we carried on the conversation that we had left off in the pub. She was on about the family that she had in the past. We eventually got around to sex and she missed not having a man in bed to make love to her.

"Well," I said, "this could be your lucky night, if you are up for it." I did not finish the words and the clothes were coming off. The sex was great and I lay back to get my breath back. Mandy was ready again; you could see she was making up for lost time. After the second bout, I was glad to get dressed and lay back to rest.

It's been a long time since I had a woman with so much energy, I thought to myself. Mandy made more coffee and she said, "I hope we can have more nights like this." I agreed with a smile. My penis was red and the time was 1 o'clock in the morning.

"Do you want to stay the rest of the night? Mandy asked.

"Well," I said, "there is no work tomorrow." We went into the bedroom and the clothes came off me again. Mandy cuddled up to me right tight and went to sleep.

I woke up and Mandy was not there. I could smell bacon and eggs on the go. I went into the kitchen. "Good morning," Mandy said. "One or two eggs?"

"Two," I said, "I got to put back what you have taken out of me." I laughed. It went down great. Mandy said that it would last me until dinner when we would meet up with Jane. She asked if we could keep our little secret for now and I replied that it was up to her. I got a kiss as I went out through the door and a big smile. I said to myself that that woman was well and truly satisfied. The Landlady was up when I got to the digs.

"We did not hear you come in last night," she said.

"I met a friend from the past and stopped there."

"Do you want any breakfast," she asked me. I declined and went up to shower and put scent on. Then I went to find a paper shop. The lady at the shop gave me a dirty look as North Wales people did not get on with the English. I found a seat at the end of the village and read the paper. I took another walk around the village and went down to the pub as it was getting towards opening time. I sat down outside on a bench and carried on with the paper. To my surprise, Jane turned up and sat down beside me. "Where did you get to last night?" she asked.

"I came down here," I said with a smile.

"Was Mandy in last night?"

"Yes," I said, "but I think she had a date." As I turned around, Mandy was there with a smile on her face. We went in and I got the drinks. We sat down and Jane asked Mandy how her date had turned out. Mandy said that it was great.

"Well, are you going to see him again?" Jane asked her.

"I hope so," she said and looked at me and smiled. The girls ordered dinner; I made an excuse not to eat just yet. The meals came and the girls ate them. The conversation was about work and the new date Mandy had got. I was glad when Jane left.

"Well," Mandy said, "are you coming around tonight?"

She said for tea but I knew sex would be for afters.

"OK," I said, "what time?"

"Around 7 o'clock."

I agreed and went to the digs and got on the bed to get some sleep. I would need it. I put the alarm on for 6 o'clock to shower and freshen up. I woke up and the clock said 5.45. I got up and showered. The half hour's sleep I got was good. I put plenty of scent on and off I went. I got to Mandy's cottage she was at the door before I got down the path. I went in. "Hi," she said, wine is all I have. White or red?"

"Any," I said. I sat down on the settee and she came in with the wine. Mandy sat down next to me and kissed me on the cheek.

"I did not think you would come. Jane phoned me for more updates on the man I met. I told her that I will take it slowly." She continued, "It is nice to have company at night, especially at weekends as the week is not too bad. I work as a carer in the old people's home outside Queens Ferry and there is plenty to do. Well, that's me and what about you?"

"Well," I said, "my mother had a lot of children; I am one of 8."

"Gosh!" said Mandy.

"So, I moved out early. I had pigs at first. I did not go to school very much that's why I cannot write very well."

"That's nothing to be ashamed of," Mandy said.

"Then I lived on a farm and learned how to drive tractors," I continued. "Then I met a paddy on a building site and that was the start of my travelling days. I move around with the jobs."

"You are a very interesting man," Mandy said.

"I am born free and I love to meet people like you."

"Good for you," Mandy said. "So, you have no proper lady friend???"

"Not at the moment," I said. "I am a bit older than you but more experienced and loving." I got a big smile.

"Is the wine chilled enough for you?" she asked.

"It is going down well at the moment," I replied. I could feel my penis twitching in my trousers. Mandy put her hand on my leg and kissed me and the clothes started to come off. I was on her like a rat up a drainpipe; the sex was good but I hoped it was over as there was work tomorrow. I would be well and truly knackered. Mandy smiled as we lay back and took a break and I got my energy back. "Are you going to stay the night?" she asked.

"Not really as I have to get up early for work."

"OK," she said. I said to myself, *Thank goodness for that.*

"What do you want for supper?" Mandy asked. "Will cheese and biscuits be all right?"

"OK," I said. Mandy went off to the kitchen still naked and my penis was roaring red.

Mandy came in with the coffee and cheese and biscuits and a big smile. "I thought you would change your mind if I did not get dressed," she said.

"The thought is there," I said, "but it's been a great weekend and more to come, I hope." That widened her smile. I got dressed, drank up, got big kisses at the door and went back to the digs. It was 11 o'clock and could do with some rest.

I was up at six, had a shower—my penis was still sore—and off I went to the power station. The lads turned up in the van. "Had a good weekend?" Fred asked.

"Great," I said. The day went well and I told the lads two pints and food and an early night and that's what I did. Tuesday was a better day and I was feeling better all around. I got on with the job in hand. The concrete was crushing down great around the first tower. Fred and I were talking about how it would be done a week from Friday and there was not a lot going on at the moment. There was talk of going to the yard for a few weeks. "Well," I said, "all good jobs come to an end and I will move on when the time comes." *Mandy would not be very pleased but there you go*, I said to myself, *you cannot win them all.* We all went to the pub and looked at the menu. I thought I would have a drink first. To my surprise, Mandy walked in and came across to me. "Hi," she said, "I guessed that you would be in here." I introduced Mandy to the lads as a friend who I had met at the weekend. I got her a drink and as I took it over to her, Mandy said, "As it's nice, would you like to sit outside?"

I agreed and went outside with a smile from the lads. "How's your day been?" Mandy asked.

"OK," I replied, "the job's going well and we won't be as long as it was stated before. Probably a week early."

"What are you doing for tea?" she asked.

"Well," I said, "I was going to order shortly."

"I make nice ham, egg and chips and I have a spotted dick pudding for afters."

I laughed at the spotted dick comment. She added, "You can have a shower first."

"Sounds good to me," I said and we drank up and walked to her cottage she held my hand. I thought to myself, *This one is going to be hard to ditch when the job is over.* Mandy went into the kitchen and came out with the coffee. "One sugar, right?" she asked. I nodded. "Homemade chips, two eggs and corned beef OK for you?" she shouted from the kitchen. I got comfortable on the settee and she came in with the food. "Hold the plate a minute," she said and put a small table in front of me. "There you are," she said with a big smile and the food went down great. I asked her what she had and she answered that she had some homemade soup early on. Mandy brought around a pudding that she had made last night. There were currants in it and that's why the name was spotted dick. It came with custard on it and it went down a treat. I lay back. "I will wash up for you," I said. She said OK and disappeared into the bedroom. I got on with the pots as I waited for the kettle to boil on the gas. When the pots were done, I strolled into the room and to my delight, Mandy was in her dressing gown. I sat down. "Will you keep in touch and come back here from time to time?" she asked. "Don't you want to settle down one day?"

"Not at the moment as I was born under a wandering star. I like to meet people like yourself. Some of the jobs I do are not that good, especially in the winter, but I get through it."

"It is so nice to have a friend like you. I know I am old," she said.

"That is not a problem," I said, "as I find you great in the sack."

"You flatter me," Mandy said with a smile. She leaned over and kissed me and that was it. The sex was good and we sat back and got our breath back.

"Are you staying the night?" she asked.

"No," I said, "otherwise I will be going out of here on my hands and knees."

Mandy smiled, "Oh well, I will catch up with you on Friday night then."

"OK," I said, "it's a date.

The next day, the lads gave me some stick over Mandy and the body she had. "Well," I said, "some people have got it." I got on with the job in hand. By Friday, the first tower was ready to be top soiled and the lads and Fred set off home for the weekend. I strolled down to the pub after a shower and a change of clothes. As I walked into the pub, Jane and Mandy were talking with concentration. I think it was me they were discussing and they both smiled as I approached them. Jane said, "It is nice that you two are an item."

"Well," Mandy said, "I would not call it that yet; just good friends."

"When will you be finished at the power station?" Jane asked.

"Well," I said, "one more week as we are not taking the concrete away. The main contractor, McAlpine's, is landscaping it. There are two new towers being built in their place and it will take two years to build. So, there will be work around here for a while yet."

Mandy said, "I have been shopping and have got two pieces of steak for tea."

"OK," I said with a smile. Jane said that she had to go as she had company coming after tea.

"I have a bottle of wine in the fridge," Mandy said.

"Sounds good to me." We drank up and went off to the cottage, holding hands again. Sex was definitely on the cards. Mandy went into the kitchen to put the steak on and came into the room with the bottle of red wine and a smile. "I won't be long," she said as I opened the bottle. The steak and chips went down great. I offered to wash the pots but she refused. The red wine got to work and the clothes came off. We went to the bedroom and the sex was great. We lay there a while to get my strength back and then I got up to wash the pots. Mandy walked in wearing her dressing gown and we sat down and watched the TV until we dropped off to sleep. Mandy was in bed when I woke up. I got into bed and dropped off again. Mandy was up when I woke up again at 8 o'clock. The bacon and eggs and tomatoes went down great. "We could go to Queens Ferry for shopping, if you like. I will drive," Mandy said. I showered to smell better. Mandy had a Ford Escort; it was clean for its age. Mandy was a good driver and she knew where the parking spaces were. I had a nosey around for socks and pants as I was getting short. Mandy wanted to pay but I beat her to it. It was going to be hard enough to leave as it was. We called in at a coffee shop and talked some more about her past, which was interesting as she was more mature than I was. I enjoyed the talk and then we drove back to her cottage. I said that I would go to the pub and she said that she would come too. "Are you hungry?" she asked.

"Not really," I said.

"When are you paid up to for the digs?"

"Until today," I said.

"Well, why don't you move in with me until the end of the job?" she suggested.

"OK, I will," I acquiesced. "I will go and get my car and gear and then we can go to the pub together. So, I walked around to the digs; the landlady was in the kitchen. "I am moving out," I said.

"OK," she said, "you are paid up to date." When I got back to Mandy's, she was more excited than ever. "Is it all right if I ring Jane and tell her?" she asked. I agreed. When she got off the phone, she was even more excited. She said that it was nice to have a man around the house again. *What have I got myself into*, I thought. But what the heck! You only live once.

The spare room was all right by me; that is, if I ever got to sleep in it, as sex was always on Mandy's mind. It was a good thing she had been doctored, at least I hoped. We went down to the pub and she held my hand like a couple. Jane was already there and jumped up to congratulate us, then went to the bar and bought the drinks to celebrate. The Guinness went down great but, in my mind, I was thinking, *What have I got into? Will it be marriage next that she will want? I am not ready for that yet*. After the second drink, it was time to go. "Are you both going out tonight?" Jane asked.

Mandy replied, "Not too sure; we will ring you if we are." We went back to the cottage. "And what would sir like for his tea?" Mandy asked.

"Beans on toast would go down OK."

"Well sir, that's what we shall," she said. It went down well. I washed the pots and the TV was on when I walked back into the room. Mandy cuddled up to me. "This is nice," she said, "and I hope it will last a while. Are you bothered to go out?" she asked.

"Not really," I said.

"Well, that's it. I will put the wine in the fridge to chill." The TV was not very good, so we talked about life. Mandy was a good conversationalist and the night passed by quickly. The wine came out of the fridge and went down with no problem. Sex was on Mandy's mind; you could see it in her eyes, but I had taken on more than I could handle with this one. Once again, the sex was good in bed and my donkey was sore.

In the morning, I woke up and the breakfast smelled good; I needed the energy. I could get used to this but at the moment, she was so demanding. The breakfast went down well. "So, what's on the agenda today?" I asked.

Mandy suggested a long walk and a drink at dinnertime.

"OK," I replied, "that sounds good to me." We washed up and then off we went in the countryside on the edge of the town. The weather was good for this time of the year. We walked for an hour or more. We found a seat beside a wall and sat down for a while, then walked back the way we had come. The pub was open and I was ready for a pint of Guinness to get my strength back. Mandy smiled as I drank it. "You needed that."

I nodded. Jane walked in. "You two had a good night?" she asked.

"OK. We mellowed out with a bottle of red wine."

I got up to buy the drinks for Jane plus for myself. The girls were chattering. I guessed that it was about me. I smiled as I sat back down. "Back to work tomorrow?" Jane asked.

"Yes," I said.

"How long to go?" Jane asked me.

"I'll pass on that one," I said. "What will happen will happen and things change day by day in life, I have found."

"Well," said Jane, "I will have to go after this because I have got company coming. I will catch up with the both of you in the week." Off she went.

"She's a good friend and she likes to know what's going on," Mandy said.

"Well, the Guinness went down well and what's for dinner?" I asked.

"Well, kind sir, what would you like?" she asked.

"Sleep first," I said, "then dinner and tea together."

We walked back home, hand-in-hand and got a few looks from Mandy's friends. We got home and went to bed. It was gone six when I woke up and dinner smelled good. I put Mandy's dressing gown on and went to the kitchen. "The steak won't be long, Billy," Mandy said.

"It smells nice; I hope it's as tasty as you,' I teased her.

"Go away with you!"

"I don't have to go red," I said and laughed. The steak went down a treat. "And what's on offer tonight?"

"There's a club not far away; it's a Working Men's club," she said, "if you would like to go."

"OK," I said, "I will shower and put my smellies on." Mandy offered to drive. "Are you sure?" I asked. "We could call a taxi if you want."

She accepted. I went to get changed. The taxi was on time and Mandy looked a picture. As we entered the club, we got a few stares from people who knew her. We found a table and I got the drinks. One man commented on how Mandy looked and I just smiled and walked away from the bar. "You seem to be well-known in here," I said.

"Yes. My husband and I came in a lot over the years."

"And," I said, "you walk in with a toy boy." Mandy laughed.

"There is bingo on shortly," she said.

"Oh," I said, "do you want to play?"

"We could, if you like."

"OK," I said, "I will get the tickets." I went across the room and got in the queue. After I got them, I sat back down just as the turn was coming on. It was a woman singer. *Not too bad*, I thought. Then it was two games of bingo and we did not win with Mandy waiting for one number. "Unlucky," I said with a smile. The turn came on again and people were getting up to dance, so I asked her and we got up to a smooth dance to looks from people on the floor. Then came the last dance and it went down well. We went back to the house in a taxi and had a big kiss on the doorstep. The drinks had made us both sleepy, which was a good thing for me as I had work in the morning and my body could do with a rest from sex.

The clock went off at six and up I got. Mandy woke up while I was in the bathroom. The tea was ready when I walked in and she was just packing a ham sandwich. I got a big kiss on the doorstep and then I drove to the power station. The lads had just arrived with smiles on their faces. As they got out of the van, Fred told me that it was not the yard for us all; it was Middlesbrough steelworks and that's where we were going for two or three weeks when we finished this job. "Great," I said, "I can meet my parents." Ogden's had started a job at the steelworks at South Bank just outside Middlesbrough and was going to be longer than I thought. I was glad. Fred said that we should be done here in one week plus as the top cover on the concrete was down to the contractor. It was smiles all around and in the pub at night. When I got back for tea, Mandy was not that pleased as she wanted me to stay a lot longer. "I will keep coming back," I said.

"You better," she said as I sat down for tea. It was a favourite of mine—spaghetti Bolognese with cheese on top. Mandy was not in a good mood for the next few days but by Wednesday, she got used to it and started to come around. The job was going well, sex was slowing down in bed and my donkey was not as sore, which was good. The weekend was nearing and I had most of the concrete flattened down and the contractor had started to cover one side of it with soil. Fred asked, "When do you want the low loader for next week as I will put it on for Tuesday." I agreed.

"It will be a change to be up north," I said. "I may see some friends I went to school with."

On Friday, the lads were away early, so I got back to the digs and surprised Mandy. "You are early today," she said.

"Well, I could have caught you in bed with a black man," I laughed. She looked at me and smiled. "Well, I am going to the pub to unwind; are you coming?"

"I could if you say so."

We went into the pub and Jane was there with a friend. The man looked well-to-do and smart. "This is David," Jane said.

I shook hands with him and went to the bar for a gin and tonic and a pint of Guinness. I was ready for it as the wind in the morning had made me dry. "So, what do you do?" I asked David.

"I work at the docks in the office," he said.

"Oh," I said, "I couldn't be inside all day long!"

"Well, it's good on wet days," he said. "Jane said that you drive cranes."

"Yes, I do and I travel with the job. My next job is up north at Middlesbrough. I was born up there and will see my parents again."

David asked where next after that and I passed on that one. "Who knows after that?" I replied. "The world is a big place and I have worked all over this county now and met some good people on my travels."

David said, "I like to stick to my own roots. Well Jane, we have to go. We may see you again before you leave next week."

"OK," I said. "Is that the boyfriend?"

"Well," said Mandy, "he's married with two kids, I heard. I am going to miss you next week. I hope we will keep in touch."

I got up for another pint. "You OK drink wise?"

"Yes," she said. The landlord asked if the job was going all right.

"OK," I said, "we have moved on to the demolition side of it and will leave it to the contactors, McAlpine's, to build the next two towers." I went back to the table and said to Mandy, "The landlord was interested in the job at the power station. So, what's on for the weekend?"

"We could stay in bed all weekend and make love; then I won't miss you so much next week," she said.

I laughed, "The poor old donkey will be sore!"

"So, what shall we do to pass the weekend?" Mandy asked.

"We could go to Chester for one night at a B&B," I suggested.

"That sounds good," Mandy said.

"OK. We will go have tea and pack a bag for overnight and leave in the morning after breakfast." We drank up and went back to the cottage. I said I would check my car over while she made the tea. I looked around at the tyres; they looked OK, so I left it at that. The tea was good—eggs, chips and beans—and a bottle of red wine to wash it down. Then we watched the TV and I dropped off to sleep.

When I woke up, Mandy was in the bedroom packing a case. "Did you enjoy your sleep?"

"It was OK," I said. "I will get a bath, if it's all right with you."

"OK," was the answer. "I will wash your back, if you want me to."

"Sounds good to me."

I went into the bathroom and got the hot tap going. I went back to the bedroom, stripped off and back to the bathroom to turn the taps off and test the water. As I got in, Mandy was at the door with a big smile on her face. "I am going to love this," she said and started to strip off; her body looked well for her age. My back felt great as she massaged me. The donkey was up at full erection. "You are well turned on by all of this," Mandy said.

"You bet," I said.

"You had better get out and I will get in; then it is my turn to be massaged," she said.

I said OK and got out and dried a bit as Mandy got hold of the donkey and washed it. I gave Mandy's back a good gentle rub and the moans sounded great from her. She got out of the bath and we both got dry and into the bedroom. The sex was great. It was 6.30 in the morning when I woke up and it was my turn to put the kettle on. Mandy walked in and wished me good morning. I said that tea was ready and toast was on. "Please don't leave me next week," Mandy entreated me. "If you do, make sure you come back or I will follow you up north."

I smiled, "I will make the breakfast today and you can get ready to rock and roll and go." The breakfast went down well and I did the pots and got myself ready. I went out to the car with my bag to look at the map book for the best way to go to Chester. When she got into the car, we were off. It was an hour's drive in the traffic. The town itself had some history connected to it with old buildings in the high street. We had to find a B&B for the night as time was rolling on and it took longer to get here. We parked the car and walked around the back of the high streets looking for signs for a B&B. We passed a couple in one street but they were full. Then we saw one which looked great outside and had vacancy on it, so I knocked on the door and a well-dressed lady came to the door. We said we wanted a room for just one night.

"OK," she said, "I will show you the only double that I have left." It was in the front of the house on the first floor. "OK with this?" she asked. We both agreed. "How much?" I asked and was told 10 pounds. I paid her then and there and got the keys.

"Well," I said to Mandy, "we will go back and fetch the car." There was a pub next to where the car was parked so we went in. The Guinness looked good on the tables as plenty were drinking it. I ordered one and a gin and tonic to go with it. We found a table to sit and I said to Mandy that I would take the car to the digs and come back. I had a job finding a carpark and I had to park two streets away, then walk back to the pub. Mandy was all smiles to see me. I told her that the car was parked a couple of streets away from the digs. The Guinness went down great and I asked Mandy where she would like to dine.

"Can we nosey around the shops first?" she asked.

"No problem," I said. "We will work up an appetite." We drank up our drinks. The high street was quite packed but then again, it was Saturday. Mandy bought herself a blouse and a jumper. I looked around and bought more socks as the boots wore them out fast. I also bought two T-shirts but before I could get my money out, Mandy paid for them. "It's a going-away present for you," she said.

"So, what would you like for dinner? I thought we would have a good meal out tonight."

"Well," Mandy said, "we could go back to the digs and sample the bed for an hour or two." I agreed and we got to the digs and the bed was not too hard and the sex was good. We had an hour's kip and it was gone seven when we stirred. When we were ready to go out, I asked Mandy what the meal was going to be. "Well," she said, "we will look around and have a drink first." We found a pub on the high street and it was quite busy. I got the drinks and Mandy found a table; the Guinness went down great. "The bed was not too bad," I said. Mandy gave me a smile. A couple sat down at our table and we said good evening to them. I asked Mandy, "So what is it going to be: Indian or Chinese?"

The couple spoke up and said that there was a good Chinese restaurant two shops down which was very good. We thanked them. We went down the street a bit and came to it. There were not many in as it was still early in the evening. We were seated near the window. "Would you like drinks first?" the waiter asked.

"What about a bottle of wine?" I suggested to Mandy.

"Your best red," Mandy said to the waiter. When he returned with the wine, he asked if we were ready to order. He poured the wine out and Mandy tasted it and said that it was OK.

"I will have prawn curry with rice," I said.

Mandy asked for scampi with a salad. The meal went down great and we both finished it off with the wine. It was getting late, so we drank up and walked back to the hotel. I could see the look Mandy gave me as we got to our room—sex was definitely on the cards.

I was up next morning as breakfast was until 10 o'clock. Mandy was in the shower first and came out with a smile on her face. "I have enjoyed my weekend so far."

"The weather does not look good for today," I said. "So, what would you like to do after breakfast?"

"We could go back a different way, Mandy said. So, when I got into the car, I looked at the map to find another route and we set off. It was a country route and it was great to be alive even if the weather was bad. We came to a nice village after an hour and the pub looked old-worldly. It was open and it was after 12 o'clock. "Do you want to try one drink?" I suggested and she agreed. I parked and we both went in. The Landlord was ever so friendly with us even though we were strangers. I could not drink as I was driving so it was a beer shandy for me and I turned and asked Mandy what she would like. She asked for a gin and tonic with ice. We sat near an open fireplace as there was plenty of brass on the wooden beams. We stayed an hour and then it was time to go as the pub was starting to fill up with people. It was another hour's drive back to Queens Ferry and I could do with a pint of Guinness. The pub was open all day, so I dropped Mandy off and put the car to bed at Mandy's home; then we walked back to the pub. There was a Guinness on the table and a big smile to go with it. "Well, here's to us and a good weekend!" as I lifted the glass.

"Thank you," Mandy said. I asked her what she would like for a meal. She suggested, "We are not cooking so it could be a takeaway." There was a menu at the bar and I brought the drinks back plus the menu.

"This is my treat," she said. I picked prawn curry with rice and Mandy picked beef curry plus rice and prawn crackers. The time was 6 o'clock. I decided to use the phone which was at the end of the bar. I asked the barman and he said OK. I came back to the table and told Mandy that it was sorted and the meal was getting delivered to the pub. The meal turned up and we got the drinks down and walked home. Mandy got the food as it was still hot and a bottle of red wine out of the fridge. The meal and wine went down great. The TV went on but we sat down with the same old conservation about when I would come back to see her. I told her that I would keep in touch on a weekly basis. "You know, I will miss you," she said, but I had heard it all before. We kissed and cuddled and went into the bedroom. Sex was on the cards and the poor donkey was sore. I said to myself that the next job I did, I would take a break from sex.

I was up early the next morning as it was going to be my last day on the job and the lads and I were going for a pint at teatime. My sandwich was on the table as Mandy had gotten up before me. "Can I meet you down at the pub tonight?" she asked.

"OK," I said and she gave me a kiss to see me off at the front door. I reached the power station and the plant fitters were there plus the low loader behind. The lads turned up in the van and Fred got out as well. He said, "Well, this is it. We have the next two days to tidy up and then go to the yard. There is another job there."

"OK," I said, "then we better get on with it." I moved the crane to where we could derig the crane and the jib went down. It was to go under the first section of the jib to be strapped up and transported. By dinnertime, it was ready to be loaded onto the low loader and it set off to the yard. I would go back to the digs for my bag and sex. "That's more like it!" Fred said.

I laughed and said, "OK. I will see you in the pub later." I parked the car outside the digs. Mandy was in and pleased to see me. "Have you had dinner yet?" she asked. I said that I had eaten my sandwich as I worked and beans on toast would go down well. I knew what would come after. "Could we have the afters first?" I asked with a smile. She agreed and we went into the bedroom. The sex was great but my penis was very sore. We lay for a while and Mandy was doing all the talking on how we could keep in touch. I just listened as I knew in my own head that I would be moving on as I was not ready to settle down. We got up and got into the shower first, then got dressed. Mandy did the same and I washed the pots. We then walked down to the pub as it was time to meet Fred and the lads. The round was on me and the crack was good. After the next two rounds of Guinness, it was time to say my goodbyes as I was driving to Middlesbrough the next day. We got back indoors and the TV went on. We laid back and I must have gone to sleep as when I woke up, Mandy was in bed. I went to the bedroom and settled down. Then an arm came across me and Mandy kissed me goodnight. The next thing I knew, it was morning. Mandy was up as I could smell breakfast, so I got dressed and packed my bag and went into the kitchen. I got a good morning and a kiss on the cheek. "So, you are not staying?" she said.

"I will be back," I said. "I will ring you tonight when I get there." The breakfast went down great and we kissed again at the front door and she waved me off. I headed towards North Wales on the M62 for a change of scenery and to see my parents again. I hoped my mother and father were OK. I drove along heading for the A1. I pulled into a garage to fill my car with petrol and then set off again north. It was a good four hours drive in traffic. I got to the A19 that headed towards Middlesbrough, then came off at the Tees Bridge turn-off. It was 12 o'clock and I decided to call around at my house first before going to South Bank steelworks. I pulled up in Bell Street at number 21. Mum got a surprise when she opened the door and shouted out to Dad, "Look who is here!"

I went in and got a big cuddle. Mum put the kettle on and I went to the back; Dad was in his chair with a bad back. I told them that there was a job at the steelworks for three weeks. They asked me where I was going to stay and I answered that I did not know yet. "Well," Mum said, "you can stay here as there is a bed in the front room; it is a pull-down and a double bed." I accepted. I drank my tea and Mum asked if I had eaten yet.

"No, not yet," I replied. "I will look after myself. I will go down to the job and show my face and will be back by teatime."

I pulled out of my parents' street and drove to the Tees Bridge, then on to the new port road and down to the centre of Middlesbrough. I went on to Ormsby on to South Bank Road towards South Bank itself. I turned left towards Dorman Long Steelworks. I was met at the gate by security and I told them I worked for Ogden's demolition; they showed me where the offices were. I met the foreman for the job—Andy. I said my name was Billy and I was sent to drive the 22RB crane with a magnet. "That's right," said Andy, "I will book you in for today and I will see you at 7 o'clock in the morning." I agreed and went back to my car in the carpark and drove back to my parents' house. Mum said, "I was just about to make tea. Would you like some? It is eggs, chips and beans."

"That would be great," I said and went into the front room where Dad was sitting and we talked about where I had been. At the end of the conversation, Mum said that tea was ready on the table in the back room so we both went and sat down and ate the meal. It went down great as I was hungry; then I said I would wash the pots for them for a change. After that, I went back to the room to talk to Dad about his problem with his back and what the doctors had told him. They told him that he had a nerve problem. The TV went on and Mum came to watch it with Dad. I went for a walk around my old school at the bottom of the street and looked at the years I had left and where I had been. But the school still looked the same from the outside, so I walked back to my house and sat down to talk to Dad and told him where I had been working for the last few years. Dad said I was very lucky to keep working. "Mind you," he said, "you always had the get up and go."

"I will walk down to the club tonight," I said. "Does Mum like the Mackeson Stout? I will fetch one for her."

"OK," he said.

"Do you want a bottle fetching in as well if you can't make it out?"

"I will have a bottle of Vaux pale ale."

I got washed and changed and walked to the club; I had my old card to get in. The doorman said, "It's been a long time since you were in here."

I said that I had been away working. I went in; the place had not changed over the years and I did not know anybody to talk to at the bar. I bought a pint of beer sat down as the TVs were on for racing and football on another TV. The beer went down well as I had looked around first to see if anybody was drinking Guinness but nobody was, so I left it alone. Then in came one of Dad's pals and he looked at me then came across and asked, "Are you Billy Rennison's son?" I said yes. His name was Bob Fleet and he lived at the bottom of the street. Bob asked if my dad was still in bad health and I said yes. "So where have you been working?" he asked.

"All over the country and I am back up here for a few weeks at the steelworks at South Bank, demolishing the old steel coke ovens .I am going to drive a crane to load the scrap and dig the old bricks out of the furnace."

Bob asked how many of us were at home as he saw Ronnie at the club. I told him that I had not seen him yet. Paul was at his girlfriend's house on Are some Road. I supposed I would meet him later. Ronnie was going out with Margaret on Archibald Street. Well, talk of the devil and Ronnie walked in and came across to the table.

"Hi," he said, "you have become a stranger!"

"Well," I said, "I am here for a few weeks and if the house is too crowded, I will find a B&B somewhere and not put a burden on Mum and Dad. How are you getting along with your girlfriend?"

"Good at the moment," he replied.

"Are you still working at the post office?" I asked. He said yes. "We will have a night out while I am here," I suggested. He agreed and went to the bar and got a pint. Bob had already got me one. When Ronnie came back, Bob got up and said that he would let us catch up with each other. I told Ronnie where I had been working in the country and the people I had met. I asked him, "Will there be a wedding or have you not got that far yet?"

"Well, I got engaged last month and we did not know where you were."

"Well, not to worry," I replied. "I can't win them all. As long as you know what you want out of life, that's the main thing."

"It's time to go," Ronnie said. "I have to get up early in the morning. I will call around at Mum's tomorrow." I went to the bar to get Mum and Dad's drinks and then walked back to Mum's house. My car looked all right parked up and I knocked on the door. Mum came to open it. I went to Dad as he was in the back room watching TV. I asked him if he wanted the beer now and he said yes. I went out to the kitchen for a glass. Mum asked if I wanted some supper and I refused. I talked to Dad as Mum drank her drink. I said that Ronnie had come to the club as I was talking with Bob Fleet. "He was asking about you both and I told him that you were not too good at the moment," I said. "So, we will be having a wedding very soon."

"Sounds like it," Dad said.

Mum said, "I have made up the pull-down bed in the front room."

"OK," I said, "I will be up early in the morning, have a cup of tea and then will be off. Tomorrow, I will find a B&B, so I won't be putting on you." I went to the front room to sleep.

I was up early, put the kettle on and went upstairs. I could hear Mum getting up as I went to the bathroom. Mum was down when I got out and the tea went down great. I gave her a peck on the cheek and I was off. The traffic was not too bad as I went through town and on to South Bank. The shifts at the steelworks started at 7.30 and I had to queue up at the gate to get in. I told the man I worked for Ogden's demolition and he told me where to park. I went to the office; Andy was there. I changed and we both went on the site. There was a 22RB with a jib on which was a magnet. It was to load the scrap onto the skips to back to the works to melt down. Then we both went across to the 38RB with a face shovel for loading fired bricks from the old furnace. "The driver has to go home in the next two days as his wife is having a baby so you can drive it," Andy said. "You will not be too busy loading scrap all day. The 22RB was filled up with dev yesterday." I went across to the 22RB, checked its oil and water and started it up. The Dorman engine sounded well for its age. There were two scraps at the side of the crane, so I started to load them. There was a big heap of scrap cut to three feet in length. At 10 o'clock, I went to the canteen; the breakfast was cheap and went down well. The food was good so if I had a late dinner, I would not need food tonight. We knocked off at 6 o'clock and thought about digs. I was not far from Redcar, which was a seaside town. I had my bag with me so I thought I would nosey around. I drove to Redcar and turned down off the seafront to look for a B&B. The season was on the way and there were not many to go to, but I spotted two in one street. I parked and knocked at the first one but it had only one double left and the price was too high for me, so I walked to the next one and this time, I was in luck. The lady was tall and slim. She showed me a room on the first floor which was a single and it suited me fine. She informed me that be breakfast would at 7.30 but I declined, saying that I would be gone by then. "Do you want a pack-up meal then?" the Landlady asked. I accepted. "These keys are yours. Will you be here for the weekends?"

"Yes."

"You pay every Friday night at 25 per week."

I was OK with that. The bathroom and toilet were next door, so I took a shower and changed as I needed a pint. As I was coming down, the Landlady came out of the kitchen. "Will you be here long?" she asked me.

"Two to three weeks," I said. "Where is the best pub?"

"The one me and my husband use is on the corner of the next road," she said.

I went and found the pub; it was called the Malt Shovel. I went in with a few stares from the regulars. I looked around and nobody was drinking Guinness so when the barmaid asked me, it was a pint of John Smith's beer and it did not taste bad. The barmaid was right chatty and asked if I had just come into town. I said yes. "Working or holiday?" she asked.

"Working," I said. "I am here for a few weeks. Do they still have dances at the Coatham Hotel on Saturdays?"

"Yes," she said. Her name was Helon.

"I may wander down there on Saturday night."

"I might go down there myself for a change," Helon said.

"So, is it a date?" I asked.

"Well, could be," Helon said. "We will know towards the end of the week if nothing else comes up." I asked for another pint and carried on standing at the end of the bar. Helon kept coming across when she could. It was a Monday and it was quiet. She asked where I came from and where I was working and I told her that I went where the work was and enjoyed travelling to meet people like her. I got a big smile from her. The night wore on and it was nearly closing time. I got my last pint as Helon shouted last orders. "I am going your way," she said as the customers started to leave. "I have to lock up as the Landlady and Landlord are out for the night." I drank up while Helon washed the last of the glasses and put them away. She locked up and we walked up the road to where she lived and said goodnight.

I was up the next morning, had a cup of tea and went downstairs. On the table was a packet of food for work. I went off to the steelworks, parked and went across to change. Andy said good morning and he told me if I would go on the 38 face shovel to get the feel of it. We both went across the site to the 38 face shovel. The driver's name was John; he said he had checked it out for oil and water and the dev was ok so into the saddle I went and moved the levers to see which worked what. After fifteen minutes, I was away with it—slow at first, then got used to it. I got a thumbs up from John. After three loads, I was into it and it was soon teatime. I went across to the canteen where the lads asked if everything was OK. Andy said that I could go back on the 22RB and load some more scrap up and tomorrow, I would be on the 38RB. I agreed. The sandwiches were not too bad and then it was back to work loading the scrap. The day went quite quickly; the meals in the canteen were good and cheap and if you went before 2 o'clock, you would not want a meal at night, which was good. At night, I showered and went out for a walk. As Helon was not working until Thursday night, I decided to try a different pub and bring back some

180

memories when I was a lad growing up here. I walked down the seafront and the tide was out, there was a good breeze about and the nights were starting to pull out. I came across the Black Horse pub, which I used to go to and it had groups on Saturday nights. I looked around; there were not many in and I got a few looks as I went to the bar and got a pint of beer. Nobody was drinking Guinness, so it had to be beer. The barman asked me if I was on holiday or work and I said work and was at the steelworks. I drank up and went back to the digs as it was getting late and I had to be up early.

I was up and out with my packed-up meal in hand. The weather was not too good. I was on the 38RB for the rest of the week. As there was no door, the 38RB was not too good so as I slewed around to load the dump truck, I got wet. I was glad when the tea break came and I covered up with a big coat to go to the canteen. Andy asked if everything was OK and I said all was good apart from the weather. The rain had stopped when I got out of the canteen, which was good, and the afternoon went well. With a big dinner inside me, another day at the mill was over with me back at the digs and showered and out. I called at the Malt Shovel and to my surprise, Helon was on and had a big smile on her face when I walked in. "Hi," I said, "I did not expect you in here tonight."

"I did not too. The Landlord had to go unexpectedly so here I am. How is the job going?"

"Great," I said, "it's like another day at the mill as they say in Yorkshire. It will be a pint and one for yourself too."

"Thank you," she said. "And what have you been up the last two nights?"

"Not much; had a walk around, called in at the Black Horse last night and there were not many people there. That's it," I said. "Is Saturday night still on?"

"I will keep you guessing until Friday night," she said. I said OK and left it at that. Then we changed the subject and when she got a minute, we talked about life in general and the beer went down well. She had been married before to a to a man in the Armed Forces but it did not work out. She had no children and in my mind, that was good as I did not want to get into children's problems again. It was soon last orders and the evening was over. Lock-up time came around and I walked her home to her flat. I got a peck on the cheek and we said goodnight to each other, then I walked to the digs and up to bed, hoping that the weather would be better tomorrow.

I was up early, dressed and looked out the window and it was fine at the moment. I went down and picked up my meal as I went out. It was Thursday and nearly a week on the job. I was looking forward to Friday night for my answer from Helon about Saturday night. If there was no work on Saturday, I would go down to Mum's place in Middlesbrough and take her shopping. I had to go back on the 22RB for the morning as the scrap was building up. I asked Andy what the crack was for the weekend and he said that he would let me know tonight. The breakfast went down well as the sandwiches were OK but I needed a change, so I gave them away. In the afternoon, Andy came across to the 38RB as I was parking and asked if I would work on Saturday morning. I said OK but not really in my mind as I could be in bed with Helon. Wishful thinking! It was the same as the other nights: digs, shower and out but go a different way so I walked towards the horseracing track and back to the seafront and the Malt Shovel. The Landlord was serving, "Hi," he said, "is it a pint?"

"That's it," I said.

"Does the job work weekends?" the Landlord asked.

"I'm not too sure yet; I will find out tomorrow."

"If it is, will you stay up here for the weekend?" he asked.

"Yes or call on my parents in Middlesbrough to see if they are all right." The Landlord called last orders and asked if I wanted another pint but I declined and drank up and said goodnight. I went back to the digs.

When I got back to work in the morning, Andy told me to move the 38RB down to the next brick kiln and start digging and loading up with fire bricks. It was hard to move the 38RB at first but I managed in the end and got started just before teatime. Again, I gave the sandwiches away as the breakfast went down great and I would have a late dinner if the dump driver agreed. The weather was not too bad but cold and windy. The day went good and the dinner went down well. Andy came across and told me that Saturday was off. "OK," I said with a smile.

"Have you scored with someone up here?" he asked.

"I may have; I'm not too sure yet," I said. "I will let you know on Monday." We finished early on Friday and I went to get changed. I had a big smile on my face as I drove back to Redcar and went to the digs. I saw the landlady and told her that there was no work tomorrow. She said that breakfast would be from 8 o'clock to 10 o'clock. "OK," I said, "I will go to the bank and get you paid. Where is the bank?" She told me and I went upstairs to shower. I then went out to find a bank, which was on the high street. I was a bit dry with finishing early and there was a pub in the high street. I did not enjoy the beer and left half of it. I walked down and spotted the bank and got the money out for the weekend. I walked back to the digs to square up with the landlady. Then I went off to the Malt Shovel, hoping that Helon was on for this date. To my surprise, she was there. "Hi," she said, "and what is your tipple this evening, kind sir?"

"You are in a good mood," I said. "A pint of your best bitter." I moved down to the end of the bar. "Well, what's the crack?" I said.

"What do you mean?" asked Helon. "I have not heard that before."

"It means, what are you doing tomorrow?" I said. "Are you working tomorrow night?"

"No," she said, "I can have the night off so it's a date."

"Well, it's a meal first, somewhere of your choice, whatever you like: Chinese or Indian. I will be going to my parents' tomorrow and will take my mum shopping as they don't have a lot of money. You can come if you want. That is, if you don't have anything else on."

She said that she would think about that and she had to serve so I stood on my own for a while as it got busy at the bar. We talked again in between serving. Then it was last orders; I had half a beer left and I did not want any more. I waited until Helon was ready to go, then I walked down with her to her flat. We got to the flat and she turned around to face me and asked if I wanted to come in for coffee. I agreed and we went in. The flat was on the first floor and Helon went into the kitchen to put the kettle on but that was a waste of time. She came into the room and we kissed for the first time and started to undress each other. The bedroom was to the left and the clothes were all over the floor. I could tell that she had not had sex for a long time for she was really going for it. My penis was really sore in the morning. I got up, put the kettle on and stood in the kitchen with my coffee. In walked Helon with a smile. I got a peck on the cheek. "That was great; you really know how to satisfy a woman," she said.

"So, what's on for today?" I asked her. "I am going down to Middlesbrough to take my mum shopping if she will go. I will go back to the digs to get a shower and breakfast and pick you up at 10 o'clock, if you are coming." She agreed with a smile.

I got showered, dressed and then went downstairs. The Landlady walked into the room. "Morning. You are back then."

"Yes," I said, "I met a friend last night and stayed there."

"Tea or coffee?" she asked. "Would you like a full breakfast?"

"Yes and coffee please." It went down well.

"Will you be back for tea?" she asked.

"No," I said, "I will eat out." I went back to Helon's flat and she was ready. We set off to Middlesbrough and the weather was not too bad—a bit of fog off the sea mixed with black smoke from the steelworks. The traffic was busy as we went through town and up the new port road towards the Tees Bridge. Mum and Dad were up as the time was 10.30. We both got out of the car and went to the door. As I knocked, my Aunt Rosy came out from next door. "Hi," she said, "long time no see." Then she shouted back into the house, "Look who is here!" My uncle Charlie came out to say hello and then my mum was at the door. I introduced Helon and we went into the house. I said to my mum, "Do you want to go shopping downtown?" She agreed with a smile on her face. "I will get ready; do you want a cuppa?" I looked at Helon and we both declined. I went outside in the garden with Dad and he did not look very good at all with his chest problems. Dad let Ronnie and Paul's pigeons out as they would be coming around shortly to feed them. I went back in the house and Mum was ready. All three of us got in the car. Mum said there was a new carpark near the town hall and a new shopping centre there. I drove down to the town hall. The carpark entrance was on the right and I found a space. We walked slowly around as Mum wanted to go in a few shops. I told Mum that I was paying for the shopping and not to worry about money. After an hour, it was coffee time, so we found a café. It was tea for Mum and coffee for me and Helon. Helon had bought a few things for herself but would not let me pay. The coffee went down well and we went around a few more shops. Mum said she had everything she needed, which was four bags. I had to carry them but it was money well spent as I did not see her very often. We got back to the car and I drove back the way we came and offloaded the bags. Dad thought we had bought the entire store. I told them that I would call before I left Middlesbrough to go somewhere else for a job and I did not know where that would be. We both said our goodbyes and drove back towards Redcar. "Is it dinner out?" I asked Helon in the car.

"You don't mess about, do you?" she said.

"Life's too short for all that," I said.

"Fancy a drink in a pub on the way?" she suggested.

"That's a good idea. We will park the car first and then walk to a pub of your choice."

"OK," she said and that's what we did. It was the pub she worked at—the Malt Shovel. The Landlady was serving and asked what she could get us. "A gin and tonic and a pint," said Helon. The Landlady said that they were on the house I thanked her.

"What did you both get up to today?" she asked us.

Helon said, "We went shopping in Middlesbrough with Billy's mother."

"So, is it the Coatham dance tonight?" the Landlady asked.

"Could be," said Helon, "but a meal first. Where would you recommend?"

"Well," the landlady said, "there's a good Chinese restaurant on the main street. It's just opened up; try that."

"OK, we will," we said and sat down in the corner. We talked and I got the same old story from Helon as I always got where was the next job and would I keep in touch. "Well," I said, "at this moment in time, I can't tell you that as I don't know myself. I will let you know before I leave. As I told you, I just follow the work and money around and I love meeting people like yourself."

"Well," she said, "I have feelings for you."

"Likewise," I said. "Let's take it one step at a time." We drank up and said goodbye to the landlady, Ann. We walked down towards main street to the restaurant. We had to wait to be seated. The Chinese man came across and asked, "A table for two?" I said yes and then we were seated. He asked us about drinks and I looked at Helon. Yes was the answer. I ordered a gin and tonic and a beer. The menus were on the table and I asked Helon, "What's it going to be?" We decided on a chicken chow mein and rice and a prawn curry and rice. The waiter came with the drinks and we ordered. We raised the glasses and said *cheers*. "Where do you want to go tomorrow?" I asked. "Or have you got other plans?"

"I have my washing to do but it can wait until Monday," Helon replied. "Have you got any washing to do?"

"I will have next week. I try to get the landlady wherever I am to wash it and pay her."

"If you have any, bring it around," Helon said. The meal turned up and we stuck in and it went down great. "I am full now," I said. "Do you want a pudding?"

"No thanks," was the answer. "I am going to look at a job I have been offered. It is in an office as a receptionist four days a week."

"Well, I hope you get it."

"I can still do bar work at night," she added. I called the waiter over for the bill and Helon offered to pay half.

"No way; it's my treat." We drank up, I paid and we walked back towards the seafront and the old bandstand was still there. We sat down for a moment and I was reminded of my memories of club trips to Redcar with the Working Men's club. Mum used to sit here as my brothers and sisters and myself would play on the sand and go and spend our ten shillings that we each got. "Well," I said, "let's talk about your life so far. Where were you born?"

"Around here," she replied.

I said, "I tell you what; let's go to the Coatham Hotel and you can tell me all about yourself."

She agreed and we walked down the seafront as it was a bit early to go into the dance hall. We went into the bar lounge and I got the drinks but Helon beat me at paying. We found a table and sat down and she told me about herself and her marriage to the bloke in the Armed Forces and how he wanted to run before they could walk regarding children and all that. She added, "With his drinking and going out with the lads, I could see that I was going to get lumbered with children, so it was a no-no on that point. It was all right for the first year; then I could see it was going tits up. I heard he was seeing another woman on the side, so I moved back to my mother's here in Redcar, got a flat of my own with the help of my mum and dad and that's it for now."

"OK," I said. We drank up as we had to go outside to get to the dance hall and line up as there was a queue. The door did not open until 9 o'clock. I looked around to see if I knew anybody but no luck. Helon spotted a friend to talk to for ten minutes and then we paid and went in. We looked around for a table and Helon found one in the far corner of the stage and we sat down. The bar was full at the moment. "The place has changed since I was here last; the stage was in a different place," I remarked. The bar had gone a bit slow, so I asked Helon if it was still gin and tonic and she agreed. The band started up and the group did not sound too bad. I got the drinks and went back to the table. We talked some more and had a few dances, which Helon enjoyed. The evening wore on and it was time to go as Helon was getting sleepy. We went out in the fresh air and walked home to her flat. We went in and the clothes came off. The sex was great and I did not need no rocking to sleep. I woke up at my normal time and went to the toilet. I went into the kitchen, put the kettle on and sat down to read an old newspaper that was on the table. I heard the noise of Helon getting up and going to the toilet. She came into the kitchen and the kettle had just boiled. "Tea?" I asked.

"Yes, thank you," she said. Her body looked well behind the dressing gown and the donkey started to rise again. She leaned over the table and we kissed and it was back to bed again without the tea. The donkey was sore again after that and I got up and dressed. Helon was full of it and I said to myself, *You have met your match with this one.* I had a cuppa and finished the paper. Helon walked back in and said, "You are some stud, aren't you? Do you want some breakfast or are you going around to the digs as it's 10 o'clock?"

"I have missed that now; I will have some toast for a change."

"I am going for a shower first; do you want one?" she asked. I said yes and got the toast down. Then it was my turn and I got dressed again. The weather outside was a bit overcast but dry and we walked around to the car and set off down the coast to Saltburn. We pulled into a layby by the sea. I wound the window down and let the breeze liven me up and it felt good. Helon did the same and we sat there and enjoyed it. After half an hour, we moved on down the coast. "Are you getting hungry yet?" I said to Helon.

"I am getting a bit peckish," she replied.

"OK," I said, "we will pull in somewhere for a bit of lunch." We pulled into Loftus and there was a pub called the Marine. We parked and went in. The time was around 2 o'clock. "What would you like to drink?" I asked Helon.

"Just a coke as it's too early for gin and tonics."

"I will have a beer shandy," I said. "The ploughman's lunch looks tasty; we could share one."

We ordered it and sat near the window. There were a lot of people eating so the pub must be popular. The lunch came in no time at all and beween us, it went down well. "Where next?" Helon asked.

"Whitby for tea."

"Oh, that's good. I have not been there for years," Helon said. We drank up and set off again and went through Staithes, which was a steep hill. It was a nice drive along the coast to Whitby. It was a job to park but we got one in the end and went shopping. I called at the bank for some beer money as I needed petrol on the way back. There were a lot of people about and we walked up the steps to the church. At the top, you knew you had done it and we had to sit down on the grass and look out at the sea. The weather was a bit overcast but dry and not too cold. We sat for a while. Helon asked, "What's the next thing in life that you are going to do?"

"Pass," was my answer. "Whatever comes along and wherever; I just don't know. There are a lot of big jobs out there at the moment and money to be made; I just follow the highest bidder."

"I admire you for what you do," Helon said.

"Thanks. I just get on with it. That's life—live it to the fullest." I added, "Do you want to walk around the harbour for shopping as we go?" So down the steps we went and back through the side streets to the bridge. We turned right along the promenade to the harbour and lighthouse and we sat down on a seat to take in the scenery. "Is it fish and chips for tea?" I suggested. "It is 6 o'clock

186

and the Mermaid is the best as it was on TV. We may have to queue to get in; it is that good."

"Well," she said, "you know some stuff."

"You learn that as you move around." We walked down the road but the queue was not too big and we did not need to stand too long before we got in. The menu was on the table and we both looked at them. "The big fish takes some eating; I will have a small," said Helon.

"That makes the two of us," I said. Tea or coffee?"

She chose tea and when the waitress came, we ordered and it was not too long before a pot of tea for two, and then fish and chips, came. It went down great and we were both full as a butcher's dog. "We will have to walk it down before we leave," I suggested.

"You are right on that," she agreed. We got the bill and paid on the way out. We walked back along the coast towards the car and found a seat to sit on for half an hour to digest the meal. We got back to the car and it was nearly dark. We set off along the coast. It was 9 o'clock when we got back. I parked the car at the digs and Helon went home to freshen up. I washed my face and we walked to the pub for the last orders. The Landlady was behind the bar and smiled when she saw Helon and I walk in. "Did you two have a great weekend?" she asked Helon.

"Great," was her answer. I got the drinks and we stood at the end of the bar. The landlord was out on a darts night. As it was work tomorrow, two pints were all I could have. Helon and the Landlady talked about the bar shifts Helon had to do this coming week as she was going for the job during the week. The day came to a close and it was time to leave the pub. We walked back to Helon's flat. We kissed at the door. Because of work in the morning, there was no sex tonight and I went back to the digs. There was nobody up, so it was straight into bed.

The next morning, I was up, dressed and down. The sandwiches were on the table. The weather was good for now; it had rained during the night. The road was busy as people were going to work. I got into the queue at the gate and it was 7 o'clock when I got parked. I went to change and met Andy in the locker room, who told me what to drive today—the 38RB until dinnertime. "If it's all right with you, then you can drive the 22RB and load the scrap."

"OK by me," I said. During break, I went to the canteen. The breakfast smelled great, so the sandwiches were going to be spare again. The breakfast went down well so it had to be a late dinner. At the end of the day, Andy asked, "How did you get on during the weekend; was it boring?"

"No," I said, "I took my mum shopping on Saturday and a barmaid at night plus yesterday."

"So, all in all, a good weekend," Andy said. "Well, tomorrow, do the same as today and I think for the rest of the week." I changed, went back to the digs, the Landlady was in the front room and asked me if everything was OK. I said OK and went up. I took a shower and went for a walk down the seafront. It was a dry night with a bit of a sea breeze. I walked to the end of the promenade, then turned up a street where there was a pub that I had noticed. It was called the White Swan. As it was only Monday, it was quiet. There were a few people in and as usual, I got looks from the locals. I went to the bar; the barmaid looked tasty: late 40s, big smile, nice tits in the right place and not too large. I ordered a pint and the barmaid said, "On holiday, are you?"

"No," I said, "working up here at the steelworks for a few weeks." The beer went down great; it was a good pint. I told myself that she was getting too friendly from the tone of her voice and I could not handle two in one week, so I drank up and bid her goodnight. I walked back to the Malt Shovel. Helon was on and I got a big smile. "So how was your day?" she asked.

"Good," I said. "How did you get on with the new job?"

"OK," she said, "it will give me some extra money to live on."

"Great," I said. "I had gone for a walk down the seafront and called at a pub called the White Swan. The beer was good but I thought the barmaid was very friendly."

Helon asked if Sally had been behind the bar.

"There was a plump-ish lady behind the bar," I said.

"That is Sally," Helon said. "I went to school with her and she has two children. The last time I had talked with her, the marriage was not going good." She added, "The new job is great. How is your job going?"

"OK," I answered. "We are getting there; a couple of weeks more. How many nights are you working this week?"

"Three," she said.

"So, we could dine out one Friday; is that OK?" I suggested.

"I will find out in a minute," she said and went to ask the landlady. When she came back, she said that it was OK.

"So, it's a date then," I confirmed. "I will call at my mum's tomorrow after work." The night ended and I walked Helon back to her flat. "I am not coming in as I have work tomorrow and my donkey is still sore from the weekend," I said. Helon just laughed so it was a kiss on the doorstep and I said goodnight and went to the digs. I was up early on Tuesday, went downstairs, picked up my sandwiches and went out. The weather was good and the traffic was busy. There was a long queue at the gate at the steelworks but I was early so it did not matter. The day was busy and the meals were good. I had a late dinner, so I did not need any food later on. When I finished, I set off for Middlesbrough. I parked outside Mum's house; my uncle Charlie came out. He had got himself a three-wheeled car and told me he could drive it on a motorbike licence. It was two years old and was a Reliant Robin. My aunt Rosy also came out as they were going shopping. I knocked on the door and Mum came. She was surprised. "You are still up this way?" I said yes and went in. Paul was in the garden with Dad and the pigeons were out. Mum came to tell me that my cup of tea was on the table and asked Dad if he wanted one. He accepted and we went in. I asked how he was and he said not too bad this week and hoped to go back to work tomorrow as he had been to the doctor's to get signed off. We sat and talked about Uncle Charlie's car. I went into the kitchen, took out 40 pounds and put it in Mum's hand. She did not know what to say but I put my finger to my lips and went *ssssh*. I said my goodbyes to them both and drove back to Redcar, parked and went to the bank for some more money. Then I called at the Malt Shovel for the last pint. The Landlord was on and asked how things were going.

"OK," I said, "it's a shame the steelworks are in a bad way with the price of steel and the jobs that had to go in the winter. It is bad around here that most pubs only open from Friday night to Sunday unless they are managers who are well-off." The night came to a close and I went back to the digs. Next morning was the same old crack: sandwiches, drive to steelworks, change and get on with the job in hand. "You could be on both machines until the end of the job as Tom's wife has got problems," Andy said.

"OK," I said.

"And how are you getting on with your lady friend?" he asked.

"Good so far."

"So is there marriage on the horizon?" Andy teased.

"I don't think so as I have already told her that I was born free and want my freedom for a long while." Andy smiled and said, "I think the 22RB will be here next as you have two more kilos of bricks to dig out." The day was soon over and I was back at the digs for a shower and went to the pub as Helon was on tonight and the donkey was feeling horny. I stood at the bar. "I am not working tomorrow," Helon said, "so if there is any washing you want me to do, then drop it off in the morning."

"I will get it tonight," I said. The beer went down well but I dragged it out as sex was in the future so it would be two pints only. Helon talked about what meal she would like to eat but she had an influx of people to serve who had just come in. It was last orders at the bar, so I drank up and went to the digs for the washing and then met Helon as she came from the pub. We went around to her flat, the coffee pot went on but before coffee could be made, the clothes came off and sex as always was good. I put the alarm on for 5 o'clock and then we kissed and went to sleep. Before I knew it, the clock went off. I got up and did not disturb her and let myself out. I went around to the digs to change and wash the donkey. I picked up my sandwiches, then went to work. Andy was in the changing room. "You looked knackered," he said.

"Well," I said, "midweek sex does not go down well." He laughed. As the day wore on, I was back to my old self again. I thought I would have an early night, but Helon had other ideas. When I called around for the washing, she asked if I was hungry. I said I was a bit. "Well, it's egg and chips for tea. One or two eggs?"

"One please, as I had a late dinner on the job." It went down good and the wine came out of the fridge. We sat and talked on the settee but not for long as we were at it like rabbits. I got back to the digs at around midnight and crashed out on the bed. Next morning, I went for a shower as I stank of sex. The Landlady was up when I got downstairs. "Good morning," she said. "Are you working on the weekend?"

"I am not sure," I replied. "I will let you know tonight when I pay you." I went off to work. I met Andy in the changing room. He said that we would be knocking off at 1 o'clock today as the lads want a long weekend. I was happy about that as I would catch up on my sleep this afternoon. I went back to the digs, parked, went to the bank, got money for the week plus digs money, paid the landlady and told her that I was not working this weekend so she would not need to make sandwiches. I called around at Helon's to see what the crack was. "Are we still going out for a meal tonight?" I asked her when she came to the door.

"Yes," she replied. "You are early today."

"The job finished at 1 o'clock today as the lads are on a long weekend."

"I'll put the kettle on if you want a drink," she offered. "I am just going to have a shower first."

"OK," I said and went into the kitchen. Helon came in with her dressing gown on and the donkey rose to the occasion, so the kettle never did get boiled. I did not know if I had any sperm left in me as we lay on the bed to get our breath back. Then we got a shower together, which was thrilling on its own. We got ready as it was teatime by then. "So where is it going to be for a meal?" I asked her as we left the flat. Helon said that the girl she had met at work had suggested a good Indian restaurant near the station. "OK," I said, "we will go there." We walked there and Helen held my hand like a couple. I thought to myself at that time, *I am getting too much involved.* We reached the restaurant and went in. There were not too many people, so we were seated immediately. The waiter brought the menus and I asked Helon if she wanted a bottle of wine with the meal. "OK," she said and looked at the wine menu. "Do you like red wine?" she asked.

"OK with me," I replied and that is what we ordered. I decided to order a prawn curry and rice plus naan breads and Helon said she would have beef curry with rice. "We can share the naan breads," I suggested. The wine came and it was good. "Cheers!" she said as she tasted it.

"What's your battle plan for tomorrow?" I asked. "And don't say sex as my donkey is sore!"

"You love it as much as I do," she said with a smile. It was a good thing nobody was sitting too close to listen to our conversation.

"Well," I said, "I don't think my mum wants any shopping this weekend so what would you like to do?"

"Well, we can just mellow out." The wine went well after the meal and I got the bill and paid. "Let's take a walk to the White Swan and see if my friend is on," Helon suggested.

We got there and the girls were surprised to see one another. "What can I get you both?" she asked.

"A gin and tonic for me and a pint of bitter for Billy," Helon said.

"So that's your name, is it? You were in the other night," Sally said.

"He told me," Helon said. It was quiet in the pub at the moment, so the girls got together at the end of the bar. It soon got busy as it was darts night; then we had to move on as people were coming in. We said goodbye to Sally. We went for a stroll down the seafront; there were a few people about as children were on holiday and the amusements were full. A good breeze was blowing off the sea. We walked along the seafront until we came to the Coatham Hotel. As it was only Friday, there was no dancing on, so we went into the lounge bar. I went to the bar—a gin and tonic for Helon and a beer for me. We sat down and talked some more but it was the same old thing: Helon wanted me to settle down but I was not ready for it.

"So, what's the crack for tomorrow?" I asked her.

"Well," she said, "I have to go to work on the new job from 10 o'clock to 2 o'clock to help with the files. Then I am at the pub from 5 o'clock until late. What will you do tomorrow?"

"I will go for a ride somewhere and catch up with school friends, if I can," I replied. The last order had gone so that was it and I did not want any more drinks. It was the end of a lovely evening and we walked home to Helon's flat. I could see in her eyes that sex was on her mind, so the clothes came off and we got into bed. Helon knew how to get her man going and the sex was great. Before I knew it, it was morning. I turned over but Helon was gone. I got up and she was in the kitchen. She heard me coming and asked, "Tea or coffee?"

"Coffee please," I said. "You are up early."

"There's a lot on my mind with the new job."

I thought, *Better to leave it at that.* "Can I have a shower here?" I asked. She said yes, so I went and had one.

"Do you want a cooked breakfast?" she asked.

"Not today," I said. There was cereal so we had porridge and it went down well for a change. I went out to the paper shop. It looked good for a ride out. I got back to her flat and read the paper with another coffee until Helon was ready to go. Then I walked back to my digs, went upstairs and got my car keys. The Landlady was in the front room. "Breakfast, Billy?" she asked.

"No thanks," I said and went out to the car. It was 9.30 by this time. I drove to Middlesbrough, then onto the Tees Bridge and over. I parked in a layby, got out and went down the side of the River Tees, where we used to play and swim in the river when nicking school. I sat down on a big rock and reminisced for half an hour about the good times. I got back to the car and drove further on to Billingham, where we used to fish as kids. I went on the A19 south and pulled off at Crawthorne, where I used to work on a farm before and after I left school. The pub where I had lived was still there. I parked in the drive of the pub; the blacksmith was still across the road. The blacksmith's name was Ernie Holsop and he was good to get on with. He knew his stuff—horses plus making things. I went to the back of the pub to see if the farmer and his wife were still there. They were also the landlord and landlady of the pub. When the man came out, it was the son-in-law and he told me that they had retired to Potto village in the North Yorkshire moors and he and the farmer's daughter had taken it over. The daughter's name was Audrey and she came out to meet me. I moved on down the village in the car. The post office was still there. I turned

191

left towards Hutton Rugby as an old mate I knocked around with lived at the Mill farm but when I asked a man at the side of the road, he told me that the family had moved on. So, I carried on to Stokesley I parked in the high street as the pubs were open at this time and I was not in a rush to get back. The Black Horse looked good and a pint of shandy would go down well. There were quite a few people as it was Saturday dinner. I drank up and moved on to Greasbrough, where I would go with the lads on a lads' night out. I drove down the main street and turned around to Sandsons Haugh yard as I knew some of the drivers but there was nobody about, so I set off back to Redcar as it was getting near teatime. As I went back, you could see Captain Cook's monument on the left on top of the Yorkshire Moors and to my right was the ICI Chemical Works, where my uncle Charlie worked. I then went down Broughton Bank and British Steelworks, where I was working at the moment. I turned right and back on the long lands to Redcar, then went to the garage to get filled up with petrol before parking the car outside the digs again. I was feeling a bit peckish, so I walked down the seafront; the smell of fish caught my nose so I went in one of the inns and sat down. The girl came over to me and I ordered fish and chips plus two rounds of bread and butter and a pot of tea to swill it down. When it came, it went down good and I was full as a butcher's dog. The time was 5.30; Helon would be in the pub by now so I walked there. I reached the Malt Shovel and went in; Helon was there talking to the landlady. I got a smile from both of them. "Have you had a good day?" Helon asked.

"Brilliant," I said and told them where I had driven to and dined in the chip shop. "Well," I said, "how's the new job going?"

"Good," Helon said, "I am getting used to it now."

"Well," said the Landlady, "I will leave you two to talk as I have the tea to get ready." She went and I asked Helon what was her name. "Ann," she said, "and John; they are all right to work for."

"Are we dancing tonight?" I asked.

"I am having too many late nights," she said with a smile. Customers started to come in, so I stood at the end of the bar while Helon served them. I said to myself that the donkey would have to stay in the stable tonight and I would have an early night. I had a couple more pints and we talked when she could. The night came to an end and I waited until Helon was ready to leave and we walked to her flat. We kissed on the doorstep, said goodnight and I went back to the digs.

I got up early as it was Sunday and walked to the paper shop and back. The weather was not too good. I sat in the breakfast room and read the paper. The Landlady came into the room after half an hour and asked if I wanted breakfast this morning. I said I would love one and in came the full works on a plate and it took some eating. I thought to myself that it was time to jib out and move on from my girlfriend as the job would be coming to an end. I sat back in the chair in the room and debated what to do: call around or give it a miss today. As Helon was working the Sunday lunch, it gave me more time to move around and I went to Middlesbrough to see Mum and Dad and call at the club. Dad was a bit better, so I took him with me and my uncle Charlie came as well. Ronnie was there too so it was two pints of shandy and a good day out. We talked about the past. I could have stayed the night but I would have to get up early to go to work. Mum had made me an extra dinner and it went down great. Dad went into the front room for his afternoon sleep, so I said goodbye to Mum and set off back to Redcar. I reached the digs and lay on the bed. I must have dropped off as it was gone 8 o'clock when I woke up. I showered and went downstairs. I walked to the pub; Helon was in with friends and looked across at me and smiled. I thought best not to get involved so I walked back out and went to the White Swan where Sally was on. She said, "Hi Billy. Are you by yourself?"

I said, "Helon has got company so I came up here for a change."

"Is it a pint you want?" she asked.

"Yes please," I replied. "I think I am getting too close to Helon and I am not ready to settle down as I enjoy travelling. I will be moving on shortly."

"Do you know where?" she asked.

"Not at the moment. I just follow the work around. Helon said that you have children?"

"Yes, two. But they are at my mother's at the moment as it's school holidays. It's quiet at the moment."

I asked, "Do you want a drink as I hate drinking on my own?"

"I will take one for later," she said.

"Do you have a boyfriend?" I asked.

"No and at the moment, I do not need one as I have too many problems to cope with."

"OK," I said. I heard a voice behind me and Sally said hi to Helon as she had just come into the pub. "I had an idea that you would be up here," she said. "My friends have just gone."

"I am sorry but I do not like to get to involved in family matters and I think it's rude just to walk into someone's company," I explained. I asked her if she wanted a drink and she accepted. I could see from the look on her face that she was not pleased with me but I can't win them all! Helon started to come around when the large gin and tonic got to work. She talked with Sally and I just stood by and let them rattle on. I got the drinks before last orders and Helon was going for it with the doubles. I heard her say to Sally that she was not working tomorrow. However, I was so when we left the pub and walked back to her flat, I gave her a goodnight kiss, but Helon had other things on her mind. No sooner did we get in the door than the clothes came off and the sex was good.

In the morning, I was up before 5 o'clock, put the kettle on, dressed, had tea, went to the digs, changed, picked up the sandwiches and then drove to work. I parked, went to change and met Andy coming out of the changing room. He said, "I have heard that Tom is coming back next week and you will be finished with the kilns this week so there will be no need for the 38RB. It will be one driver only."

"OK with that," I said.

"I will keep you informed as the week goes on," Andy said.

"OK," I said. "Is there any more work on the grapevine for Ogden's?"

"I will find out today," Andy said. I said to myself, *It's time to move on.* Helon would not be pleased. It was a long day as I did not get much sleep and the donkey was sore. The saddle of the crane was not the best of seats to sit on at the best of times. I was glad when the shift was over. I would have to ring around and buy the construction news at the paper shop and see what's about in case Ogden's are quiet. I got back to the digs, paid the Landlady for a week and told her it could be my last week. I would let her know on Thursday. I went to the White Swan to have a couple of pints before bed and an early night. Sally was on. "Hi," she said, "Helon was really putting the drink away last night."

"Yes," I said. "Can a man get raped by a woman?" I asked with a smile on my face. Sally just laughed. "I have heard that this could be my last week and I will be finished on Friday. I will have to break it gently to Helon." I got my second pint and got one for Sally; then it was bedtime.

"You could come around my house for tea tomorrow, if you like," Sally offered.

"I don't think Helon would like that," I remarked.

"Live dangerously!" Sally said.

"OK," I said, "you are on." She gave me her address and number. "What time should I come? I will bring a bottle of wine. White or red?" Red was the answer and I drank up and said goodnight as it was gone 8 o'clock. I showered and went to bed. I was up early and went to the paper shop and ordered a construction newspaper. "It will be in on Friday," the man said. I read half the local paper before 7 o'clock and then drove to work. The lads were in the changing room and said, "You may be leaving us on Friday."

I said, "That's the name of the game: last in, first out. Something always comes along; I am never stuck." I went to the canteen and had breakfast. At dinner time, I had only a cup of tea as I was to go for dinner at Sally's at night. The shift got over, so it was back to the digs, parked, showered, called at the shop for a bottle of wine and went to the address Sally had given me. I rang the bell and she came to the door. She looked good and the donkey twitched in my pants. The table was set. I gave Sally the wine to chill. The meal was my favourite: Spaghetti Bolognese. When she served it, it went down great. I helped her wash the pots and we sat down and she told me about her ex and the children and how old they were. The wine got to work on Sally and we kissed on the sofa. Donkey rose to the occasion and the sex was out of this world as Sally had not had sex for four years and oh boy was she up for it. I had the marks on my back to prove it. I just hoped I would not have to have sex with Helon as a going-away present. I got dressed and told Sally that I was going back to the digs as it was 10.30 and I had to get up early in the morning. "OK. Can we meet up for Friday night?" she asked.

"I will call at the pub and let you know as I am not too sure what's happening on the job." We kissed and I left.

I showered in the morning. I reached work and got the verdict from Andy that it was quiet at Ogden's so I had to go job-hunting again. It was another bad day as the girls had drained me. I got myself a bottle of energy drink to liven myself up from the canteen at breaktime and another at dinnertime. Andy came to the machine during the afternoon. He had a few telephone numbers for me to call for a job and I thanked him. "You look knackered," he said.

"It's what you call burning the candle at both ends," I said.

He laughed, "Well, I hope you find a job."

"I have not failed yet," I remarked. It was Thursday night and I got in early after a couple of phone calls. I got the construction newspaper and sat in the TV lounge to read it. There were a few jobs going in the south and one for Malta with Wimpy's for six to ten weeks for a navy driver plus plant operator. I decided to ring that one tomorrow during breaktime as there was a phone in the canteen. I rang at breaktime; I got through to the plant manager and I told him that I was single with no ties. He sounded interested and asked where I was at the moment. I told him the job was at an end with no more work at the moment. "Can you come down to the yard on Monday?" he asked. I agreed and he gave me the address. I was pleased when I put the phone down. *I can only try*, I said to myself as I went to the machine. I cleaned the last of the bricks out and parked the 38RB. The lads came across as I was leaving; it was their long weekend. I said goodbye and I got my gear together. Andy came over to say goodbye and I told him about the job in Malta. I said that I had to go for an interview on Monday. I said my goodbyes and left and drove back to the digs in Redcar. I went to the bank to get the money to pay the Landlady the rent. I would leave on Sunday morning and not get caught in the traffic to London. I looked at the map in the car to refresh my memory on where I was going to go. I got the address book out of the drop-down in the car and looked at where I could stay for a couple of nights if need be. There was a B&B outside Victoria station. *I will give them a ring*, I thought, and looked for another address if I could get somewhere near where I could use the tube train. I left the car parked and walked to the telephone box near the White Swan. I called for a pint at the same time. I rang the B&B and was lucky to get a single room from Sunday night. I was pleased with myself and went into the pub. I got a big smile from Sally and I told her what I was up to and where I might be going. The pint went down well and I got Sally one too. To my surprise, Sally asked me what I would like for supper if I would call around. "Well," I said, "I will have to call and tell Helon what the score is first as she is also a friend, then I will come back." I drank up and went around to the Malt Shovel pub but Helon was not on. The Landlady told me she had gone to her friend's place for a few days, which she would have told me if I had stopped in the other night.

"OK," I said. "Just give her a message when she comes back that I have moved on and will be going down to London this weekend, tomorrow in fact. There is a job in Malta and I have to go for an interview this weekend."

"Good luck with the job," the Landlady said. I drank up as it was only a half pint and walked back along the seafront to think before going back to see

Sally. I thought, *tomorrow I will call at Mum and Dad's to tell them I am done at the steelworks and am moving on*. Then I thought about my passport and was it still in date; if not, I would blow the job. Fingers crossed as I had not thought about that until now because it will take a week or so to get it updated. By the sound of the man, he wanted someone straightaway. I went back to the digs and looked in my case. It had one year more to go so that cheered me up. I walked back to see Sally at the pub. "So, what's the verdict for tonight?" she asked me.

"Good, as Helon has gone to stay with friends for the weekend," I answered. Sally passed me the menu for pizza as I could do with one. Sally picked a cheese and tomatoes pizza and I ordered the same. We did not have to wait long—half an hour—and it was there. Sally wanted to pay. *Well*, I thought with a smile, *services rendered*. It went down well with the beer. You could guess what was on the menu for dessert—sex. The night wore on and it was soon last orders. I had my fill and I stood aside while Sally cleaned up. We walked back to her flat and the kettle went on and we sat and talked for a while. We kissed and that was it; clothes off and bed. As there was no rush to get up early, she wanted sex again before I could get out of bed. Eventually, I got up and dressed and went out to the paper shop. As I was walking, I saw Helon up the road, so I went the long way back to Sally's. I told her that Helon did not see me. The breakfast smelled good and went down great. I said to Sally that I would go to my mum's tonight, so I said my goodbye now. I said I would ring at the pub on Monday night. "OK," she said, "look after yourself."

I went to the digs and told the Landlady that I was going so it was goodbye for now. I put my bag in the car and headed for Middlesbrough to Mum. As it was Saturday the town was busy as I came through and drove up the Newport road to the Tees Bridge. Memories of past Saturdays came back to me as I would be out on the street when the football team played at home and get two shillings or half a crown for looking after the cars. Mum came to the door. I went in the room and Dad was in the chair. "Well," I said, "the job has come to an end and I have to move on. I am going to London tomorrow as there is a job in Malta and I have an interview on Monday morning with Wimpy Construction." I asked if it was all right to stay the night here. Dad said yes and they put me up the bed in the front room. Mum asked if I had eaten and I said that I had had a good breakfast before I left and would get fish and chips later on. "No," Mum said, "I am doing egg and chips for tea; you can have some. I was OK with that. Mum gave me a list and I went to the Co-op shop at the top of the road and got some shopping in for her. It was a change to walk around the old hornets. I was reminded of the memory of the pub as you got money back on the bottles if you took them back so we would climb over the wall and get them out of the crates and take them back to the shop. I got back to Mum's with the groceries and Mum wanted to pay but I refused. Margaret and Kathy were still at home with Dennis. Paul was at his girlfriend's. Malcolm and Dad had taken over the allotment and were still growing vegetables for the table. Mum brought the egg and chips to the room and we all sat down around the table. We had to pull the leaves out of the table as we used to do when we were young. I was asked about the places I had been and worked at. Ronnie came around and he asked if I wanted to go to the club. I washed up for Mum; then we asked Dad to come and all three of us went to the Newport Working Men's club. Dad got me signed in as I was not a member yet. I was in the chair to buy the beer and with it being Saturday night, there were a lot of Dad's friends. He was not on the committee now as it was too much for him with work and all. It was a good evening out with Dad. I got Mum two Mackeson Stouts as Mum loved them. We got back indoors and Mum asked if we wanted supper. I declined and went into the front room and the bed was already made up. Sleep was what I wanted with no sex.

I was up early and heard a noise upstairs; it was Mum in the bathroom, so I got up, put the kettle on for her and washed my face. The tea was good. The milkman was at the door, so I sorted the bill and then went to the paper shop at the bottom of the street. Next to the paper shop was Brady's Butchers and the memory of my mum sending us down here to get two shillings of meat bones to put in the stew all came back to me. Dad was up. I glanced at the paper and drank my cup of tea. I got my bag together to put in the car; I checked the oil and water in the car as I was going on a long trip today. Mum made me have breakfast before I left so it was porridge, which was not as lumpy as it was years ago. I said my goodbyes and promised to keep in touch. I drove to the A19, then down to the A1. The weather was good—dull but dry—and the traffic was not too bad as it was Sunday. I was looking forward to the job in Malta, that is, if I got it. I was thinking how Mum would get a shock when she went to the pantry as I had put forty pounds under the breadbox; it would help them along. I got down the A1, then pulled into a café to give the car a rest to cool down. I bought myself a cup of tea and as had I left the paper with Dad, I picked up one from the counter and spent half an hour reading it. I paid and went back to the car and got the map out again to see which side of the Thames river I wanted to be—the south side. The hotel I had booked into was on Victoria Road, so I had to go through the Blackwall tunnel and head towards Victoria embankment onto Victoria Street. Then it was down to the station. Wilton Road was just off it. The Abby Hotel was there and it had a carpark to drive into. I got my bag out and went around the front into the hall and rang the bell. A man came out. "Hi," I said, "I have booked a room for a few days." He looked at the book on the counter and asked my name. "Rennison," I said.

"Yes. I have you here. Room 3 on the first floor," he said and gave me the key. I went up to the room, which was small but would do. I was hungry so I went out and found a café. I ordered steak pie, chips and peas and a cup of coffee; it was good and went down well. Then I went for a walk and found a pub, it was teatime, so there were many people in. I went to the bar; I looked around and no one was drinking Guinness, so I asked for a pint of lager instead and sat down in the corner. I thought about the job I might get tomorrow in Malta with Wimpy's. There was a phone in the corner of the room and I rang Sally at the Malt Shovel pub and left a message with the Landlord to pass on to Sally that I had reached and would ring in the coming week if I got the job.